THE HARBRACE CASEBOOKS IN POLITICAL SCIENCE
Under the General Editorship of
ALAN F. WESTIN, *Columbia University*

The Uses of Power (1962)
The Third Branch of Government (1963)
The Centers of Power (1964)
Power and Order (1964)
Politics in Europe (1965)

Politics in Europe

5 Cases in European Government

CONTRIBUTORS

H. H. Wilson
PRINCETON UNIVERSITY

Stanley Hoffmann
HARVARD UNIVERSITY

Otto Kirchheimer
COLUMBIA UNIVERSITY

Constantine Menges
UNIVERSITY OF WISCONSIN

Michael G. Duerr
THE CHASE MANHATTAN BANK

Harold J. Berman
HARVARD UNIVERSITY

A HARBRACE CASEBOOK IN POLITICAL SCIENCE

Politics in Europe

5 Cases in European Government

W 99

EDITED BY

Gwendolen M. Carter NORTHWESTERN UNIVERSITY

Alan F. Westin COLUMBIA UNIVERSITY

NEW YORK · CHICAGO · BURLINGAME

Harcourt, Brace & World, Inc.

Library of Congress Catalogue Number: 65–17351

PRINTED IN THE UNITED STATES OF AMERICA

CONTENTS

INTRODUCTION

Selecting cases to illustrate politics in Europe is a hazardous but exhilarating experience. Each of the four countries considered in this volume is commonly looked on as a "type": Great Britain, the classic, stable two-party parliamentary democracy; France, an unstable multiparty system; Germany, the administrative Rechstaat; and the Soviet Union, Communist totalitarianism. The European Common Market seems no less distinctive as the most successful supranational organization of the postwar period.

The cases were selected in part with these characteristics in mind. But they also illustrate unexpected as well as expected features of national and intergovernmental politics. In the commercial TV case we see the traditional process of decision-making manipulated by minority interests inside and outside parliament. The de Gaulle campaign for direct election of the President at least temporarily defeats the old parties and establishes presidential supremacy. In the *Spiegel* case the prized impartiality of German administration is undermined by an ambitious politician who seeks to silence a biting organ of the fourth estate. In the Common Market, despite the resistance of national farm groups, a crucial step forward is taken through intergovernmental negotiations. The Khrushchev efforts to establish fixed standards of law ultimately founder on the need to protect the regime but do accomplish impressive changes in the process.

Each case deliberately focuses on a different feature of political society: for Great Britain, pressure groups; for France, the Constitution; for Germany, the press; for the Soviet Union, law; for the Common Market, European integration. Yet it is not difficult to see in the cases that each of these issues also affects the other political arenas. Pressure groups operate under different circumstances in a totalitarian state such as the Soviet Union, but they exist and can be strengthened by changes in policy as the growth in importance of Soviet lawyers clearly indicates. A constitution can be changed by manipulation in a democratic as well as a totalitarian state, as we see when France's imperious political leader exploits his own indispensability. The press can alert the public to executive arbitrariness, as did the *Spiegel*—and suffer for it—or leave the issue to clashing pressure groups, as in the commercial TV case.

The similarities of many features in all political societies, however, should not blind us to some fundamental differences. To manipulate parliament and public into accepting commercial TV is different in kind from de Gaulle's rejection of prescribed constitutional procedures in forcing through his constitutional revision. And both of these differ in kind from the continuous struggle between terror and legality in the post-Stalin era.

The very writing of a case study reveals another dimension of the comparative study of political systems. Cases about the American system are ordinarily quite simple to write. In a nation with power divided between the federal and state governments, a separation and conflict of powers within the national regime, well-organized and multifold interest groups, a competitive and muckraking press, and a tradition of harsh frankness in political exposure, the insides of politics are usually revealed for all to see and probe. At the other end of the spectrum the analysis of Soviet politics is handicapped by closed meetings, secret records, severe penalties for disclosure of information, a one-party controlled press, and restrictions on full and free access to events and information by foreign observers. All of this can be overcome to some extent by the learning, insights, and circumscribed sources of talented reporters and professional observers, but even the most dedicated Kremlinologist admits that true "case studies" of Soviet politics are only possible for those rare events that lead to published "inside commentary" and "factual data" such as in the Soviet decision to intervene in Hungary and the Khrushchev denunciation of Stalin.

Between the "open" and "controlled" extremes of political systems for case-study analysis lie the intermediate arenas of Great Britain, France, and Germany. Each system throws up a different kaleidoscopic arrangement of data for case-study analysis of politics. The press is no less vigilant and energetic in these three European nations, but it does not often have the same degree of "inside" access to government as in the American system. Interest groups are not as numerous and openly combative as in the United States. The respect for government secrecy is greater in Europe, despite debates over its limits; and the law limiting disclosure is generally more strict, as the *Spiegel* case demonstrates so graphically. Thus the cases presented in this book are, both naturally and by design, "typical" of the informational levels and analytical modes possible for each of the political systems portrayed.

These five cases provide windows through which to see the workings of formal and informal factors in government. They do not replace a text but supplement it. A text lays out the whole political system, describing each part in sufficient detail to make its function clear. It puts the parts in the context of the whole. A case is sharply focused on a particular issue and omits those details that are not specifically relevant to it. Nonetheless, politics being what it is, these cases provide not only lively, immediate ways of seeing the interaction of factors, forces, and personalities but also insight into the policies, problems, and potentialities—both constructive and disturbing—of some of the most important of modern political systems.

GWENDOLEN M. CARTER
ALAN F. WESTIN

1

GREAT BRITAIN

Pressures
on Parliament
The Commercial TV Affair

H. H. Wilson

Commercial television came to Great Britain on July 30, 1954. It came in
the form of an act to create an Independent Television Authority that would
own and operate a second television channel, financed by advertising revenues, to compete with the BBC. Those in Britain who understood the potential for private profit in this new institution knew that, in the words of
one of them, there had been nothing like it "since Charles II doled out pat-
ents for making soap."

To most Americans the event, if noticed, was of minor significance, except
perhaps to some employees of certain soap companies and advertising agencies. Indeed, most Americans, if they thought about it at all, probably wondered at the delay and the fuss. Drawing on their own experience, they were
hard put to understand Britain's hesitation to exploit what they knew was a
"pitchman's paradise," the greatest adjunct to free enterprise since advertising itself was invented.

To most Britons, however, the bill breaking the monopoly of the British
Broadcasting Corporation and placing a cash nexus on the airwaves constituted a radical change. The BBC was not merely an august, respectable
institution but, especially during World War II, it had become a symbol of
the nation itself—along with tea and the royal family. It had become Britain's
face to the world; it had become invested with Britain's pride in its capacity
to create institutions unique in the world. Who could believe that its hegem-

ony in the field of television broadcasting—a field in which it had been the world's pioneer—would be so rudely shattered?

But if it was a jolt to most Britons, the successful challenge to the BBC was a complete shock to the corporation itself and to what has become known as the "Establishment"—an elite group made up of the aristocracy, the leadership of the Conservative party, the top clergy, the Oxbridge dons and fellows, and the lords of the press. The Establishment was almost solidly behind the BBC and opposed to the idea of commercial broadcasting. Nevertheless, in spite of its powerful opposition, the change took place, having been engineered within the Conservative party and passed into law by a Conservative government.

Thus, the introduction of commercial television into Great Britain acquires significance on many levels, aside from mere interest in "how it was done." It was a defeat, one of the few, certainly, for the power of the Establishment within its own precinct, the Conservative party. It was a defeat also for the Establishment philosophy of paternal government, which had regarded the airwaves as public property, to be used in trust for the education and edification—and occasionally the entertainment—of the nation. Behind the successful campaign for commercial television was the rising power of a new group within the Conservative orbit, dedicated to removing the dead hand of the Establishment—its class rigidity, its patronizing superiority, its façade of anticommercialism, its fuddy-duddy ways. Representing new businesses, new money, and employing a public relations approach, these men were the alchemists of a new image for the Conservative party. They believed that television was an ideal way of selling products and politics, and they stood ready to reap the profits of both.

At no time did a majority of Conservative party members support a commercial television channel; nor, until the very last stages of the fight, did more than two or three of the top party leaders publicly favor such an innovation. Thus, the passage of the commercial television bill raises serious questions about the capacity of orthodox and traditional political institutions such as the Conservative party to resist infiltration by powerful groups representing a minority of the party's coalition. Further, an analysis of the campaign for commercial television challenges previously held beliefs that pressure groups did not exist in Britain, or that their influence was operative only in matters of minor "fiddling" and could not affect major policy. Surely the decision to introduce commercial television was more than a minor fiddle. In the words of Anthony Sampson, it was "an innovation more sudden and dramatic than the nationalized industries . . . still having repercussions on parliament, the monarchy, the Church, the press, and even the position of the Prime Minister."[1] It was a decision of major significance, affecting not only the future of the communications media but the nature of political discourse and the character of society itself.

---

[1] *Anatomy of Britain* (Harper and Row, New York, 1962), p. 600.

Background: The BBC

The British Broadcasting Corporation received its first charter and license in January, 1927. After several years of experimenting with various degrees of private, commercial, and government control, the BBC was created as a public corporation by the Conservative government, following the advice of its investigating commission that "the control of such a potential power over public opinion and the life of the nation ought to remain with the state, and that the operation of so important a national service ought not to be allowed to become an unrestricted commercial monopoly."

The formal organization of the BBC has not changed since its inception. The administrative officer is the Director-General, chosen by the Board of Governors, which is itself chosen by the Queen in Council (i.e., the cabinet). The corporation is financed through license fees paid by owners of radio (and now television) sets. Although the corporation operates under a royal charter, it is licensed by the Postmaster-General and, in theory, his power (and, through him, the power of the government) is absolute. In practice, however, the corporation early succeeded in establishing itself as a semi-autonomous organism whose operating independence has been respected by governments whatever their political persuasion.[2] This development was due largely to the efforts of its first Director-General, J. C. W. (now Lord) Reith, who remained with the BBC until 1938. It was also Reith who inculcated the belief that a monopoly was necessary, not just for technical reasons (which have always limited the number of available broadcasting frequencies in Britain), but to maintain the highest standards of British culture. To maintain those standards—to inform and educate, not merely to entertain—was his conception of the BBC's fundamental purpose. Under his regime, the BBC broadcast two programs—a uniform national service and a regional service for local programs—giving the public "something slightly better than it now thinks it likes."

There is no question but that Reith stamped the corporation with his personality. As one of his staff put it, "he was Queen Victoria, Genghis Khan, Leonardo, rolled into one. He was Headmaster, Field-Marshal, Permanent Secretary, Commoner, Captain of the Ship, Father wielding a cane . . . around him we were all dwarfs."[3] Concern with moral and cultural standards led to a high degree of public responsibility but also to a high degree of stuffiness. The corporation became known as "Auntie BBC." Many chafed at the "Reith Sunday," when only sermons and solemn music could be on the air. Employees resented Reith's domination of their personal lives, from his insistence that the evening news announcers (radio) wear tuxedos to his firing of anyone with a divorce or other personal "scandal" in his background. The impartial way in which news was presented led Harold Laski in

---

[2] It has been suggested that the mere *existence* of government control, not necessarily its use, is sufficient to act as a check on the corporation.

[3] Quoted in Sampson, *op. cit.,* p. 601.

1946 to describe BBC policy as "the principle of maximum inoffensiveness." One of the sharpest digs came from playwright John Osborne who attacked the "staff of highly trained palace lackeys with graveyard voices, and a ponderous language stuffed with Shakespearean and semi-Biblical echoes."[4]

During the war, all existing radio services were combined into one, the home service, but a second national service, the General Forces Program, was introduced. This concession to public taste was continued after the war as the Light Program. Sir William Haley, appointed Director-General in 1944, added in 1946 the remarkable Third Program. This network offered as radio fare, "without regard to length or difficulty, the masterpieces of music, art, and letters which lend themselves to transmission in sound." There was much opposition to this program as too esoteric and limited in appeal and a waste of a valuable frequency. Ironically enough, Lord Reith concurred in this latter view, adding that the program was a mere sop to the conscience of the corporation, a benighted effort to make up for a general lowering of standards.

Some competition for the BBC always existed in the form of radio relay exchanges, that is, broadcasts sent over wires to a loudspeaker in the subscriber's home, which were serving about one million subscribers by 1950. These exchanges distributed programs culled from foreign sources as well as the BBC, thus providing greater variety than the latter alone. Licensed by the Post Office, the exchanges were opposed by the BBC as a threat to its balanced program approach, by newspapers afraid that the use of foreign commercial programs would cut into advertising revenue, and by radio manufacturers because the wire service did not require receiving sets. Eventually stringent controls were applied, severely limiting the proportion of foreign programs and restricting the type that could be broadcast in English.

More serious for the BBC was the competition from abroad, especially from Radio Luxembourg and Radio Normandy. These companies, beaming commercial programs in the English language, ultimately attracted four to six million listeners; by 1938 British firms were spending £1.5 million a year advertising consumer goods on such stations. Radio Normandy did not resume operations after the war, but Radio Luxembourg continued to attract British advertisers sponsoring light music, light drama, and American religious revivalists, though to a somewhat reduced audience.

The BBC emerged from the war with an enhanced reputation and a newly varied, more attractive fare of programs. There were, however, a few weak spots that indicated some trouble ahead. Among these were a degree of rivalry with the Post Office, dating from Lord Reith's battle to make the corporation more independent, and an increasing restiveness over the BBC's monopoly. Also, there was the start of a boomerang reaction to the wartime identification of the BBC with the state. Not only its close ties but its "tone

[4] *Ibid.*

of reverence" toward British institutions was making the BBC, according to one observer, "the most visible and disliked symbol of the Establishment."[5] From the other side, some Conservatives blamed the BBC for Labor's decisive victory in 1945, calling the BBC's impartiality a pro-Labor bias.

Evident also was a reawakening of interest in radio advertising as an effective marketing technique. Having witnessed the response to Continental commercial broadcasts and to the wartime American Forces Network, interested observers concluded that many Britons were responsive to commercially sponsored programs.

1946: The Demand for Inquiry

The BBC's charter was due to expire at the end of 1946. Expansion of radio services during the war and the development of television called for a general review of the status and financing of the corporation. Rising interest in advertising and doubts about the wisdom of monopoly led to the association of competitive broadcasting with charter renewal.

The Labor government announced early in 1946 that it intended to renew the BBC charter without an inquiry and to increase license fees as a means of obtaining greater revenues with which to sustain and develop the new services. This announcement met with dissatisfaction both inside and outside the Labor party. Churchill proposed a joint select committee of both houses of parliament to consider the renewal of the BBC charter "with or without amendment." The motion was unexpectedly popular, and some 211 members gave open support. Though only one Labor M.P. put his name to it, some twenty were believed in sympathy.

The government's White Paper on broadcasting policy, when it appeared on July 2, 1946, suggested the time was not ripe for a full-scale inquiry into broadcasting policy or improvements in broadcasting because there had been too little time to evaluate the postwar programs. Although both the government and the BBC praised the advantages of competition and promised that toward this end the BBC would strengthen its regional organization and offer more local broadcasts, the White Paper rejected sponsored programs on the ground that they would be resented by many people. Since the government felt there was not time for thorough investigation of the BBC before the expiration of the charter on December 31, 1946, it proposed a five-year extension of the BBC charter.

But there was overwhelming demand within as well as outside parliament for an inquiry before this extension was approved.[6] The magisterial *Times*

---

[5] *Ibid.*

[6] The debate in the House of Lords followed the government's announcement on June 26 of the forthcoming White Paper and was an attempt to modify it. The debate in Commons followed publication of the paper in July, 1946.

of London could not "understand why the demand for an inquiry should be regarded with such suspicion and reluctance." The main issue in the debate was that of monopoly. Fears were expressed concerning the real or potential political control of the BBC by the party in power and the deleterious effect this could have on the formation of public opinion. The refusal of the Labor government at that time to consider even a limited inquiry served to create resentment and sharpen suspicion. Had an inquiry been undertaken in 1946, however, the charter might well have been renewed by 1948 when the Labor government still possessed an impressive parliamentary majority, and the BBC might today be in control of all British broadcasting.

The Beveridge Committee Investigation

Although a Labor spokesman had referred in the July, 1946, debate to "powerful, and not always disinterested, voices pressing the claims of commercial broadcasting in this country today," politically significant voices in its favor were few. The Manchester *Guardian* commented that "there is no demand for commercial broadcasting in this country." Henderson Stewart, Liberal-Unionist M.P. and a leading opponent of charter renewal, denied any connection between competitive and commercial broadcasting.

Moreover, there was no reason to suppose the status of the BBC might become a party issue. The demand for an inquiry had been nonpartisan, while criticism of the BBC had been, if anything, strongest within Labor's own ranks. Conservative no less than Labor leadership seemed committed to the public service role and philosophy of the BBC. The Labor government had no reason to suppose its defense of the BBC to be crucial to its tenure. When it finally promised an investigation, it felt no particular urgency to get on with it. Difficulty in finding a chairman added to the delay in announcing a committee of inquiry. It was not until June 21, 1949, that Herbert Morrison, Lord President of the Council, announced in Commons that Lord Beveridge had agreed to become the chairman; the rest of the committee was named at that time.

The Beveridge Committee as finally constituted was made up of the usual assortment of clerics and earls, liberals and ladies. It included three members of parliament and at least one intellectual. Beveridge himself was a distinguished public servant, author of the famed Beveridge Report of 1942, and for several years head of the London School of Economics.

For the next eighteen months, Lord Beveridge led the most complete and thorough investigation that had ever been made of the operations of British broadcasting. Subcommittees visited the United States as well as BBC installations throughout the British Isles; some sixty-two meetings of the full committee were held, and more than two hundred memoranda of evidence were submitted. Testimony was taken in private to allow for greater freedom of expression and to avoid the influence of newspaper reporters on the deliberations of the committee.

In the beginning, the committee, and especially its chairman, refused to regard the monopoly problem as settled. Beveridge directed the investigation along lines that were intended to root out evidence of what he called the "four scandals" of monopoly: bureaucracy, complacency, favoritism, and inefficiency. Not surprisingly, the committee reported that "we found a substantial body of serious opinion challenging monopoly itself," and considered a variety of proposals for the establishment of competing broadcasting corporations. It rejected them, however, not "because we reject the aims of these critics; very largely we agree with all the aims," but because it concluded that what was good in British broadcasting could only be safeguarded if the BBC retained its monopoly. The committee saw its task as that of devising internal controls to avoid the attendant evils of monopoly. For this purpose, it made more than a hundred recommendations, most of which were ignored during the discussions that followed.

The committee examined the issue of commercial broadcasting and found it the most difficult problem to resolve. The main testimony on behalf of commercial sponsorship of programs was presented by the Institute of Incorporated Practitioners in Advertising. It was based largely on a pamphlet that had been distributed to members of parliament during the 1946 debate (the pamphlet had been prepared by J. Walter Thompson Company, Ltd.). At that time, monopoly had not seemed an important issue to spokesmen for advertisers. Their case was that "commercial broadcasting would provide industry with a powerful weapon for selling its goods, and that in return, industry would provide greatly increased resources, both in money and opportunity, by which public entertainment could be improved." The memorandum presented to the Beveridge Committee was a calculated elaboration of that argument at points thought to be politically strategic. An effort was also made to scotch critics of "Americanization," which had become a synonym in Great Britain for vulgarity and bad taste. The advertising practitioners were certain that British programs would never resemble commercial radio in America.

The Incorporated Society of British Advertisers, representing some four hundred firms that regularly purchased advertising, submitted to the Beveridge Committee the results of a poll of its member and nonmember firms. Of the 1,330 receiving the questionnaire, only 382 firms replied, and of that number only 291 companies were concerned with consumer advertising. A majority (58.1 percent) supported commercial broadcasting, but 41.9 percent opposed it. Generally firms dealing in products bought by the consumer (medical, cosmetic, toilet, food, drink, grocery) and firms with American connections favored commercial broadcasting. Some of them submitted independent proposals suggesting that the BBC be supplemented by a commercial system.

The committee could not agree and a majority were content to leave the issue of commercial broadcasting to be resolved by the government and the BBC. All but one of the members concluded that "dependence upon sponsors for the means of broadcast communication is in the last resort dictated for the wrong aims and often takes forms which public opinion in this country would reject." However, only seven of the eleven members agreed to the outright rejection of all forms of broadcast advertising. Beveridge himself, with the support of two other members, saw no reason why "a public service broadcasting agency should not set aside or name specific hours for programs admitting advertisement" so long as there were appropriate safeguards to see that broadcasting remained financially independent of the advertisers.

What was destined to become the most influential part of the Beveridge Report was written as a dissenting, minority report by the one member willing to embrace the tenet of commercial sponsorship of broadcasting—J. Selwyn B. Lloyd, in 1949 a relatively unknown Conservative backbencher, but later Secretary of State for Foreign Affairs. During the course of the committee's deliberations, Lloyd had visited the United States and had been very much impressed by the large number of small local stations. In the end, he could not agree with his colleagues on the Beveridge Committee and concluded that only private sponsoring of programs could provide an effective method for the elimination of the potential dangers of monopoly. Although he criticized the American practice of placing public service broadcasting at the mercy, in effect, of the controllers of the private stations, and although he found "much of the advertisement matter . . . boring, repetitive, and rather offensive to British ears," he thought it not impossible "to devise rules which would make it more tolerable." Besides, he concluded, advertising was "a price to be paid, and must be faced as such."

As far as the BBC was concerned, he criticized its size as a hindrance to technical development, and its excessive power, but he was especially critical of the notion that "it is the BBC's duty to decide what is good for people to hear or to see, and that the BBC must elevate public taste. . . ." While accepting his colleagues' suggestions for internal restrictions on the power inherent in monopoly, Lloyd felt that in the end something more would be required, namely, competition from independent sources. He therefore recommended that the BBC continue to operate as a noncommercial public service system financed by license fees, that it be paralleled by one or more private commercial systems, and that a Commission for British Broadcasting be established with full regulatory power over all aspects of broadcasting, including the power to enforce standards and rules for advertising.

When the Beveridge Committee Report appeared in mid-January, 1951, the BBC greeted it as a great victory and assumed that its constitutional place would remain substantially unchanged. The government did not proceed with any sense of urgency; Herbert Morrison, responsible for broadcast policy, stated in the House of Commons on February 22: "I should not think that there was a great hurry about that. The charter runs to the end of the year. Folks outside the House will want to think and talk about it, which they are doing. The government, naturally, wants to consider it with great care. I would ask that we should not be pushed too hard about it just now, because we are not ready."

In truth, the Labor government had many problems that seemed much more pressing than broadcasting policy. The general election of 1950 had resulted in a very slim majority, and the government was hampered by the relentless political activities of the opposition, as well as by a bitter internal, ideological revolt led by the Bevanites. The party leadership was plagued with ill health: Sir Stafford Cripps was out completely by October, 1950; Clement Attlee was out with ulcers during the spring of 1951; Ernest Bevin had to resign from the Foreign Office in March (where he was replaced by Morrison), and although he took over broadcast policy in exchange, Bevin was too ill to be effective in the few weeks remaining before his death. Responsibility for broadcast policy then fell on Patrick Gordon Walker, a relatively junior minister who did not possess the influence of either Morrison or Bevin.

The Labor government's White Paper announcing its response to the Beveridge Committee's proposals finally appeared in July, 1951, and stirred renewed controversy. As expected, it recommended continuing the BBC's monopoly and continuing the clause prohibiting advertising without the written consent of the Postmaster-General. The government rejected the committee's proposal for a charter with no fixed term and proposed instead a fifteen-year limit, postponing the question of periodic review for future governments. Resistance centered on two other government proposals—one to establish national broadcasting commissions, a majority of whose members would be drawn from county councils and major urban and local authorities, and the other a Treasury proposal to deduct 15 percent of the net license revenue for general purposes for three years. For the first time in its history, the BBC submitted a formal protest to parliament, claiming that the national commissions would subject the corporation to local political control. These protests were echoed by the parliamentary Labor party when it met on July 16, 1951, and condemned the government's proposals.

Thus when Patrick Gordon Walker defended the government's scheme in the House of Commons on July 19, 1951, he tried to assure the members that it was intended only as a basis for discussion. He took a firm position, however, on the question of advertising, arguing that the matter should be settled on principle. "One has to decide whether broadcasting should be controlled by those who have broadcasting interests and broadcasting interests only at heart, or whether broadcasting should be controlled as a sort of by-product by those who have other interests at heart."

Among the most active of Gordon Walker's challengers on the issue of competition were several members of the Conservative Broadcasting Policy

Committee, which had been formed by the opposition chief whip in February, 1951, but which had been meeting informally since February, 1950. They included John Rodgers, a director of J. Walter Thompson, Ltd., and Charles Orr-Ewing of A. C. Cossor, Ltd., a radio and electronics firm, as well as Lord Dunglass, Brendan Bracken (who later resigned when it became clear the group favored commercial broadcasting), Geoffrey Lloyd, Selwyn Lloyd, Kenneth Pickthorn, John D. Profumo, and Duncan Sandys. Peter Goldman from the Conservative central office served as permanent secretary. This group made an effort to agree upon a report to the Shadow Cabinet and to the 1922 Committee[7] by May, 1951. The group invited representatives of the interested parties, including the BBC and advertising agencies, to appear before it and agreed on a recommendation to introduce some form of competition into both radio and television for a trial period. Its members stressed the importance of conducting this experiment while the BBC was still developing new wave lengths and completing its television coverage. Otherwise, they warned, the monopoly might become permanent. The 1922 Committee held a meeting to formulate the party's position on the Labor White Paper; about fifty other Conservative members were also present. Only one of twelve speakers—Brendan Bracken—supported continuation of the BBC monopoly.

Nevertheless, the party leadership selected W. S. Morrison, later Speaker of the House, to reply for the Opposition. His speech, though somewhat ambiguous, was favorable to the BBC. He approved the fifteen-year charter extension, opposed regional councils, and recommended that the BBC continue to receive all the license proceeds on the ground that the funds were needed to catch up in television and that advertising was the only likely alternative source of revenue.

There was little indication in the Commons debate that a fundamental change was desired in the pattern of British broadcasting. Only two members indicated a dedication to commercial broadcasting. Objection to monopoly was again the primary feature of the debate, though there were side skirmishes about whether a majority of the British people opposed commercial broadcasting. John Rodgers expressed the view that "there is a real difference of opinion here between—if I might use the phrase—what the best people think and what the people think."

The debate in the House of Lords on July 25, 1951, seemed to be domi-

---

[7] The Shadow Cabinet consists of those M.P.'s whom the opposition party has designated to fill cabinet positions should the government fall. Although they may not necessarily be appointed in the event of victory at the polls, they are responsible for following problems and policy in their respective areas, making vital and responsible the concept of "Her Majesty's Loyal Opposition." Cabinet and Shadow Cabinet face each other across the front benches of the House of Commons; behind them sit the ordinary M.P.'s, the "backbenchers." Conservative backbenchers, meeting formally, comprise the "1922 Committee," a name which originated from a revolt of Conservative backbenchers in that year.

nated by spokesmen for the BBC. Exceptional was Lord Woolton's speech —the significance of which was not fully appreciated at the time—revealing his personal commitment to commercial broadcasting, though he emphasized that this was not Conservative party policy. While the election of 1950, which returned Labor to power with a majority of only six, might have pacified Conservative fears that the government was using the BBC to create a political monopoly, Woolton stressed this theme in his address, comparing the role of the BBC with that of the Nazi broadcasting system. He went on at considerable length about his objections to monopolies; he wound up explicitly denying party commitment to this position but went on record with the view that "within a reasonable distance of time from now, some station should be either leased or created that would permit of sponsored programs."

Despite the repeated urging of the BBC, no action was taken before adjournment in August. The announcement of a general election in October, 1951, ended the Labor government's chances for controlling the future of the BBC.

Backbench Persuasion

At the time of the Conservative victory in 1951 there was little reason to suspect that a major change in the organization of British broadcasting would take place within the foreseeable future. The future of the BBC had not been an issue in the 1951 campaign. Very few of the elder statesmen whom Churchill's appointments had brought into the cabinet favored ending the BBC monopoly, much less introducing commercial television. Furthermore, widespread debates among young Conservatives during 1946–47 had demonstrated that there was little enthusiasm in those circles for drastic change. It seems fair to state that as of 1951 both political parties agreed on preserving the BBC monopoly. All of this, however, reckoned without the influence of the "new boys" of 1950—one hundred new members of parliament, men who were remote from the front benches, but who were beginning to define the new tone of the Conservative party and who would shortly become influential in it.

As the BBC charter was to expire December 31, 1951, the Prime Minister named a cabinet committee including Lord Woolton, Sir David Maxwell Fyfe, Home Secretary and Minister for Welsh Affairs, James Stuart, Secretary of State for Scotland, and the Marquess of Salisbury, Lord Privy Seal, and announced a six-month extension of the charter. On the face of it, the committee named by Churchill seemed calculated to ensure the continuation of the BBC without basic alterations.

A hint of trouble might have been observed in a November meeting of the 1922 Committee, the tone of which strongly suggested hostility to the BBC's leading place in broadcasting. A rough estimate, however, would have shown that one-third of the party—the newest and presumably least influential—favored commercial broadcasting; one-third was opposed; and one-third seemed indifferent. How, in these circumstances, was the change brought about?

Great credit must be given to the activities of a few men, members of the parliamentary class of 1950, who had, after their election, organized a group that concerned itself with changing the policy of the Conservative party toward broadcasting. Members of the group represented the new generation of Conservative politicians in Great Britain, and they heralded a new style of life as well. Able and ambitious, brilliant and brittle, cultivated and commercial, they stood for the new higher democracy of the cash register. And on this issue, at least, they could indulge themselves in a political luxury—the identity of moral conviction and personal interest. Whether they opposed BBC operations in the name of antimonopoly, in defense of the people's freedom to be debased, or in opposition to semiofficial inculcation of cultural values, most of them had, or acquired, solid financial interest in the outcome of the controversy over the future of the BBC. Activists included the employees of radio manufacturing concerns, professional public relations consultants, and the director of an advertising agency. One member of the parliamentary group had become enthusiastic about the political potential, for the Conservative party, of a commercialized media.

The group found natural allies in several older Conservative members of parliament who had extensive interests in the communications industries, or who felt that restricting television to educational and cultural purposes unnaturally confined "this great piece of educational and selling machinery."

After the Conservative victory, a Broadcasting Study Group replaced the Broadcasting Policy Committee and the new men and their allies became the hard core of this official organ of the Conservative party. Though somewhat unrepresentative of Conservative feeling, they were in a position to formulate and present their views as Conservative policy and to attempt to win the commitment of the party not only to the disestablishment of the BBC but to a green light for commercial broadcasting.

The Broadcasting Study Group moved cautiously at first, fearing a clash with Churchill and the cabinet. They asked only that private sponsors be permitted to establish an autonomous television service that would use BBC facilities during the evening hours of six to eight. They also proposed the establishment of a body of censors to control sponsored television programs. The Group agreed not to disclose its existence and operations to the press. This tended to neutralize members of the Conservative party who might have been aroused to oppose the activities of the Group had they been informed of them. As it turned out, these members rarely attended meetings at which broadcasting policy was discussed and seemed to know little of the extent of the activities of the Group, especially its efforts to influence ministers and to keep its views about appropriate broadcasting policy before the cabinet.

The Group's first triumph occurred at a private meeting in December, 1951, with a number of Conservative leaders. Present was the Postmaster-General, who appeared to be sympathetic and receptive and suggested the Group submit their proposals to him. Acting on this invitation, the Group prepared a pamphlet, *The Future of British Broadcasting,* which was circulated to the cabinet and the 1922 Committee in February, 1952.

While this policy statement echoed the Beveridge Committee's objections to monopoly, it went considerably further and warned the government that "on this issue we are not prepared to compromise." Six points were made against the continuation of the BBC as the dominant broadcasting influence in Great Britain:

1. Unified control over such potential power is undemocratic.
2. The government of the day controls the policy of the BBC.
3. The BBC's growth has made it clumsy, rigid, overcentralized.
4. Competition would stimulate technical developments (which would lead to valuable exports of electronic equipment) and develop the cultural resources of the nation while providing choice for the public.
5. One employer encourages complacency and inefficiency.
6. Home-grown commercial broadcasting was necessary to fend off "uncontrolled" commercial stations on the Continent and in Ireland.

For the BBC they proposed to substitute a commission that would be responsible, through a minister, to parliament, a proposal that had been rejected by the Beveridge Committee on the ground that it might lead to political interference.

The report was supplemented by assiduous missionary work among Conservative M.P.'s. By the time the proposals were formally presented to the 1922 Committee on February 28, 1952, the Group claimed that approximately 95 percent of the Conservative backbenchers supported some change in the BBC. At this same meeting, however, Lord Salisbury presented a report from a cabinet committee that opposed any change in the status of the BBC. Lord Salisbury conceded that, in theory, monopoly was obnoxious but argued that there was no public demand for altering the BBC and that the Conservative party had no mandate to introduce such a change. Besides, he added, the materials that would be required for additional broadcasting facilities would have to be diverted from vitally important export and armaments industries. His report ended with a stirring plea for national unity by claiming that a debate on the BBC issue would produce bitter controversy and that the avoidance of such a disturbance should outweigh theoretical considerations like opposition to monopoly. The case for commercial service was hardly improved when Lord Woolton suggested that the Communist party might buy commercial time, or that the cooperative movement could become a sponsor, thus damaging the small shopkeeper.

The broadcasting group returned to the attack with a detailed refutation of the cabinet committee's position. They cited public opinion polls showing that 52 percent of the people were critical of the BBC while 66 percent believed that competition would improve BBC operations. They denied that an irreconcilable controversy would be triggered by the proposal to introduce commercial television; indeed, they suggested that the public might welcome additional service which came to them without the imposition of additional license fees or taxes. Through it all, they managed to imply that they were closer to public opinion than either the press or the cabinet.

A small subcommittee was appointed to represent the 1922 Committee in negotiations with the government; shortly thereafter, Lord Woolton assumed responsibility for formulating the cabinet's broadcasting policy. Within a remarkably short space of time—that is, by May 15, 1952—a compromise was reached by allowing the BBC to retain a monopoly over radio but introducing a competitive element into television. This plan was announced in the White Paper published May 15, 1952. On its face, the promise ". . . that in the expanding field of television provision should be made to permit some element of competition when the calls on capital resources at present needed for purposes of international importance make this feasible," appeared innocuous and cautious. It lay swathed and concealed in reaffirmations of love and respect for the accomplishments of the BBC. Some thought this promise of competition was merely a feeble sop thrown to a determined parliamentary minority, but in truth it meant that the Churchill government was now solidly committed to commercial television.

Central Office Support

Although the work of the young backbenchers was impressive, they could hardly have achieved this victory alone. While they had mobilized support behind their limited proposals, those who favored commercial television in the party were still in a minority. The fact is, the group had a powerful ally in Lord Woolton, Lord President of the Council and Chairman of the Conservative party. Woolton skillfully created the impression that he was reluctantly forced to retreat from defense of the BBC in the face of overwhelming backbench pressure. Yet it is known that Woolton had personally opposed the BBC before his entrance into politics in 1946, and that he had been determined to break its monopoly and introduce sponsored programs before this became a matter of government policy.

This remarkable man had assumed the party chairmanship on July 1, 1946, entering politics late in life for the express purpose of saving his country from socialism. In the process, Woolton remodeled the party organization, vastly increasing the power of the central office and introducing new research and propaganda techniques from the fields of advertising and public relations. He encouraged the entrance of figures from the advertising and public relations worlds into the activities of the party at all levels, especially in the central office, and as candidates. Every technique in the armory of manipulative politics was used in attacking the Labor party, and these led eventually to the Conservatives' electoral victory of 1951. Woolton shoved aside the old in favor of the new, opened up avenues of advancement in the party to those who might have had to wait for years to be considered, if indeed they could have been considered for leadership at all under the rules of the old Conservatives. He stood for a new Conservatism—active, competitive, modern, and practical.

After the Conservative victory in 1951, Woolton was offered his choice of cabinet position. He chose to become Lord President of the Council and in his memoirs recorded that "the Lord President is able to greatly influence policy through the operation of cabinet committees; such work behind the scenes was much more attractive to me than the more obvious role and the power that comes from making parliamentary speeches."[8] He also retained the chairmanship of the Conservative party organization.

As his right-hand man in the Conservative party, he employed Mark Chapman-Walker, a former socialist who had become an advertising and public relations man. The task of fashioning the party's propaganda fell largely to the latter. Perhaps his most memorable achievement was the *Popular Pictorial*—as the name suggests, a picture magazine, presenting the Conservative cause by means of strip cartoons and bathing beauties. His talents were valuable in creating a new "image" of the Conservative party as he suggested televising party conferences and cultivating political "personality" rather than principle.

With characteristic enthusiasm, Woolton's aide credited the achievement of commercial television to the party professionals and the central office. "All the top leadership of the party was opposed," he recalled, "with the exception of Lord Woolton. We wouldn't have got our program through without him." With Woolton's tacit approval, the bureaucracy not only ran ahead of the party rank and file, but endeavored, often successfully, to commit the party leadership in Commons to advance positions.

The procommercial militants were favored in their campaign by the dire economic circumstances of the country, which absorbed almost totally the energies of the Prime Minister and his most important cabinet ministers. As Britain was still suffering from a negative balance of trade, the government felt compelled to extend rather than relieve the austerity program of the Labor party, and was accused of betraying the free enterprise expectations of their supporters. Pressure built up within the party for the Conservatives

---

[8] *Memoirs of the Rt. Hon. the Earl of Woolton* (Cassell, London, 1959), p. 365.

From *Signs of the Times* by Osbert Lancaster, published in 1961 by John Murray

British Press Cartoons on Commercial TV

"Some of you who have been privileged to hear Canon Fontwater may have been asking what makes his surplice whiter than the Archdeacon's."

Vicky in the London *Evening Standard* (Ben Roth Agency), June 29, 1962

". . . And, we must as always, listen to the voice of the common people!"

Jensen in the London *Sunday Telegraph* (Ben Roth Agency), July 1, 1962

Low in the London *Daily Express*, November 24, 1953

Another Fake?

to make at least one positive gesture in the direction of enhancing competition and strengthening private enterprise. The BBC charter loomed more and more as the one thing that could be changed, television as the one expendable industry which could be "denationalized."

Churchill was preoccupied at this time also with problems of world peace. Basically indifferent to the fate of the BBC, he seems to have regarded the matter as one of personal preference rather than of high political principle or of consequence to the highest national interest. While he did not favor commercial television, neither was he friendly to the BBC, because he believed it had denied him access to broadcasting facilities in the 1930's. Possibly also, like a great many other Conservatives, he held the BBC partially responsible for the Conservative defeat of 1945. As it was, he moved slowly into an accommodation with the ginger group of backbench Conservative M.P.'s. By the time the critical debate took place he, too, supported the basic decisions and expressed the opinion that "the present complete monopoly should not continue."

An additional factor was the narrow majority by which the Conservative government held the Commons. On the surface, such a margin of control in politics may mean that concessions to the opposition are necessary. In British politics the discovery made by the broadcasting group was that the opposition need not come from the outside. Nor was this discovery confined to broadcasting policy; the leaders of this revolt were the same persons who forced a reluctant government to denationalize steel and road transport and to end the Supply and Services Act.

It is difficult to overestimate the importance of the dedicated activities of the members of a coherent group that knew what it wanted, had a good idea of how to get it, and was determined to win. Changing the BBC never became a public political issue in the usual sense of the word. Policy formulation took place internally, quietly, and out of sight. The important meetings were not meetings at all but conversations in private places—committee rooms, dining rooms, House of Commons smoking rooms, clubs. The activist group also had as an ever-present ally the indifference or inertia of a considerable portion of their colleagues. In the absence of strong feelings, many members may have been sympathetic to the rebels simply because they were rebelling against the party leaders, another indication of the growing gulf between the intellectual, moral, and social outlook of the old party leaders and that of the rank and file of the new M.P.'s.

Conservative Proposals

With the publication of the White Paper in May, 1952, the controversy that had been going on within the Conservative party behind closed doors came into the open. The government's proposals were cautious enough, stating simply that the BBC charter would be renewed for a ten-year period and that the government would "propose alternative arrangements" for the development of television that would include "some element of competition." But debates in the House of Commons and in the House of Lords, especially the comments of those eager for sponsored television, clarified the government's real intention beyond a doubt.

In the Lords, debate was one-sided, both numerically and in terms of the prestige, status, and presumed influence of those who spoke against the government's proposals. Lord Reith led the attack on May 22, 1952, reminding his colleagues that somebody had introduced Christianity into England, "and somebody introduced smallpox, bubonic plague and the Black Death. Somebody is minded now to introduce sponsored broadcasting." Reith reviled the government for its "clever" document—"one can imagine the stresses and strains, the pullings and pushings behind the scenes, arguments and counterarguments, drafts and redrafts"—and insisted that it was the fundamental principle of public service broadcasting that was "scheduled to be scuttled." Urging the government to reconsider, he asked: "Need we be ashamed of moral values or of intellectual and ethical objectives? It is these that are here and now at stake."

These sentiments were echoed by Lord Macdonald of Gwaenysgor, formerly Postmaster-General in the Labor government, who asked, "Is it wise for this country to follow up the craze that we find growing rapidly in some countries to commercialize everything? Is it really wise, will it add to the dignity of this great country of ours? Surely there are some things which are too sacred to be commercialized." Lord Brand, a member of the General Advisory Council of the BBC, took the same ground, objecting that commercial broadcasting spreads "the idea that everything is for sale." Advertising, he felt, would debase standards, since "every advertiser does everything that he thinks is best needed to sell his product." This led to the central question:

> Must we give the people exactly what they want, or what they are supposed to want? . . . Are the public always to be flattered and followed, as they certainly will be, if we give way to advertising? Or do the community try to use this great instrument, not only for entertainment, but also for enlightenment? If so, we shall reject on principle any commercial advertising.

Opposition to this point of view was voiced by what one noble lord referred to as the "adventurous young Peers," who claimed to speak for the younger generation of Conservatives as well as for the people as a whole. They rejected the notion that it was anyone's business to set standards and impose controls. They called for freedom—freedom for the listener to choose for himself the kind of entertainment he preferred, freedom for the parent to decide for himself how much time his child should spend watching television, freedom for the broadcaster to attract the largest circle of customers he could. They objected to the view of men like Lords Hailsham, Halifax, and Brand that broadcasting, as part of its public service, should preserve values and standards, should raise public taste and not merely reflect it. Impatient with the moral tone, they rejected any standard but the one of success.

Those who favored the government's plan were impatient with its caution. Opponents, also, were most bitter about its ambiguity on the point of commercial development. The Postmaster-General tried to pacify both sides, stating that while "it is clear that under our proposals commercial television is possible . . . it is equally true that there are other possible ways of providing competition. For this reason the word 'commercial' was quite deliberately left out, and not because we were either shy or coy about its use."

In the end, the government spokesmen admitted only that the "door is kept open for sponsored television" and stated that "it cannot be but *several years* before any licenses can be granted" for sponsored television broadcasting. (Italics added.)

Debate in the House of Commons began May 28, 1952, with the government again bending over backwards to appease the opposition while holding the leash on backbench critics. Sir David Maxwell Fyfe, Home Secretary, who moved the adoption of the government's proposals, set the tone of moderation, tolerance, courtesy, and understanding toward real and justified differences of opinion. As Sir David talked, the introduction of sponsored broadcasting seemed to become more and more remote in time. In any event, he assured his audience and the nation it was not the government's intention to permit British television to be marred and scarred by copying American methods. Far from it, he thought that sponsored television in Great Britain "may prove to be the way in which sponsoring can earn its revenue and acclimatize itself to British taste, which is quite different from American taste."

The supporters of commercial broadcasting were hardly placated by this speech. They disliked the report with its many loopholes and lack of guarantee that commercial broadcasting would begin immediately, and they expressed dismay at Sir David's implication that a change would be far in the future. Denying any private interest in commercial broadcasting, they championed the people's right to be entertained. As one of them explained, "We are doing this, not because of any monetary gain, but because we have fought ever since 1945 in our constituencies on the theme of trust the people—set the people free to choose their own programs."

The government had made the motion the subject of a three-line whip, the strongest possible request for party members to be present and vote. A Labor party countermotion was defeated, and the government's report was approved by a vote of 297 to 269. The license debate which took place on June 23, 1952, was, in the light of this success, anticlimactic. Patrick Gordon Walker cautioned the newly created Associated Broadcasting Development Company that a Labor government, when it came to power, "would certainly not carry on the policy implied in this nonexclusive license." It was more significant that the formation of this company assured the government that its commitment to "introduce some element of competition" was taken seriously by the powerful financial and manufacturing interests which would invest in the new broadcasting scheme.

Interested Parties

With all due credit to the half dozen or so Conservative backbenchers who worked day and night on the project, we would miss the opportunity for insights into the operations of pressure politics were we to to confine our attention to the activities of Conservative politicians or even to the political parties and their organizations alone. Nor is it sufficient to take into account the formal statements of private associations with an interest in the matter. Once the formal curtain is penetrated, it soon becomes clear that not only were powerful financial and manufacturing interests prepared to invest money in the new broadcasting scheme, but they were vitally involved in winning the first commitment from a timorous Conservative government and, even more, in wringing from that government after a two-year siege the right to begin operations.

With the Conservative party forming the hub, the interests fanned out through British society. As might be expected, the groups most involved were those selling goods to a vast consumer market, advertising agencies, market research organizations, and those manufacturing equipment for the television industry. While these groups were, in fact, the interests that supplied the motives, the people, the money, and the rationale behind the case for a commercial alternative, they were not unanimous. Thus one major motion picture producer gave financial support to the National Television Council—a pressure group formed in 1953 to fight against commercial television—while the other major British producer appears to have taken no action. Some interests that were initially opposed jumped quickly on the bandwagon when it began to roll; others, like Lord Beaverbrook's powerful *Daily Express,* changed to become critics of the movement.

The Radio Industry Council insisted, at its annual meeting on November 18, 1953, that there should be more programs "but it is not our job, here or in the Council, to say what methods should be used." This led one commercial advocate to ask scornfully, "Why all this sitting on the fence? Why the attitude that it really hasn't got anything to do with you? I am amazed that in a young and great and virile industry such as yours there should, in certain quarters, be such hesitation and timidity in putting the competitive television knob on the set."[9]

[9] Sir Robert Renwick, quoted in London *Daily Recorder,* November 25, 1953.

Among the most difficult of the positions to sort out were those of the various segments of the advertising fraternity. The leading trade association —the Institute of Incorporated Practitioners in Advertising (IIPA)—declared a policy of neutrality, though it had supported commercial broadcasting in testimony before the Beveridge Committee and had advocated commercial radio throughout the 1930's and 1940's. In the postwar world, however, the IIPA apparently decided to proceed cautiously out of respect for the Labor government's antipathy to advertising and the fear that a premature attempt to introduce commercial broadcasting would redound unfavorably to the sponsors and to advertising. Some of the largest advertisers, such as Lord Moyne of Guiness, opposed commercial broadcasting on the ground that it would increase expenses without creating new business. Those favoring commercial broadcasting included, in general, the large British firms, the American-connected firms, and firms familiar with commercial broadcasting through use of Continental facilities before the war.

The IIPA's neutral stance was offset in part by the formation of a private committee of interested agency executives which began meeting regularly in the board room of S. H. Benson, Ltd., a large British agency. Recollections differ as to whether the group began meeting in 1948, in July, 1952, or early in 1953. Cyrus Ducker, then director of the London Press Exchange, was, it is agreed, the prime mover. He had returned from the United States in 1948 convinced that British advertising could not afford to miss out on the new medium. The early meetings included representatives of J. Walter Thompson, Ltd., S. H. Benson, Ltd., Mather and Crowther, Erwin Wasey, and, somewhat later, Frank Dowling. With the passage of time, the group moved to the IIPA headquarters and eventually became a subcommittee of the Committee on Radio, Cinema, and Television of the IIPA.

Considerable attention was given at these meetings to devising a formula which would make advertising acceptable to the public, advertisers, and the government. As the government had not yet formulated its policy, this group was in a position to be influential. In any case, they were able to obtain private meetings with Lord De La Warr, the Postmaster-General, with Captain Leonard D. Gammans, the Assistant Postmaster-General, and with Sir Ben Barnett, the post office civil servant directly in charge of television. The group seems to have had two primary objectives in its discussions: to prevent the capture of the new medium by more aggressive and brash outside interests and to establish a form of operation that would not mimic the American pattern of sponsorship. But they were dealing largely with men who had no experience with commercial broadcasting, and they found that a great deal of their discussions were spent in educating these men.

Although the melange of interests behind commercial television hardly constituted a unified group, there were three men who emerged as the central figures and effective leaders of the campaign. These three remarkable men bolstered flagging spirits, cut off retreats, and renewed the offensive on behalf of sponsored television when some of the most respected voices in Britain were raised against it following the government's decision to find an alternative to the BBC. The BBC itself had turned one of them, Norman Collins, into a powerful opponent by a decision not to promote him to the newly created post of Director of Television. Lord Simon, then chairman of the BBC Board of Governors, said that Collins asked for two hours to think over this action. "Like damned fools we agreed, with the result that Collins filled the afternoon papers with the story of his 'resignation' because the BBC wasn't interested in television."[10] A pleasant and personable individual with first-hand knowledge of television techniques, great enthusiasm for commercial television, and resentment against what he felt was the BBC's subordination of television to sound broadcasting, Collins is credited by some observers with being the key figure in keeping the issue of commercial broadcasting before the country.

The two other men with whom Collins became associated after his resignation from the BBC in 1950 were Sir Robert Renwick and C. O. Stanley, who joined him in founding High Definition Films, Ltd., and the Associated Broadcasting Development Company. Renwick possessed far-flung industrial interests, including fourteen directorships in the electrical industry. He also had considerable experience in communications at the Air Ministry and the Ministry of Aircraft Production, where he established a firm friendship with Charles Orr-Ewing. He supported the expansion of television service in Britain as president of the Television Society and as early as 1947 recommended that government either support television more adequately or permit sponsored programs for a trial period of five years. To his connections in the radio equipment industry and the financial world he added wide acquaintanceship with Conservative party leaders, and especially with Lord Woolton. Some assumed that his influence in the party derived from what was presumed to be large-scale aid to the Conservative election fund.

Stanley, the chairman and managing director of Pye, Ltd., was also directly interested in both the manufacturing and advertising aspects of television. As a member of the television committee of the Radio Industry Council, Stanley had frequently expressed discontent with the pace of television development proposed by the Labor government. During these years, the most powerful single restraint on the development of television was the restriction on capital investment imposed by both the Labor and Conservative governments. Cabinet rulings, unknown to outsiders, permitted the BBC to build only one television transmitter at a time. Proponents of commercial television tended to blame the BBC's Television Advisory Committee, and in October, 1952, backbench complaints and deputations resulted in the appointment of Stanley and of C. Darnley Smith, chairman of a radio company, to this advisory committee.

---

[10] Interview, November 17, 1958.

The Debate Widens

Another phase of the struggle over the future of British television was carried on by two pressure groups organized for the purpose: the National Television Council to defend the BBC and the Popular Television Association to demand freedom of the airwaves. These two groups made manifest the latent alliances on either side of the contest. While generally they resembled each other, there were significant divergences in origin, organization, finances, and strategy.

The moving spirit behind the National Television Council was Christopher Mayhew, Labor M.P. for East Woolwich, freelance producer, and writer for the BBC, who was unhappy with the desultory opposition to commercial television. Accordingly, during the spring of 1953 Mayhew met privately with several prominent individuals, including Lord Simon of Wythenshawe, former chairman of the BBC Board of Governors, and Mary Stocks, who had served on the Beveridge Committee, in an effort to secure support for a nonparty organization of opposition. Shortly after, Mayhew submitted a draft of a pamphlet, *Dear Viewer,* to Lord Simon, members of parliament, officials of the BBC, and other potential supporters. It won the enthusiastic endorsement of Lady Violet Bonham-Carter, whose ability and position as a Liberal in touch with most of the prominent Conservatives made her an important acquisition. Also, sometime during the first weeks in April, Eric Fletcher, Labor M.P. for East Islington and a vice president of Associated British Pictures Corporation, Ltd., offered the part-time services of the corporation's public relations officer to direct the campaign, an offer that caused some internal difficulty to the new organization but was finally accepted out of sheer financial necessity—though with the understanding that the organization would be under no obligation to promote the policies of the movie industry.

Lady Violet Bonham-Carter became the center of the organizational effort when, on May 19, she acted upon the suggestion from Mayhew and (now Sir) Gerald Barry that the organization be formed by inviting fifty distinguished people to a private meeting at her home. She was joined by Lords Brand, Halifax, and Waverly and by Tom O'Brien, Labor M.P. and chairman of the Trades Union Council; though the Archbishop of York declined the use of his name, he expressed his support and his willingness to speak on behalf of the council.

The organizers were thrown into a state of alarm when the Assistant Postmaster-General stated that commercial television would be the subject of a government announcement when parliament reconvened in October, 1953. Indeed, it was feared that he intended to announce the licensing of commercial stations. At this point, the sponsors decided that they had no choice but to announce immediately the formation of the council by means of a letter to the *Times.* Sir William Haley, editor of the *Times,* suggested that publication of the letter be delayed until after the coronation on June 2; it was published on June 4 over the signatures of Lady Violet Bonham-Carter, Lord Brand, Lord Halifax, Tom O'Brien, and Lord Waverley. The letter announced the formation of a National Television Council "to resist the introduction of commercial television into this country, and to encourage the healthy development of public service television in the national interest." It asserted the sponsors' belief that "the development of this new medium of information and entertainment calls for the exercise of the highest sense of social responsibility in all those engaged in it, and that commercialization—now imminently threatened—is fraught with dangers to those spiritual and intellectual values which the BBC has nobly striven to maintain." Although the letter would hardly stir adrenalin in a neutral reader, its timing was a stroke of genius. Reports of the treatment of the coronation by American commercial television had outraged everyone, and the prestige of the BBC had suddenly soared. (The Americans had spiced the coronation with advertising comment that was dubious in both taste and timing—despite assurances to the contrary—and one station had even managed to put J. Fred Muggs, a chimpanzee, into the act.)

Hundreds of letters of support from prominent people were received. An organizing committee was formed which represented the "best" people of Great Britain. Apart from the motion picture corporations, producers, exhibitors, and technicians, and to some extent the press, the individuals concerned appear to an outsider to have had no direct economic stake in the outcome of the controversy. Those who directed activities, conducted public meetings, and bore the brunt of routine work did so without expectation of gain and, in some cases, at a personal sacrifice. Speakers for the council were not paid, and examination of the financial records does not reveal any remuneration for those who wrote pamphlets. Mayhew, indeed, gave the royalties from the sale of his pamphlet to the council.

The council appears, however, to have been handicapped in its opposition to commercial television by its own beliefs. Apparently, it never considered a mass appeal, believing that it could count on the "weight of authority." Its campaign was restrained in the extreme. In sharp contrast to common practice, all publications, letters to newspapers, press releases, and meetings were identified as originating with the National Television Council. Scruples about undue influence led to a self-denying financial policy—the largest donation was two hundred and fifty pounds and there were few to match it.

Despite the self-imposed handicaps of approach, the council enjoyed considerable advantages. For one thing, its members were talented, a good many of them having been drawn from universities and other educational bodies, skillful in debate, and enjoying ready access to debating forums. Under its sponsorship, some forty-five meetings were addressed at university debating societies, political clubs, youth centers, citizens' organizations, chambers of trade, workers' educational association groups, and Rotary Clubs. The council and its representatives found an open road to the national press, especially to the *Times,* the *Observer,* and the Manchester *Guardian.* Council members monitored the press and replied to the vital points raised by the opposition.

The organizational affiliations of council members afforded considerable advantage in the distribution of the three major pamphlets produced to argue the case against commercial television. These connections stood the council in good stead likewise in its efforts to persuade other groups to send resolutions opposing commercial television to the government, and a flood of these came in from religious and educational bodies.

Efforts were made to persuade individual Conservative members of parliament to oppose the government, or at least to argue for a free vote when the subject came up. Before the debate in the House of Lords, November 25–26, 1953, a letter went out on behalf of Lord Halifax, requesting all peers to attend and support his motion condemning the government's White Paper. Members of the organizing committee of the council attended the debates, and the office staff was available for the assistance of the participants.

The inhibitions that crippled the work of the group opposed to commercial broadcasting had little effect on the Popular Television Association, which was organized formally in June, 1953, to support the introduction of commercial television. Everything about this group, from its origins to its operations and finances, is a subject of controversy. Ronald Simms, the association's full-time secretary, informed the press on July 22, 1953, that the Earl of Derby had originated the association and had agreed to serve as its president. Simms, a former advertising man, took pains to inform the reporters that "we have no financial connection with commercial TV." Another version of Popular Television's creation was recalled in 1959 by Lord Woolton. "We created the Popular Television Association—you know, ex-central office—" he told the writer, "and put Lord Derby at the head of it." The creation of a nonparty organization was, he said, "a common practice in the Conservative party. It was done before and has been done since the television controversy."

The association was organized at a time when the fortunes of commercial television seemed at a low ebb. The National Television Council had been formed in a burst of publicity amid the vehement reaction to the unsavory handling of the coronation by American television. Some promoters lost heart when they saw the lords, archbishops, and university chancellors in the ranks of the opposition. The anger of the backbenchers seemed to be having no impact as the government's cautiousness appeared to increase. At a meeting on July 3, 1953, the backbenchers decided it was necessary to build up pressure on the cabinet to counteract what they felt was the influence of "the prudes, the prigs, and the priests." C. O. Stanley, Sir Robert Renwick, and Norman Collins supported this decision, and Lord Woolton asked the

Earl of Bessborough to ask the Earl of Derby to head a new organization. This was done, and in a very short time the Popular Television Association was formed with Lord Derby, later to become president of Television Wales and West, as president.

The organizational meeting was held at St. Stephens Club, and a fund of twenty thousand pounds was raised to finance the campaign. While details are not known, it was an open secret that the Popular Television Association was supported by those with an economic stake in breaking the BBC's control of British broadcasting. A letter to the *New Statesman* acknowledged that money for Popular Television came from "C. O. Stanley and other radio equipment manufacturers" but saw no reason not to use it in "a good cause."

The declared object of the Popular Television Association was "to awaken the national conscience to the dangers, social, political and artistic, of monopoly in the rapidly expanding field of television, to provide the public at the earliest possible moment with alternative programs which are in keeping with the best standards of British taste and to open up steadily widening opportunities of employment for artists, writers, producers, and technicians in all fields of the entertainment and electronics industries." The association proclaimed its dedication to "the task of setting television free. For all who value freedom of the mind there is no more important task today." Pamphlets delicately described commercial broadcasting as "competitive television," and hammered at the theme of something for nothing—an alternative program, more viewing time, a greater variety of programs all "at no cost to the public." Depending on the audience to which the speaker was addressing himself, television was to become the vehicle of religion, education, local news, or culture. Speakers for the association asserted, and its leaflets repeated, "There will be advertising announcements at the beginning or the end of a program, but there will never be any interruptions."

Lord Derby, Sir Robert Renwick, and others who represented the association pounded home the theme that commercial sponsorship would somehow bring on a vast expansion of British industry. It was seen as the source of an unprecedented export market for British cameras, studio equipment, control rooms, transmitters, and other technical equipment. The building industry would gain because of the demand that would be created for regional studios and transmitting stations. And, of course, the programs themselves would require the services of talent which would be substantially British. The support of every professional association with any tangible connection with the television industry was solicited through letters from the association. In addition, special materials were prepared for inclusion in the trade journals such as one article headlined "Song Writers Ready for the Rush," which continued: "In anticipation of sponsored television, the Popular Television Association is preparing a list of composers and lyric writers which will be made available to *bona fide* advertisers." The titillation of material interests was carried so far by Ronald Simms as to let him write for the Dublin *Sunday Express* that "television organizations are looking for more Irish people . . . Irish people who can write, who are artists, musicians, producers, entertainers, designers, or actors."

In 1959, when asked what use had been made of these various lists of talented individuals, Gordon McIver, Simms' successor, said they "might" have been passed on to the program companies, "but really they were just a gimmick to win support."

Press releases and handouts from the Popular Television Association were not identified with the association but were distributed as news to a mailing list of fourteen hundred newspapers. These materials were prepared in the form of feature articles signed by well-known figures; in fact, a panel was created containing the names of those willing to write such articles or simply to sign them. The BBC was accused of being unable to afford the services of the most popular performers, of plotting an increase in the license fee, of "flogging foul films and boosting bawdy books," while wide publicity was given to the claim that dull BBC television had been found soothing for mental patients. With its feature and news story service and its canned editorials, the association claimed to have "secured a total of just over a thousand column inches of editorial space in a recent week."

Letters to the editor were encouraged, including an offer of assistance to any volunteer who could not compose his own. The result produced letters with identical paragraphs, signed by people widely separated; one favorite appeared in at least twenty-two newspapers, signed variously, but dispatched from the same address. Another nineteen identical letters signed "Leonard London" gave the address of a secretarial bureau.

How to get the most out of a situation was demonstrated by Simms, who refuted the contention of a correspondent that there had been no popular demand for commercial television by observing "I disagree wholeheartedly. I receive a large number of provincial newspapers and have noticed in the past few weeks a tremendous increase in the number of letters in these papers putting the case of people who genuinely desire to have alternative services."

In contrast to the National Television Council, the organizational supporters of the Popular Television Association remained in the background for the most part. Advertising agencies and some individual officials contributed financially but did not endorse the association publicly. John Rodgers, a Conservative M.P. and a director of J. Walter Thompson, recalled later that he had nothing to do with the Popular Television Association because "that was set up by vested interests." The PTA, however, did establish close working relationships with Aims of Industry, a public relations firm which had conducted the sugar antinationalization campaign in 1950. Kenneth Mason and Gordon McIvor were sent to the Popular Television Association from Aims, and ultimately McIvor succeeded Simms as secretary of the association when Simms became chief publicity officer of the Conservative party. Aims also cooperated in the distribution of material and made available the services of its speakers' bureau panel; for the duration, the members of this panel were billed as experts on television. Specially prepared films arguing the case for commercial television were also made available by Aims of Industry and are estimated to have reached an audience of at least 225,000 indoors and perhaps another 200,000 during a six-month outdoor film tour.

Through this campaign the general public remained apathetic. It did not respond to invitations or exhortations to attend meetings and listen to the speakers for the rival groups. The National Television Council, of course, did not attempt to become a mass organization and cannot, therefore, be said to have failed. But the Popular Television Association, despite its claims of a membership of ten to twenty thousand and its avalanche of publicity, could effect no more than a simulation of public interest and activity.

Undoubtedly, however, the organization and activity of both pressure groups were worthwhile from the standpoint of those who organized them. The National Television Council was probably the crucial factor in making certain that British television would not develop from the start along American lines. Its existence and activity were necessary to bring about the creation of a public authority to own the transmitting facilities and license the program companies and were responsible for the inclusion of many of the safeguards in the final Independent Television Act. The Popular Television Association, on its side, was able to convince the government and hesitant Conservative M.P.'s that even if the public was not excited about commercial television, there would be no disaster at the polls following its introduction. Paradoxically, probably a majority of Conservative voters opposed commercial television in 1953, while perhaps a majority of Labor voters favored it. It could be that rank-and-file Labor was in closer sympathy to the entrepreneurial-democratic philosophy of the procommercial Conservative leaders than their own members, sharing their anti-Establishment bias and their indifference to or resentment of standards set by their "betters." What the debate of the pressure groups established was that a majority of set owners (and potential viewers) preferred a second channel and did not much care how they got it.

The Final Phase

From the outset of the discussion among Conservative backbenchers, it had been assumed that commercial TV meant sponsored broadcasting with the sponsor selecting the program. However, the White Paper, when it appeared on November 13, 1953, emphasized two basic principles: a public corporation would own the facilities and there would be no sponsoring by advertisers—"the responsibility for what goes on the air shall rest with the operator of the station and not on the advertiser."

It was a compromise that hardly satisfied anyone. Those who dreaded the introduction of commercialism into British television continued to see in the government's White Paper proposals the thin edge of evil. Advertisers rankled at the thought that "the strongest selling medium that has yet been devised" would be put in a strait jacket. Backbench Conservative supporters of commercial television were dismayed, and one of them went so far as to describe the White Paper as "probably the most depressing document I have ever read in my life."

The bill to create an Independent Television Authority was finally introduced on March 4, 1954, and for another five months the government was buffeted by the opponents of commercial television and its disgruntled advocates. One significant deviation from the White Paper was the provision that as much as £750,000 per year be provided on the request of the public operating authority, and that the Postmaster-General, with treasury consent, be permitted to lend the authority up to £2 million. This effort to strengthen the authority against the advertisers by providing them with an alternative means of operating was a response to the criticisms of the National Television Council. The backbench group that had originated the idea of commercial television tended to label the ultimate form of the measure as the conception of "sloppy minded people who do not wish to get on with the job."

The debates in the House of Lords (November 25–26) and the House of Commons (December 14–15, 1953) did not produce new arguments but did indicate the strength of the various pressures on the government. In the House of Lords a motion by Lord Halifax disapproving the government's proposals precipitated a heated debate that attracted the largest attendance in years. In a remarkable performance Lord Hailsham, speaking for the ailing Lord Halifax, attacked his own party leadership for practicing "shoddy, disreputable politics" and described the effort to compromise as "a passport to chaos and confusion and a convenient cloak for complete muddleheadedness." In the end the government defeated the Halifax motion by a majority of seventy, but there were eighty-seven votes against the policy, and an estimated one hundred Conservative peers abstained from voting. There is a possibility that the opposition would have been greater had the intemperate Hailsham not alienated so many Conservatives.

The government found the course rougher in the House of Commons. A Labor party request for an all-party conference was rejected unless it would agree in advance that the BBC's monopoly should be broken and the alternative system supported by revenue from advertisements.

The advertising industry as a whole, however, was pleased: "At long last . . . a British government has recognized that there is a place for advertising in the field of broadcasting. . . . The science of selling has established its right to a share in a medium which it has for too long, and quite unreasonably, been denied."[11]

In the House of Lords a few changes were made which tended in the direction of increasing the powers of the authority: the maximum penalty was increased for a breach of contract by a program company; a portion of performances were required to be British; and an advisory committee on children's programs was added. The government also reluctantly accepted an amendment giving the Postmaster-General the power to specify the hours of day in which the authority could broadcast.

With the whips in action and an adequate government majority assured, there was never any doubt that the bill and its amendments would be approved, despite the lack of enthusiasm among both those M.P.'s who first conceived the plan for commercial television and those who had had reservations all along. On July 30, 1954, after twenty days of debate and bargaining spread over five months, the bill to create the Independent Television Authority became law.

Aftermath

In the fall of 1955, the first television advertisement—for toothpaste—appeared in Britain, signaling the formal launching of commercial operations. The first Director-General of the new Independent Television Authority was Sir Robert Fraser, a former socialist intellectual and, during World War II, head of the Central Office of Information. A self-styled liberal and Benthamite, a believer in democratic choice, he has likened commercial television to "people's television," since it reflects the people's "likes and dislikes, their tastes and aversions, what they can comprehend and what is beyond them."

Fraser's most important job in the beginning was to hand out contracts to the companies that would actually produce the programs and sell the advertising. As some hint of the potential profits became known, the competition became intense. As one investor put it, getting a contract was like getting a license to print money. Although parliament had hoped to avoid centralized control, and the television act itself stipulated that the companies be "independent of each other both as to finance and control," early losses weeded out the smaller contenders, leaving a few big groups in control. Although there are at least fifteen companies with contracts for the various regions and for weekend or weekday broadcasting within those regions, four companies—the "big four"—dominated mainly by big showmen, have effectively monopolized the field.

The Authority supervises the operations of the program companies to see that the act is enforced and standards are maintained. Advertisements from money lenders, marriage bureaus, undertakers, and the *Daily Worker* are

---

[11] *World Press News,* March 12, 1954.

forbidden; but most pressure is exerted in secret, and it is difficult to gauge its extent. There is increasing pressure from advertisers to extend the amount of advertising time, and the original promise of no interruptions in programs has long since been abandoned. Abandoned also were the great promises about the encouragement of local talent, as the air was promptly flooded with Hollywood westerns and American (or American-style) detective stories and quiz shows.

The BBC quickly entered the battle for viewers in order to combat the initial popularity of independent TV. The corporation managed to outbid its rival for the privilege of showing "Wagon Train" and developed a program of its own called "Compact," a twice-weekly half-hour on the sex life of the staff of a women's magazine. If the competition with commercial television had the effect of lowering the BBC's standards, it also shook it out of much of its stuffiness and complacency. Except in the north, where ITV holds 66 percent of the viewers, both channels have a nearly equal share of the audience. Although ITV has always been influenced by popularity ratings and general advertising pressures, the desire to curry favor with parliament in regard to future additional channels has led it to assume a more responsible voice. The difference between the two channels has become more and more a question of tone, of "class." The BBC still tries to lead as well as reflect public taste; it has never quite got over the aura of cricket and sopranos in chiffon. ITV rarely does more than reflect public taste and, as Anthony Carthew has written, "on the odd occasions when it tries something adventurous or experimental the approach is self-conscious, the attitude one of 'look at us being cultural.' "

The more general effect of commercial television is harder to pin down. Anthony Sampson has described it as the "indirect, insidious power of projecting images, ways-of-life, and associations of ideas . . . such that no institution can afford to ignore it." Commercial television "projects a classless, Americanized, competitive world, full of mid-Atlantic accents and sleek cars, into the remotest villages where TV aerials stick up with the regularity of chimneypots." Its effect in politics has not necessarily been to make discussion freer or more spirited; desire not to offend a mass audience has the same deadening effect on ITV as overidentification with established authority did on the BBC. If anything, the irrational and the manipulative have been stressed and materialistic, consumer values have been emphasized.

As many in the Conservative party were aware, this development could not help but redound to the benefit of the Conservatives. As one procommercial Conservative M.P. wrote in 1953, "The advantage should lie with the Conservative Party, because the more vulnerable Labor voters will be exposed to a new form of persuasion." A Conservative party official confirmed this prediction when he observed, in 1959, that commercial television has "done us incalculable good" by bringing goods and services into people's homes, providing distraction by directing desires and imagination toward products, giving people a stake in things, making them conservative. In this sense, one can see the introduction of commercial television as part of a larger pattern of Conservative policies which include reduced restrictions on installment buying, lower down payments on homes, and the encouragement of stock ownership.

This kind of program represents a departure in Conservative policy. In 1946 R. A. Butler could say that "quality is as necessary as equality," and that Conservatives should be guardians of tradition, bringing "all that is most inspiring in our past to serve the ever altering needs of our present." By 1950 Conservatives were rejecting what the "best people think" in favor of what the "people think." A cynical pseudoegalitarianism was replacing the older commitment to preserving standards. In part this change represents a shift in personnel in the Conservative party, the recruitment to positions of power of men from the new industries connected with the mass consumer market. In part also, it reflects what has been called the "upper-class colonization of business." The traditional ruling class has been entering into more active commercial careers, with the result that there has been a decline in "nonbusiness-class living," a disappearance of nonbusiness standards of conduct and systems of values.

This development, especially as evidenced in the campaign for commercial television, calls for a reexamination of traditional thinking about the relationship between business interests and the political process. It is no revelation that the Conservative party relies on and is relied on by business and takes many of its policy cues from business interests. But in this case certain business interests, working together with a small group of dedicated M.P.'s (and in some cases indistinguishable from them), and party professionals were able to push their program through against the wishes of the majority of their leaders and constituents. The formal declaration of interest which M.P.'s are supposed to make was neither inhibiting nor significant, nor did parliament itself act as a "countercheck" on any one lobby. The "pitiless floodlight" which the Opposition is supposed to cast was also ineffective in limiting the influence of outside interests. For one thing, the alliance of interests working for commercial television never came fully to light until the very last stages. Labor party people never seemed aware, until it was too late, of the seriousness of the threat to the BBC; one may speculate that their effectiveness in opposition was limited by their lack of access to the circles in which policy was formed: the clubs, the meeting places, the country homes where informal discussions were held. The BBC, as part of the Establishment, had no such excuse; its innocence may perhaps be laid to its bureaucratic isolation and partly also to complacency.

The role played by the party chairman and the central office in bringing the Conservative party to heel also deserves some comment. Supposedly the professionals, the chairman included, are agents of the party and its leaders. But in this case the commercial interests worked directly through the professionals who, in turn, used the central office for propaganda purposes outside as well as inside the party, forcing the party into more extreme positions. The professionals seem to have held the rank and file in low esteem, counting on party responsibility to ensure their loyal support once the line had been laid down.

One cannot help but conclude by speculating on the effect of manipulative techniques, such as were used in this campaign, on the operation of a political democracy. At no time did the British voter, let alone the rank-and-file Conservative, have a chance to vote on the issue. By and of themselves a free press and an opposition party seem inadequate protection against the techniques of pressure employed by modern public relations.

One may wonder whether the British form of party organization, assuming it has been correctly described by British and American scholars, is able to contain and control such pressure, subordinating it to the demands of public policy.

Selected Bibliography

Most of the information in this case study was culled from interviews with active participants, personal papers, and the files of the National Television Council. For background material consult the following:

COASE, R. H. *British Broadcasting: A Study in Monopoly,* The London School of Economics and Political Science, Longmans, Green & Co., London, 1950.

ECKSTEIN, HARRY. *Pressure Group Politics: The Case of the British Medical Association,* Stanford U. Press, Stanford, 1960.

FINER, S. E. *Anonymous Empire: A Study of the Lobby in Great Britain,* Pall Mall Press, London, 1958.

PAULU, BURTON. *British Broadcasting in Transition,* U. of Minnesota Press, Minneapolis, 1961.

RICHARDS, P. G. *Honourable Members: A Study of the British Backbencher,* Faber & Faber, London, 1959.

WALLER, IAN. "Pressure Politics: M.P. & P.R.O.," *Encounter,* vol. XIX, no. 2, August, 1962, pp. 3–15.

WILSON, H. H. *Pressure Group: The Campaign for Commercial Television in England,* Rutgers U. Press, New Brunswick, 1961.

WILSON, H. H. "Techniques of Pressure," *The Public Opinion Quarterly,* vol. XV, Summer, 1951, pp. 224–42.

Study Questions

1. What does this case show about how a pressure group can succeed in putting through its policies within the tightly organized British parliamentary system? Do you think the same techniques would work in relation to (a) nationaliz-

ing sugar refining, (b) closing off West Indian immigration, (c) securing a decision to join the Common Market?

2. What light does the case cast on the new character of the Conservative party and on the ways in which it formulates policies? Is the Conservative party as susceptible to business pressure groups as the Labor party is to the trade unions? Would you expect a Labor government to eliminate commercial broadcasting?

3. What arguments in support of and against commercial television were decisive? And with whom?

4. To what extent does the relationship between government and television broadcasting reflect the character of a given political system? Where would you place Great Britain in the spectrum of American, French, German, and Soviet systems of television control?

2

FRANCE

Presidential Power and the Constitution

De Gaulle Appeals to the People, 1962

Stanley Hoffmann

On the evening of Wednesday, August 22, 1962, General Charles de Gaulle was being driven from the presidential Elysée Palace to the airport of Villa-coublay. He was returning to the country home in eastern France that he had left in order to preside over a cabinet meeting in Paris. As his car was coming through the streets of Le Petit Clamart, a suburb of Paris, it was ambushed by a gang of French terrorists dedicated to the lost cause of French Algeria. Over one hundred and fifty bullets were fired. Some hit the tires of the General's car; one missed his head by a mere couple of inches. The problem of de Gaulle's succession had been posed in the most spectacular and frightening fashion.

What was actually at stake was the determination of France's political institutions. This had been one of de Gaulle's main concerns since the fall of the Third Republic in 1940. When he restored the Republic in 1944, France's political leaders established new institutions as impotent as those of the Third Republic: the National Assembly was the most powerful body, and the cabinet, entirely dependent on an Assembly split into numerous parties, was condemned to instability and paralysis. De Gaulle, who had resigned early in 1946, waged a campaign for constitutional reform and founded a party, the Rally of the French People (RPF); both failed. But in May, 1958, when the Fourth Republic had proved unable to repress an insurrection in Algeria of French settlers and veterans supported by the army, de Gaulle was called back to power. His first decision was again to push constitutional reform. In September, 1958, the French people approved by referendum the Constitution of the new Fifth Republic. While it maintained a parliamentary regime—i.e., the existence of a cabinet responsible to the National Assembly—it curtailed the political and legislative powers of parliament and created a powerful presidency of the Republic.

The first President, elected for seven years in December, 1958, by an electoral college of eighty thousand notables—members of parliament and of France's local government bodies and representatives of France's municipalities—was General de Gaulle. From 1958 to 1962 his chief problem was the war in Algeria. In March, 1962, despite violent resistance from French settlers (helped by terrorists in metropolitan France), Algeria was granted its independence. The stage was thus set for the next drama: the fate of France's institutions. Now that the emergency of the Algerian war was over, would these institutions remain dominated by the presidency, and particularly by the present occupant of that office, General de Gaulle? Or would France's old parties, whose role he had so stringently reduced, try to get rid of his heavy tutelage and return to a political system comparable to that of the Third and Fourth Republics? From April to August, 1962, these parties became increasingly restive. The shots that were fired on that August evening opened the battle, the parties vs. the President.

This case analyzes the way in which that battle was fought from September to November, 1962. In order to consolidate both his achievements and his interpretation of the President's role, de Gaulle took the intiative in constitutional change. The old parties fought this change but were defeated, first in a referendum on the new constitutional provision proposed by de Gaulle, then in elections to a new Assembly that would succeed the National Assembly he had dissolved after it had overthrown the cabinet. What started as a simple altercation between de Gaulle and all the old parties ended, because of the twists and alliances of the election campaign, as a rather more complex and traditional contest between the left and the right. The immediate stakes of the battle were whether General de Gaulle would remain in office and whether the Gaullist party would preserve or lose the power it had gained in 1958. A slightly more distant but highly significant issue was whether, after the expiration of de Gaulle's term as President, his successor would be elected by universal suffrage. The biggest, if most remote, problems in question were whether the French political system would be so transformed as to provide permanent political stability and strong government, and what kinds of political alignments would henceforth dominate the French scene.

De Gaulle's Political Blitzkrieg
Act One: The Referendum

De Gaulle's Choice
A week after the attempt on his life, General de Gaulle announced to the cabinet that he was determined to propose a constitutional revision designed

to "ensure the continuity of the state and to preserve the Republican institutions." The battle had started. It did not develop rapidly. In the first days of September public attention was distracted by the arrest of the terrorists who had attacked the chief of state, and by the spectacular visit of de Gaulle to Germany. But matters came to a boil as soon as he returned, buoyed by the "plebiscite" of enthusiastic German crowds.

The real object of the battle was the nature of de Gaulle's revision: the election of the President of the Republic by universal suffrage. For it confirmed and tended to make irreversible the trend that had—in the eyes of the old parties—completely distorted the Constitution of 1958 over the previous four years.

The Constitution of 1958 tried to reconcile the need for representative government—i.e., a system in which the various tendencies of public opinion, represented by parties, would participate in the policy-making process —and the need for stable and strong executive authority. The tragedy of French political history had been the inability to establish such a reconciliation. Representative government allows—indeed makes for—executive authority whenever there is a parliamentary regime with a two-party system; for the party that wins the majority of seats in parliament then gives its support to a cabinet headed by the party's leader, as in Great Britain. The same result can be achieved in parliamentary regimes in which there are more than two parties when there is a stable coalition of parties united in support of a cabinet and of a program, as for instance in Holland.

A different approach, leading to a comparable result, is that of a presidential system: here, executive authority is assured by the direct popular election of the President, who is not responsible to Congress. However, when the President's party does not control Congress, or when the President's party lacks cohesion, the power of the chief executive may be severely limited, even though he has a fixed term in office. In France's political experience, the only attempt, made in 1848, at establishing a presidential system led to dictatorship: the President elected by universal suffrage, Louis Napoléon, the nephew of Napoléon I, staged a *coup d'état* against the Legislative Assembly and proclaimed the Second Empire. As for parliamentary democracy, the confusion of France's party system had led, from 1875 to 1940 and from 1946 to 1958, to the crippling of the executive.

The Constitution of 1958 tried to strike a balance, not by repudiating parliamentary democracy, but through two types of provision. The first device was the result of a compromise between those leaders of France's political parties who had agreed to serve in de Gaulle's cabinet after having been the unhappy dignitaries of the Fourth Republic, and de Gaulle's Minister of Justice, Michel Debré, also a parliamentarian but a fervent Gaullist. Together they agreed on what might be called "reformed parliamentarism." The cabinet was responsible to the National Assembly, but because of the chaotic situation of French parties measures had to be taken to ensure cabinet stability and efficiency despite the probable absence of a coherent and lasting majority in the Assembly. Thus, on the one hand, the overthrow of the cabinet by the National Assembly—which had happened incessantly in the Fourth Republic—was made much less likely by the new Constitution, which regulated quite stringently the conditions under which the Assembly (whose sessions were considerably shortened) could force the cabinet to resign. On the other hand, although parliament retained the power to vote laws, the scope of its legislative powers shrank. In other words, in the absence of the "organic" conditions for an effective parliamentary system, the Constitution resorted to "mechanics"—i.e., to "legal engineering" provisions designed to protect the cabinet.

There was, however, a second set of provisions in the Constitution of 1958, those relating to the presidency. They bore the mark of General de Gaulle's own thinking. Since cabinets, however well protected from parliamentary assaults, nevertheless remained susceptible to them, governmental impotence was still to be feared. Hence the need for what de Gaulle called "a national arbiter far removed from political struggles"—i.e., a man who would combine in his own person the advantages of executive authority and the virtue of being representative: for he was to be elected by the broad college described earlier, and he was to ensure "the regular functioning of the governmental authorities, as well as the continuance of the state . . . national independence, the integrity of the territory, respect for . . . treaties." In order to carry out his task, he received the power to turn to the people as the final judge, through dissolution of the Assembly and (in somewhat more restricted circumstances) through resorting to referendums on bills "relative to the organization of the governmental authority." He also received important emergency powers under article 16.

Now it is clear that the conception on which the presidency is based is totally different from that which inspires the provisions dealing with the government and its relations to parliament. The latter tries to reach stability *through* the classical parliamentary system that makes the popularly elected Assembly the effective source of political power. The Gaullist conception of the presidency, on the contrary, tries to *short-circuit* the traditional representative channels. De Gaulle's presidency was a step on the road to what has been called "direct democracy": the direct selection by the people of an executive leader who has the power to appeal to the people. In the Constitution of 1958, the President's *powers* exceeded even those of an American President (i.e., in respect to dissolution of the Assembly, referendums, emergency powers), but he was not *elected* directly by the people. There was something unfinished about this part of the construction.

Thus the Constitution was a hybrid whose most startling feature was the dual executive—the coexistence of the President and of the cabinet's Prime Minister.[1] The irony of the four years that followed the adoption of the Con-

[1] See S. Hoffmann, "The French Constitution of 1958: I. The Final Text and Its Prospects," *American Political Science Review,* vol. LIII, no. 2 (June, 1959), p. 344, for a discussion of the dual executive.

stitution lies in the fact that although a strong majority appeared in the first Assembly of the new Republic, it was not the parliamentary element of the Constitution—i.e., cabinet preponderance within a context of party government—that developed.

The elections to the first National Assembly of the Fifth Republic in November, 1958, showed the wide extent of popular dissatisfaction with the parties of the Fourth Republic. The beneficiary of this wave of revulsion was a new party, the Union for the New Republic (UNR), rapidly organized by de Gaulle's supporters but differing from the late RPF in that de Gaulle was not its titular head. It captured 17.6 percent of the votes on the first ballot and 26.4 percent on the second (see p. 64); it won 206 seats in the Assembly. This was some seventy seats short of an absolute majority, but the UNR parliamentary group was by far the largest in the Assembly. The first cabinet of the new regime was headed by Michel Debré, a leader of the UNR. His support included the UNR, French deputies from Algeria, and the bulk of the deputies of two of the old parties: the MRP, a Christian Democratic party that represented a largely conservative electorate (although the party's ideology was socially progressive), and the much more deeply conservative Independents.

The Dominant Position of the President

Even though the Constitution stated that "the Government shall determine and direct the policy of the nation," it was the President of the Republic who became the dominant power in the executive and in the regime. De Gaulle interpreted his role in the most sweeping way, thus ensuring the predominance of the "presidential" over the "parliamentary" aspect of the Constitution. He proceeded first by reducing the importance of the cabinet. The most important issues of policy were decided not at the Hôtel Matignon, the seat of the Prime Minister's office, but at the Elysée Palace. The President of the Assembly, UNR leader Jacques Chaban-Delmas, once referred to this practice as the creation of "reserved sectors," off-limits to all the "parliamentary" organs—i.e., the cabinet as well as the Houses. Thus foreign policy, military affairs, and the handling of the Algerian war became de Gaulle's preserve: the Prime Minister (and the other ministers) could only execute de Gaulle's decisions, or try to influence their execution. There never was any doubt that the cabinet was actually the President's agency functioning with the Assembly's support and not the Assembly's executive body functioning with the President's toleration. The other branch of the parliamentary machinery, parliament itself, also suffered from the President's conception of his role. As guardian of the Constitution, the General took it upon himself to interpret that document, and his interpretation always went against parliament's claims.

Finally, the President, having thus reduced the role of the parliamentary organs, bolstered his notion of "direct democracy" by addressing himself constantly to the people over the heads of ministers and parliamentarians alike. This appeal to the people took two forms: presidential tours of French provinces, and referendums in which the people were asked, formally, to approve bills concerning the fate of Algeria and, quite explicitly, to endorse the person of General de Gaulle (January 8, 1961, and April 8, 1962). This was, for the General, both a way of bypassing parliament and a way of consolidating his predominance over the cabinet. For, although article 11 says that referendums are called by the President "on proposal of the government," there was no doubt that the government proposed what de Gaulle had already decided. It was also a way of demonstrating the spectacular efficiency of de Gaulle's conception of government by a leader who leans directly on the people, unencumbered by any "intermediaries." De Gaulle had always been convinced that government means action, that assemblies can deliberate but not act, and that French assemblies were too divided and too unruly to be anything but obstacles to action. He also believed that whereas French "intermediaries"—deputies, representatives of interest groups, intellectuals—had been corrupted by fights and doubts, the mass of the people still had a nostalgia for the common good and a longing for a leader who could define it.

The formidable development of the presidential part of the Constitution would perhaps not have sufficed to shape the future of France's institutions if the other part had not failed to exhibit the signs of political health and vigor that Debré had hoped for. "Reformed parliamentarism" proved too fragile for comfort. As long as the Algerian war lasted, parliament's docility remained on the whole assured. Nevertheless, despite the existence of a majority behind Debré, parliament frequently showed its impatience with the restrictions imposed by the Constitution on both its legislative and political powers. If Debré's hope had been one of orderly and trusting cooperation between a chastened parliament, respectful of constitutional limitations, and the cabinet, his expectations were disappointed. Even during the Algerian emergency, parliamentary discontent boiled so vigorously that the cabinet had to clamp the lid down tightly. In particular, the Senate, in which the old parties had a predominant majority, behaved as an opposition chamber which had to be overridden by the Assembly at the request of the cabinet.

Growing Parliamentary Opposition to de Gaulle
Things got much worse with the end of the war in Algeria in 1962. Parliament was in its fourth (i.e., next to last) year; under France's electoral law, new elections would have to take place before the fall of 1963. Michel Debré would have liked de Gaulle to dissolve the National Assembly right away so that new elections would take place at a time when the General's prestige was particularly high. He resigned when de Gaulle rejected his advice. He was replaced in April by Georges Pompidou, a personal adviser to de Gaulle, a former high school teacher and subsequently general director of the Rothschild bank, a man who had never been a member of parliament or

of a party. His appointment was resented by the Assembly, which saw in it
—quite rightly—one more step toward the complete victory of de Gaulle's
conception of the Constitution. Debré, for all his loyalty to de Gaulle and
stern rejection of parliamentary encroachments, had at least been a "member
of the club," a sincere believer in parliamentary government, and not merely
an amiable reflection of the General's ideas. Immediately, a climate of opposition developed—vigorous enough to reduce Pompidou's majority on the
vote of confidence on April 27, to 259 votes against 128 and 119 abstentions. The subsequent resignation of the MRP ministers in May over foreign
policy made matters worse. It provided the opposition with a theme: European integration. It was clear that there was a majority in parliament for a
policy of supranational integration, rejected only by the UNR and the handful of Communist deputies.

Thus, gradually all the old parties came to oppose de Gaulle. They had
remained as numerous as ever (indeed, a small new party, the Unified Socialist party [PSU], had appeared in between the Socialists and the Communists); they had made no effort at merging or at changing either their structure
or their outlook. Once the settlement of the Algerian war was achieved,
two of the parties that had supported de Gaulle as long as the war had lasted
abandoned him. The MRP did so with reluctance, but it could stomach
neither de Gaulle's foreign policy nor his extension of the role of the president. The Independents also criticized de Gaulle's constitutional and foreign
policies, but the main reason for their disaffection was their resentment of
Algerian independence; de Gaulle and his Prime Minister succeeded in "selling" this policy to the Independent ministers in the cabinet, but not to the
deputies in parliament. Thus these two forces moved over to join the three
parties already in opposition: the Communists, bitterly opposed to de Gaulle
since 1945 and isolated from all other parties since 1947; the Socialists,
who had hesitatingly (but decisively) rallied to de Gaulle in the troubled days
of May, 1958, but who criticized all his policies except with respect to the
now resolved issue of Algeria; and the Radicals, France's main party and
"vital center" under the Third Republic, ideologically left-wing and anti-
clerical but socially moderate, badly weakened by endless splits under the
Fourth Republic, crushed at the polls in November, 1958, but still influential in the Senate and in some parts of France.

As for the UNR, the old parties expected it to be a passing fad, whose
popularity would fade with the end of the de Gaulle era just as the old RPF
had vanished. The fact that the UNR failed to give itself a strong organization or to formulate a program going beyond endorsement of de Gaulle, and
that it behaved as a "mass of brute votes" at the disposal of the executive
rather than as a genuine political force inspiring the government, seemed to
justify such calculations.

The Constitution itself fed the hopes of many of the old political leaders:
after de Gaulle, a President who was elected by a relatively sedate electoral

college in which small villages and small towns were overrepresented might well be a cipher who would fail to make full use of the powers of the presidency. Indeed, this had happened under the Third Republic. If the presidency were thus to wither on the vine, the paper obstacles designed to save the lion tamer (the cabinet) from the lions (parliament) would not last long. Similar obstacles (less drastic, to be sure, but just as artificial) had already failed to stop parliament under the Fourth Republic. Maybe one did not even have to wait for the next President: should the next National Assembly have a majority hostile to the General, the deputies could make it impossible for him to form a cabinet and oblige him to choose between resignation, capitulation to the wishes of the majority (which would mean the end of his conception of government), and the use of his emergency powers (which would entail a highly risky quasi-dictatorship); for in the first year of a new parliament elected after a dissolution, the Assembly could not be dissolved again.

The Issue of Constitutional Change

Given those possibilities, it appeared to many observers that there were only two ways of safeguarding executive authority after de Gaulle. Both required constitutional changes. One, which had the support of France's Premier of 1940, veteran conservative deputy Paul Reynaud, now in his eighties, was the idea of "a single government for each legislature." The newly elected legislature would select a Premier, theoretically for the duration; should this government be nevertheless overthrown, new elections would have to be held. Automatic dissolution would thus serve as a deterrent to parliament's appetites. This was a method for reinforcing the executive while maintaining (or rather restoring) the preponderance of the parliamentary part of the Constitution as against the presidential one, for the cabinet's Premier would not be elected directly by the people; he would be taken from parliament. The other way, which was advocated by some of France's leading specialists in public law, such as professor Maurice Duverger, was the adoption of a presidential system more or less fashioned after that of the United States: the President would be elected for a fixed term by the people. This would have marked the preponderance of the presidential element in the Constitution, although Duverger and his supporters carefully pointed out that in a truly balanced presidential system, parliament ought to recoup some of the powers it had lost and the presidency lose some of the powers it had gained under the Fifth Republic.

De Gaulle himself had hinted at the need for reform. The change he suggested was, as could be expected, in the second direction. He was not concerned with asserting the cabinet's power as opposed to that of parliament, but rather with asserting the President's power over both. Thus he mentioned in his press conference of April 11, 1961, that "one could envisage" the election of the President by universal suffrage so as to reinforce his personal authority. He, de Gaulle, had not needed such an election in order to benefit from "a national and popular mandate": although technically elected only by the notables, he had obtained such a mandate "through exceptional events which will not necessarily be repeated after me"—i.e., the circumstances of history and popular endorsement through the various referendums. He warned that "should I have the time and the opportunity, I could, at the right moment, put this most important item on the agenda."

This warning could hardly be well received by the old parties, for should such a change occur, it could dash the hopes of those who thought that a weakening of the presidency after de Gaulle might prepare a return to undiluted parliamentarism. Moreover, such a change, by reducing even further the importance of the cabinet vis-à-vis the President, would have resulted in a parliament and a President that were both elected by universal suffrage, but with the latter having decisive advantages. Whereas the former could hit only at the Premier but not at the President, the President could always bypass parliament through referendums, intimidate parliament through the threat of dissolution, and get whatever legislation he desired by having the cabinet resort to all the devices of the Constitution. In other words, he could do things no American President could do: he would combine the assets of the presidential type of executive—popular election and stability—with the assets given to the cabinet in Debré's scheme of "reformed parliamentarism." Thus one can understand why the old parties, already in the spring of 1958, posed as the defenders of a "strict application" of the Constitution of 1958 as it was, and why the announcement in September of the proposal for direct election of the President provoked their indignation.

The Main Battleground

Yet the main battleground was not the substance of the change, but the method of revision decided on by the General and announced after the cabinet meeting of September 12, for this method deliberately avoided the amending procedure set up by the Constitution itself four years earlier. Under article 89, which constituted part IX, *On Amendment,* the Constitution could not be revised without the participation of parliament:

> The initiative for amending the Constitution shall belong both to the President of the Republic on the proposal of the Premier and to the members of Parliament.
>
> The government or parliamentary bill for amendment must be passed by the two assemblies in identical terms. The amendment shall become definitive after approval by a referendum.
>
> Nevertheless, the proposed amendment shall not be submitted to a referendum when the President of the Republic decides to submit it to Parliament convened in Congress; in this case, the proposed amendment shall be approved only if it is accepted by a three-fifths majority of the votes cast. The Secretariat of the Congress shall be that of the National Assembly.

De Gaulle decided instead to submit his amendment directly to a referendum, without asking parliament to vote on the proposal first. His decision raises two questions. First, was there any legal basis for his action, or was it a cynical violation of the Constitution? This point was to be fiercely argued throughout September and October. Legalism is quite characteristic of French political discussions. In a country in which many of the parliamentarians are lawyers, and in which there are few political scientists but many law professors concerned with the interpretation of the Constitution, a first-class legal row was both inevitable given the circumstances and an obvious object of relish for the initiated.

De Gaulle seemed to be satisfied with a few elementary arguments. The article he invoked—as against article 89—was article 11, which he had used already in 1961 and 1962 when he had submitted bills on Algeria to the people:

> The President of the Republic, on the proposal of the Government during [parliamentary] sessions, or on joint motion of the two assemblies, published in the *Journal Officiel,* may submit to a referendum any bill dealing with the organization of the governmental authorities, entailing approval of a Community agreement, or providing for authorization to ratify a treaty that, without being contrary to the Constitution, might affect the functioning of [existing] institutions.

It could be argued that a constitutional amendment is "a bill dealing with the organization of the governmental authorities"—to which the critics of the General replied that since article 89 was the only one that dealt with amendments, article 11 obviously concerned ordinary bills only. A second argument that the General's defenders were going to exploit was derived from article 3:

> National sovereignty belongs to the people, which shall exercise this sovereignty through its representatives and by means of referendums.
> No section of the people, nor any individual, may attribute to themselves or himself the exercise thereof.

But one could object that it was the Constitution itself which determined when sovereignty was exercised through representatives and when it was exercised through referendum. In the case of amendments, representatives did not necessarily have the final say, but they had at least the first say.

Thus the arguments the General could find were shaky. The meaning of his action was clear: whereas the text of the Constitution organized a procedure of revision that belonged essentially to the "parliamentary" part of the document, de Gaulle—consistently acting so as to undermine that part and to bolster his own conception—decided to create, even on a flimsy legal basis, a procedure more in agreement with "direct democracy"—a dialogue between the President and the people, short-circuiting parliament.

This raises the second question: why did he do it? Could he not have pushed his change through the orderly procedures of the Constitution? The answer is obvious. De Gaulle could expect implacable hostility from the Senate. In the National Assembly itself, he could count only on the support of the UNR; the other parties were likely to be either opposed to the change or willing to accept it only with amendments that would have clipped the powers of a President elected by universal suffrage. To submit the bill to parliament meant either ignominious defeat or a long drawn-out battle in which the chief of state risked losing his prestige through attrition. In other words, since the door was locked to a reform that gave a more presidential flavor to the Constitution, the General decided to break through anyhow by piercing a hole in the wall. On such issues as the maintenance of the Atlantic alliance and Europe's political integration, the parties could easily have put him on the defensive. Instead, he put them on the defensive by obliging them to fight the idea of a President by popular election. To be sure, they would accuse him of violating the Constitution, but the battle would take place on a field of his own choosing. It would not be easy for the parties to convince the French that they were not fit to elect their own chief of state.

Nevertheless, it was a gamble. In order to obtain a change that would consolidate constitutional *practice* since 1958, de Gaulle had to take serious liberties with the constitutional *text;* in reply, the parties, to preserve their chance of reversing after de Gaulle the *practice* he had built up, merely had to pose as the holy defenders of the *text*—both against the substance of de Gaulle's amendment and against the procedure he had chosen. It was he who had insisted for many years on the need for political stability; they could show that it was he who was now creating turmoil and undermining respect for law. The majority that had been supporting the cabinets was slipping, but it had not disintegrated. Now it was likely to melt, and the Assembly was likely to overthrow Pompidou. Should de Gaulle then dissolve the Assembly, the next one might not be any more likely to provide him with a majority. He could thus be forced to give in to the will of parliament or to get out. De Gaulle was convinced that his reform was indispensable to the solidity of French institutions after him, but was he not risking a situation that could prepare a return to the past more decisively than if he had done nothing at all?

When on September 19 the General asked the members of the cabinet for their opinion on the change and its procedure, he found some of them reluctant to follow him all the way. The Minister of Housing, a young and dynamic civil servant, Pierre Sudreau, resigned; others suggested that the General try at least to get the measure through parliament, or that he accept restrictions to the President's powers. But he refused to budge. All the advice he accepted was to send on October 2—the day of the opening of parliament's new session—a message to both Houses informing them of his decision. The debate that would follow could lead to a dissolution of the Assembly, should it overthrow the cabinet.

Mobilization

The old parties reacted swiftly and vigorously. As early as September 6 the National Council of the Socialist party unanimously denounced de Gaulle's projects. Its secretary-general, Guy Mollet, had waged an opposition full of nuances against de Gaulle ever since Mollet's refusal to enter Debré's ministry in January, 1959 (following his participation in de Gaulle's cabinet in 1958); he had had to face within his own party the sniping of a much more consistently anti-Gaullist minority. He now seized this opportunity to reassert his authority. In the following week, the National Political Committee of the small PSU, two prominent leaders of the Independents, Paul Reynaud and the chairman of their parliamentary group in the Assembly, Bertrand Motte, the assistant secretary-general of the Communist party, Waldeck-Rochet, and the president of the Radical party, Maurice Faure, all expressed their hostility. Representatives of the Socialists, the Radicals, the Independents, and the MRP got together to discuss the possibility of a counterproposal.

There was something new in such a rallying of forces. Socialists and Independents had recently joined in criticizing the regime, but they had never tried to work together: Mollet had once called the French right "the stupidest in the world," and the Independents had no love for the Socialists, whom they considered to be financially irresponsible and demagogic. Now Reynaud and Mollet found themselves agreeing that the best constitutional solution would be the concept of a single government for each legislature. What was also new was the participation of MRP representatives. Even so, many of the MRP leaders hesitated to declare war on the General, in part because of their fear of losing some of their voters, as had happened at the time of the RPF in 1947–51, and in part because they were not basically hostile to a President by popular election—as long as he was not too powerful.

The pace quickened after September 20. On the evening of that day, President de Gaulle, for the first time, addressed the nation on the subject. He could hardly have provoked the old parties more overtly. He stated that ever since "the French people called me back officially to be their leader" he had felt "naturally obliged" to ask the people a question about his succession. "The keystone of our regime is the new institution of a President of the Republic" who is no longer, as before, "confined to advice and representation," but is, on the contrary, in charge of "the destiny of France and of the Republic." He then gave the President's role the most extensive interpretation it had ever received—one that went far beyond the 1958 theory of "arbitration," and that covered all the practices of the past four years. The President "answers for France and for the Republic." He needs "adequate means" to carry those "supreme responsibilities."

The Constitution gives him those means. It is he who appoints the ministers, and selects the Premier. It is he who calls and presides at their meetings. It is he who . . . takes . . . all the important decisions of the state. It is he who appoints the civil servants, the officers, the members of the judiciary. In the vital areas of foreign policy and national security, he has to take direct action, for according to the Constitution he negotiates and signs treaties, for he is the commander in chief, for he presides over defense. Above all, should the nation and the Republic be in immediate danger, the President gathers in himself all the duties and all the rights which public safety requires.

Of course, he added, the Prime Minister determines policy (but "on the basis thus set" by the President); of course parliament votes laws and can overthrow the cabinet, "which shows the parliamentary nature of the regime." "But, in order to preserve, in all circumstances, the acting capacity of and the balance between the branches, and in order to mobilize popular sovereignty when necessary, the President permanently holds the possibility of calling upon the nation either through referendum, or through new elections, or through both means." This was an extraordinarily broad reading of article 11, as well as a clear warning to the Assembly.

He then explained that men coming after him might "not have received from events the same national mark" that he bore. Hence his proposal.

On this subject, which concerns all Frenchmen, how should the country express its decision? I answer: in the most democratic fashion, through referendum. It is also the most legitimate way, for national sovereignty belongs to the people, and first of all, of course, in the constituent area.

He reminded his listeners that it was through a referendum that the Constitution had been adopted, and invoked the text of article 11. There could be only one meaning to such a speech: de Gaulle had chosen quite deliberately to fight it out with the old parties now.

The parties and their press reacted strongly. The Socialists denounced de Gaulle's interpretation as being "in contradiction with the intentions of the drafters and with the very text of the Constitution." They called for a "reply by parliament" (September 21). The Political Bureau of the Communist party confirmed its opposition to "personal power" on September 23. Paul Reynaud of the Independents tried to get the presidents of all the parliamentary groups of the opposition, except the Communists, to agree on a counterproposal along the lines of a "single government for each legislature." They met on September 26, but there were two significant snags: the MRP was not officially represented, and Mollet objected to the idea of an automatic dissolution of the House each time the cabinet was overthrown.

The opposition risked wasting its chances if it gave the appearance of proposing a return to the old system or if it failed to present a united front. By September 29 it looked as if the opposition was making both mistakes: two counterproposals were submitted to parliament, not one. Moreover, the main proposal replaced "automatic dissolution in case of a cabinet crisis" with "automatic dissolution except when serious circumstances make it unadvisable."

Preparing for Battle

Over the weekend of September 29, the opposition's prospects began to improve. The only support for de Gaulle came from his former Prime Minister, Michel Debré, who justified de Gaulle's procedure in terms of "the seriousness of the times"—not a very legal argument. Two events showed that the battle the General had provoked would be fierce. The first was a series of statements by various local branches of the MRP. They opposed the procedure as well as the substance of the reform (although many accepted the idea of a "true" presidential system). The second was the yearly congress of the Radical party, which met in Vichy. It was marked by a fiery speech by Gaston Monnerville, a Radical representing a department in southwestern France but born in the West Indies, who was the President of the Senate. As such, according to the Constitution, he was the third highest authority in France—after the President and the Prime Minister. Should the President die or resign before the end of his term, the President of the Senate is supposed to become Acting President of the Republic. He now accused de Gaulle of deliberate violation of the Constitution and exalted "the sacred duty" of opposing it. He called for a "common front of Republicans . . . in parliament, in the cities, in the municipalities, in the villages, wherever Frenchmen understand that the future of their liberties is at stake and that they ought to sacrifice themselves for liberty in case of need." Many of the delegates were in tears. Having reached a high pitch of revolutionary fervor, the party which prided itself on its links with the men of 1789 adopted a motion calling on parliament to censure the cabinet and asking for a "single Republican candidate" in every district should new elections take place after a dissolution.

The bill changing the Constitution, as prepared by the cabinet, was submitted on Monday, October 1. It provided for the direct election of the President by the people for a term of seven years. It also stipulated, in order to strengthen the President's authority, that he needed an absolute majority of the votes on the first ballot to be elected; if no candidate obtained such a majority, a second ballot would take place two weeks later. Only the two candidates who had the greatest number of votes on the previous ballot (or, should some contenders have withdrawn their candidacies in the meantime, the two candidates with the greatest number of votes among those remaining) would be allowed to run. Thus no President would be elected with less than a clear majority. Also, in accordance with de Gaulle's concept of a President who rises above parties, the bill organized a procedure for the presidential election designed to reduce the campaign to a minimum of time

—about two weeks. Finally, in what looked like retaliation against M. Monnerville, the bill sharply curtailed the powers an Acting President could use in the interim preceding the election of a new President.

The cabinet submitted the bill to two important bodies. One was the Council of State, France's highest administrative organ, which serves both as the government's legal adviser and as France's top administrative court. In its capacity as legal adviser, it is obligated by the Constitution to give its opinion on all bills prepared by the executive. With only one exception, its members found the procedure derived from article 11 unconstitutional. A sizable minority also voted against the substance of the bill, and the majority that approved its principle nevertheless objected to the imbalance between executive and legislative powers which would result from it. This opinion was not binding on the executive, but the opposition of this select group of France's senior civil servants, on whom the Gaullist regime had heavily relied for the execution of its policies and for staffing the ministers' brain trusts, could not but encourage the political opposition. The Gaullist state had been an example of the "administrative" tradition of French political systems, as opposed to the "representative" tradition of the Third and Fourth Republics.[2] Here was important evidence of dissent among the administrators themselves.

The other body to which the bill was sent was the Constitutional Council. Although it had no formal jurisdiction in this particular question, it was invited to give an opinion. Usually the Council, which judges the constitutionality of parliament's rules and regulations, supports the executive against parliament. This time, however, it gave a negative opinion.

This was bad news for the cabinet, which met on the morning of Tuesday, October 2, to approve the text of the bill.

Battle: In Parliament

When the National Assembly met in the afternoon, the various opposition parties had reached a decision: rather than submit a bill on constitutional reform in reply to that of the President, they would present a motion of censure against the cabinet in conformity with article 49 of the Constitution:

> . . . The National Assembly may question the responsibility of the government by the vote of a motion of censure. Such a motion shall be admissible only if it is signed by at least one-tenth of the members of the National Assembly. The vote may only take place forty-eight hours after the motion has been filed; the only votes counted shall be those favorable to the motion of censure, which may be adopted only by a majority of the members comprising the Assembly. Should the motion of censure be rejected, its signatories may not introduce another motion in the course of the same session. . . .

---

[2] See A. Nicholas Wahl's interpretation in S. H. Beer and Adam Ulam, eds., *Patterns of Government* (Random House, New York, 1962), ch. 12.

The motion was signed by fifty-three deputies, ranging from the Socialists to the Independents, and including the MRP. Here was its text:

> The National Assembly,
> considering that democracy entails respect for law, and above all for the Constitution which is the supreme law;
> considering that whereas the French people is sovereign, the Constitution's object is precisely to define the manner in which sovereignty is to be exerted, either through the people's representatives, or through the people;
> considering that the Constitution, whose author is General de Gaulle and which he submitted to the people's approval in 1958, formally prescribes in a special section that a bill for amendment must be (1) voted by the two Houses of Parliament, (2) approved by a referendum, after the French people has been enlightened through the debates in Parliament;
> considering that, in pushing aside the vote of the two Houses, the President of the Republic violates the Constitution whose guardian he is;
> considering that he thus opens a wedge through which an adventurer might pass, some day, in order to overthrow the Republic and abolish liberties;
> considering that the President of the Republic has been able to act only on the "proposal" of the Government,
> censures the Government in accordance with Article 49 of the Constitution.

The government that according to the Constitution controls the legislative agenda of the Houses could have objected to the inclusion of a counterproposal in the agenda; it could not, however, prevent a debate on a motion of censure. The adoption of and priority given to this motion by the opposition leaders had an important meaning. They had decided to fight the President's move immediately and directly rather than open a debate on the substance of constitutional reform, for such a debate would have revealed that they were far from united on the specifics of a revision. To centure the cabinet meant to avoid an embarrassing battle of proposals and counterproposals. However, it also meant staking the ultimate success of the opposition's campaign in the country on the hope that the people were sufficiently aroused by de Gaulle's cavalier treatment of the Constitution to endorse a purely negative, if united, opposition. Negativism—i.e., rejecting de Gaulle's procedure and saying little about the reform's substance—was the price of unity. This was not the first time that a procedure of de Gaulle's had been rejected, but it was the first time that the opposition took de Gaulle himself as a target, even though legally it could hit only Prime Minister Pompidou.

As had happened so often before under the Third and Fourth Republics, negative unity proved at least sufficient to destroy. The Senate on Tuesday, October 2, reelected Monnerville as its President with 212 votes for him, 3 against, and 29 white ballots (i.e., abstentions)—those of the UNR. It was a vote of defiance of de Gaulle, and Monnerville, in his brief acceptance speech, interpreted it as such. The debate on the motion of censure was to start at 3:00 P.M. on Thursday, October 4, in the National Assembly.

De Gaulle, who had announced that he would speak on radio and television on Thursday evening, decided on Wednesday to make his speech instead at 1:00 P.M. the next day—i.e., just before the opening of the debate. It was hardly an attempt to change the deputies' minds: it was even more of a provocation than his speech two weeks earlier had been. Not only did he say that "ever since the beginning" he had known that he would propose this reform to the people, not only did he not even bother any more to buttress his position with legal arguments, but he turned the referendum once again into a plebiscite. This time what he was asking the people's "direct proof of confidence and encouragement" for was an equally direct defiance of their representatives, and he hinted that he would resign if the people did not support him: "Your answers will, on October 28, tell me if I can and shall pursue my task in France's service."

The debate took place in that old and familiar atmosphere that ever since May, 1958, had deserted the "House without Windows"—i.e., the Palais-Bourbon, where the Assembly meets—the atmosphere of a bullfight, in which the ministerial bullfighter had a good chance of being gored, and in which the bull and the spectators smelled blood. Ever since the adoption of the Constitution of 1958 and the appearance of a majority that had supported de Gaulle's Premiers, the Assembly's debates had become so tame that all the efforts of these former champions of the Fourth Republic who led the assault against the cabinet could not quite succeed in making the debate great. But now it was vivid and passionate enough (especially when the opposition leaders protested during the evening the way in which France's official television system had presented the afternoon debate, devoting thirty minutes to Pompidou and three to the opposition!). Paul Reynaud, one of the most polished parliamentary speakers, was the first to speak. In an address that sounded like a prosecutor's indictment, he inveighed against the President and adjured the Assembly to defend its honor as the spokesman of the people: "France is here and not elsewhere . . ."; the Assembly must not be degenerate enough to renounce the Republic.

The other non-Communist opposition leaders emphasized that which united them: a common refusal to accept the violation of the Constitution, the danger of the precedent such a violation would constitute. They were in a buoyant mood and talked as if they wanted to exorcise at last the heavy hold the absent General had exerted over the Assembly for so long. Waldeck-Rochet announced that the Communists not only would vote against the cabinet and against the change but also would be willing to discuss a common program with the other forces of the opposition. Thus they tried to use this issue as a means of getting out of the ghetto in which they had been kept for fifteen years.

As for de Gaulle's case, it was presented with much polemical vigor by a series of UNR deputies and, with shaky results, by Pompidou in two speeches. His first address presented a lengthy, intricate, and utterly unconvincing legal defense of the procedure of revision, as well as a spirited defense of de Gaulle's record against those who had accused him of betraying his task—a direct allusion to Monnerville. His second speech, later in the debate, was an attempt to dampen the fires that UNR spokesmen had uncautiously fed: he tried to minimize the implications of the change, stressing that it did not increase the President's powers and thus aimed not at "modifying" but at "reinforcing" the Constitution. He stated that the change would help the parties "overcome their divisions," and rejuvenate their activities; some day perhaps a "real presidential system, as in America" could result, although it was too soon for France's habits. Meanwhile, a return to the past could only lead to chaos, and he accused those who wanted such a return of playing into the hands of the Communists. The latter line was clearly an effort at dissuading the MRP, if not from overthrowing him, at least from voting no on October 28.

But Pompidou's appeal had no immediate effect: 280 deputies—39 more than the absolute majority—voted the motion. This included all 10 Communists, all 43 Socialists, 33 out of 37 Radicals and other center deputies, 50 out of 57 MRP's, 109 out of 121 Independents, 31 other deputies of the right, and even 4 UNR deputies. At 5:00 A.M. on Friday, October 3, the first cabinet crisis of the Fifth Republic had begun.

Battle: In the Country

General de Gaulle showed little emotion over the fall of the government. While the battle was going on in the Assembly, he was in the country, attending military exercises. It was only on Saturday, October 6, that he saw Pompidou, received his resignation, pronounced the dissolution of the Assembly, and asked the cabinet to stay in office until after the election of the new legislature.

Despite this show of serenity, however, the Elysée had reason to be worried about its gamble. Although many of de Gaulle's enemies were skeptical about their chances of getting the French people to reject a constitutional proposal that increased the people's political role, they had at least a fighting chance of obtaining enough votes to make de Gaulle lose face—especially if the MRP decided to vote no. In this case, parties representing approximately 80 percent of the votes cast during the elections of 1958 would stand against de Gaulle and the UNR. Over the weekend, the National Committee of the MRP by a vote of 110 to 23 "recommended" a negative vote. The resolution was not all the more tenacious enemies of de Gaulle would have liked: it was a "recommendation," not a "request." Also, convinced that the next Assembly would have a majority of deputies who had voted against de Gaulle's proposal, and wishing to avoid a destructive battle between the new Assembly and the General—i.e., to postpone a definitive break with him—

the MRP delegates asserted their determination to do all they could "in order to avoid an irreparable split in the country." Finally, they did not condemn the idea of a President by popular election if it could be "in the framework of a regime that would ensure a real balance of powers." This hesitation reflected both the presence of a sizable "Gaullist" minority, many of whom had been the General's ministers, and a desire even among the others not to associate too intimately with parties that might be open to the charge of wanting to return to past chaos. However, the outcome of the meeting was a major success for the "no's."

Whatever enthusiasm may have been lacking at the MRP meeting was provided on Tuesday, October 9, in the Senate, by a vitriolic speech by the indefatigable Gaston Monnerville—a speech that pleased the senators so much that they decided to have it posted in France's town halls. He explained that the people were being "abused" by de Gaulle, that parliament defended the people's real interests and, quoting de Gaulle, who had said in a recent speech "I have the right" (to propose a reform), he exclaimed: "No, Mr. President, you do not have the right, you are taking it." In his hostility to the idea of direct popular election of the President, he even mentioned the United States as a country in which the President is elected "indirectly." Direct democracy, which had existed in ancient societies, had according to Monnerville been gradually superseded by representative government, and plebiscitary democracy was not direct democracy anyway, since it abolished all the "relays between the citizen and the state—local bodies, political parties, unions, professional or ideological associations," and thus amounts, at best, to "enlightened Bonapartism."

Even if the executive could win the battle of the referendum, it was considered by political observers to be likely to lose the elections. There was a debate among de Gaulle's advisers as to the best date for those elections. Members of the UNR wanted them at the same time as the referendum, so as to benefit from the approval they expected the voters to give to the proposal itself. The Prime Minister thought that it would be better to have the elections later, in November: in this way, a "yes" vote having already been registered, the voters would be more likely to be consistent than if they had to vote for a party without knowing the results of the referendum. It was not until Wednesday, October 10, that de Gaulle made his decision: the elections would take place three weeks after the referendum. The General was obviously determined to separate as clearly as before the role of the President —in direct "dialogue" with the people—from the parliamentary, "partisan" side of politics, and also to exploit the "yes" vote he expected on October 28 as a wedge that would divide his opposition. At a recent conference, the heads of the so-called *cartel des non*—a four-party alliance of non-Communist anti-Gaullists (Independents, Radicals, MRP's, and Socialists)—had begun to show the tenuousness of their alliance, and this was a portent from which de Gaulle could take heart.

Nevertheless, the executive found lined up against it all parties—with the

exception of the UNR, the small party of left-wing Gaullists (UDT), and a
dissident fraction of the Independents that rallied around Independent cabinet ministers who protested the party's decision to back only those candidates
who would vote no on October 28. Also, a host of civic groups, labor and
farm unions, and local government bodies denounced de Gaulle's referendum, even though the two large non-Communist unions (in contrast to the
Communist-led CGT) did not formally request a negative vote, for they had
little love for the parliamentarians of the Fourth Republic. Fourteen distinguished writers and intellectuals, such as Jules Romains, the biologist Jean
Rostand, and the philosopher Gabriel Marcel, signed a manifesto attacking
"personal power." Most newspapers were equally critical. With most of
France's "intermediaries" mobilized against the President, it was not surprising to hear the Minister of Information, who spoke on television on October
9, describe the issue as one of "political ethics," i.e., should the people have
the final say about their affairs, or should the "notables" and parliament
(which, he said, had never been able to draft solid Constitutions) remain in
charge?

The opponents of de Gaulle, thus taxed with a nostalgia for paralysis and
impotence, retaliated with charges of plebiscitarian dictatorship. A series of
events provided them with new ammunition. First, General de Gaulle on
October 18 made another appeal on radio and television. His themes were
not original, but his language was harsher (the previous regime was "the
system of decadence"), and the threat to resign unless backed by the people
was made more ominous:

> If you answer no, as all the old parties would like so as to restore their
> regime of disgrace, as well as all the plotters who want to promote subver-
> sion, or even if the majority of "yes" is weak, mediocre, risky, it is obvious
> that my role will be over, immediately and forever. For what could I do
> without the warm confidence of the nation?

The reactions to this speech among de Gaulle's opponents were violent: a return to monarchy, said Mollet; the organization of panic, charged Reynaud.
What did this blackmail mean, asked many newspapers: would de Gaulle
leave if he received less than half of the votes of all *registered* voters? In that
case, all would depend on the number of abstentions.

Second, the highhandedness of the executive seemed demonstrated anew
when the government collided head on with the Council of State. On October
19, in its capacity as France's highest court for administrative matters, the
Council invalidated an *ordonnance* (i.e., a bill originating from the executive in accordance with the emergency powers of article 16) which had been
used during the Algerian crisis in 1961. This bill had set up a Military
Court of Justice to try the authors of "crimes perpetrated in connection with
the Algerian war." The Council, which has no jurisdiction over laws, can
pronounce on all acts of the executive. It found that this particular measure

was null and void because the composition and procedure of the Court violated general principles of law concerning the rights and guarantees of the defense. Coming so soon after the Council's stand on the referendum, and having been decided in the midst of the campaign, the decision was sure to be exploited politically. This became even more certain when the Prime Minister's office immediately denounced the verdict as an encouragement to subversion, and when the cabinet, on October 24, accused the Council of having overstepped the limits of its jurisdiction. In the midst of a battle with parties and parliament, the executive seemed to want to take on France's administrative courts too.

Third, the opposition's campaign was provided with another instance of governmental unfairness. Ever since World War II, the French broadcasting system, which is, as in Great Britain, a public monopoly, has been—in contrast to the BBC—treated by every government as an agency at the service of the executive. This total lack of objectivity did not matter much under the Fourth Republic; there were too many fleeting cabinets, and they depended too much on parliament for them to be able to use the radio as an effective instrument for their support. But under the Fifth Republic, executive stability and the development of television made of the RTF (French Radio and Television) a formidable weapon in de Gaulle's hands. The Ministry of Information, which supervises the RTF, presented the government's case and regulated the opposition's access to the RTF in such a way that the Union of Radio and Television Journalists struck in protest on October 17. Despite this protest Monnerville, who wanted to speak as President of the Senate, was rebuffed. The six parties whose representatives were allowed to come before the cameras (the UNR and five opposition parties) were given only ten minutes each on October 22–23. This meant that the opposition received only fifty minutes altogether, whereas the government enjoyed, of course, far more than the ten minutes of the UNR, since de Gaulle and the ministers could speak at will. This did not mean that France's voters were being brainwashed, for even though the RTF is a state monopoly, there exist so-called peripheric radio stations (Radio Luxembourg, Radio Monte Carlo, and Europe I) on which campaigning was far less restricted and slanted, and which have many more listeners than the excessively state-controlled French radio. Nor was the regime's argument that it needed radio and television since most of the newspapers were hostile or cool completely without justification. What it did mean was that the regime was determined to exploit what power it had, and it had more power over television than over radio. The opposition parties were not alone in protesting: an impressive list of writers and professors petitioned for "honest information."

The Eve of the Referendum

During the last week of the campaign attention was brutally diverted by the Cuban crisis, which provided the Gaullists with a new argument for a positive vote. Nevertheless, the week of October 22 to October 28 was marked by high political tension. The opposition, whose leaders did not shine during their brief television appearances, was reinforced by a strident attack on de Gaulle written in the influential Radical daily *La Dépêche de Toulouse* by the crusty first President of the Fourth Republic, Vincent Auriol. Also, on October 26 former Premier Pierre Mendès-France—the man whose brief government in 1954 had temporarily galvanized France and put an end to the war in Indo-China, and who, since his resignation from the Mollet cabinet in May, 1956, over the Algerian problem, had been a lone wolf in French politics, as hostile to the Fifth Republic as to the parliamentary leaders of the Fourth—strongly condemned the referendum and proposed a detailed program of constitutional and political action should the "no's" win and de Gaulle resign. Thus, according to him, "no" would not mean chaos or a return to the Fourth Republic, as the Gaullists charged. On the same day, the leaders of the *cartel des non* published a joint program. It was extremely vague; it requested a "democratic statute" for the RTF, educational reform, an integrated Europe, a consolidation of the Atlantic alliance, a "government for each legislature." This may not have been enough to give a negative coalition a constructive look; but to find anticlericals and pro-Catholics, partisans of parliamentary rule and partisans of a "true" presidential system, enthusiasts of planning and defenders of free enterprise signing the same document was, as *Le Monde* pointed out, no small event.

The executive stepped up its own campaign. On October 24 the Prime Minister was interviewed on the RTF. He repeated what he had said to the Assembly: the proposal aimed only at bolstering the President's prestige, not at modifying the relations between the various branches. But he added a sharp attack on France's former leaders: he, for one, was not "a professional politician" like those he had seen ever since 1918 "wasting France's victory" after World War I and dragging the nation to humiliating defeats in 1940 at Dien-Bien-Phu and at Suez. Two days later, General de Gaulle made his last appeal. He alluded very briefly and indirectly to the Cuban crisis: "In our world, which is so dangerous—one sees it right now—France could not survive if she fell back into her past impotence." He repeated his threat: "If the French nation, in its own presence and in the presence of the world, came to reject de Gaulle or even gave him only a vague and dubious confidence, his historical task would be immediately impossible and thus ended."

De Gaulle's appeal for personal support had placed many Frenchmen in a highly embarrassing situation, reflected in the contradictory stands of various public (but nonpartisan) figures, as reported in newspapers and weeklies. Many of them had no sympathy for the leaders of the "no's," and had only disgust for the performance of the parliamentary system of the Fourth Republic. But they resented de Gaulle's authoritarian conception of the presidency and the tactics he had followed in this instance. Some, like the director of *Le Monde,* decided regretfully that they could not support him. Others, like Duverger, pleaded for a reluctant "yes," arguing that a positive vote would at least bar a return to parliamentarism and make a more democratic version of the Fifth Republic possible later. What the voters felt was not easy to guess. The camp of the "no" did not expect to win: it hoped to be strong enough to impress the electorate, so as to win decisively in November. But the campaigners had found little popular excitement; they had resorted to written propaganda rather than to rallies, and did not really know how much headway they had made.

The Results

Here are the results of the vote in metropolitan France:

registered voters	27,582,113		
actual voters	21,301,816		
abstentions	6,280,297	22.76%	
blank or void	559,758	2.02%	
yes	12,809,363	46.44%	of registered votes
		61.75%	of votes cast
no	7,932,695	28.72%	of registered votes
		38.25%	of votes cast

SOURCE: *L'Année Politique,* 1962.

The number of abstentions, while much higher than for the referendum of 1958 which approved the Constitution (15.06 percent) was lower than for the referendums on Algeria of January, 1961, and Apirl, 1962. But the proportion of "yes" votes was the lowest ever obtained by the General. It was the first time that less than half the registered voters had approved a measure proposed by him. It was the first time also that the "no's" outnumbered the "yes's" in any of the French departments: fourteen out of ninety. Twelve of those fourteen departments constituted a kind of continuous arc going from southwestern France to the Italian border (with the exception of the Alpes-Maritimes at the southeastern corner). This was an area in which the newspapers—especially *La Dépêche de Toulouse* and the dailies of Marseille —had been particularly violent in their opposition. Essentially, the vote reflected a special political culture, "formed under the Third Republic, in which the magic of words and the prestige of ideologies are more weighty than the concern for effective achievements" and in which the ideological left (Radicals, Socialists, Communists) had been dominant ever since the establishment of the Third Republic.[3] In those departments, opposition was strongest in the villages and small towns, which had been the very base of the political system of the Third Republic. There was no strong correlation between the level of economic development and the vote, nor can it be proven

---

[3] François Goguel, "L'electorat gaulliste," *Nouvelle Frontière,* no. 5 (January, 1964), p. 30.

that the voters were deeply influenced by television: the Bouches-du-Rhône —the department of Marseille—had both the highest proportion of negative votes and the highest number of TV sets, whereas the Vendée in western Franch had 77.36 percent of its voters approving de Gaulle, but one of the smallest number of TV sets. One correlation of significance was that of the votes and of the birth rate: the greatest proportion of positive votes coincided with the areas with the highest birth rate.

The map of the high "yes" areas shows that there were three Gaullist bastions. Two coincide with traditional French conservative votes, and show that here Gaullism had become the heir of the conservative tradition even to the point of offsetting the anti-Gaullist appeal of the conservative parliamentarians: this was the case in western France (Brittany and Normandy) and eastern France (Alsace and Lorraine). But the third area was one in which, throughout the Third and Fourth Republics, the left had been very strong—the large, industrial area of northern France. The city of Arras, whose mayor was Guy Mollet, gave a clear majority to de Gaulle.

The interpretation of the referendum was far from easy. On the one hand, de Gaulle's opponents pointed out that he had obtained results which were rather meager, when weighed against the pressure he had put on the voters. The Gaullist myth was hurt, said Le Monde. And in many areas that had sent UNR deputies to the Assembly in 1958—such as the area of Bordeaux —the rise of the "no's" was a bad omen for the Gaullists in November.

On the other hand, if one considers the referendum of 1962, not from the viewpoint of Gaullist "mythology," but "as a contest between the 'guide' of France and the 'old parties,' the results take on a rather different significance."[4] Seventy-three percent of all mayors were reported to be in favor of "no"; political forces that represented 82 percent of the vote at the elections of 1958 had obtained only 38 percent of the vote in 1962. In 1958 the Socialists, the MRP, the Independents, and (more grudgingly) the Radicals had supported de Gaulle. The referendum of 1962 showed that when they opposed him they lost more than half of their support. Whereas Communist voters, according to opinion polls, appeared to have followed the instructions of their party, one-third of the Socialist voters, half of the Radical and Independent voters, and no less than 85 percent of the MRP voters had deserted into the "yes" camp. Except in the south, the old political class—the parliamentary leaders in Paris, the traditional notables in the small towns and villages—was losing its hold on the population. The fact that the "no" vote was especially strong in leftist areas showed only that, paradoxically enough, it was mainly the left that now stood for France's traditional political system; the right had been thoroughly revamped by the Gaullist revolution.

Jacques Fauvet, the political editor of Le Monde, wrote that there had been "no winners, no losers." This was not quite accurate, for the constitutional

---

[4] Henry W. Ehrmann, "Direct Democracy in France," American Political Science Review, vol. LVII, no. 4 (December, 1963), p. 895.

revision had been adopted by the people, thus making a return to parliamentarism more difficult. But the opposition, badly beaten by de Gaulle personally, could nevertheless take heart in the rise of the "no" vote. Moreover, it could hope that when it was confronted not with de Gaulle but with lackluster Gaullist candidates, the voters would support it and send to Paris a National Assembly hostile to the General and thus capable of undoing what the referendum had just done. A Gaullist defeat on October 28 would have marked the end of the Fifth Republic. The Gaullist victory merely left the future in doubt, and made the elections of November the decisive test.

Act Two: The Elections

The Circumstances

General de Gaulle, who was at his country home the day of the referendum, delayed his return to Paris for one day in order to reflect on the significance of the referendum's results. He came back on Tuesday, and at the cabinet meeting of Wednesday, October 31, he "stressed the great significance of the positive answer given by the people."

There was one last skirmish. Monnerville had warned the Radical congress that, in accordance with the Constitution, he would refer the government's measure to the Constitutional Council should it be approved by the people, so as to get a ruling from the Council on its constitutionality.[5] He did so on November 3. The Council met on November 7. By a vote of 6 to 4, however, the Council returned to its position as supporter of the executive by denying its own jurisdiction in the matter. The Council defined its position as follows:

> Although Article 61 gives the Council the task of ruling on the constitutionality of organic and ordinary laws . . . without specifying whether its jurisdiction extends to *all* legislative texts, i.e., both those that have been approved by the people through a referendum and those that have been voted by Parliament, it follows from the spirit of the Constitution . . . that the laws to which the Constitution has wanted to refer in Article 61 are *only* those voted by Parliament, *not* those which have been adopted by the people through a referendum and which are thus the direct expression of national sovereignty.

Having decided it had no jurisdiction in the matter, the Council, according to article 60, "announced the results of the referendum" after it had certified "the regularity of the referendum's procedures." The same day de Gaulle promulgated the bill. Monnerville wrote an angry letter in which he accused the Council of having committed suicide. From de Gaulle's point of view, the battle was won. What remained was to win the war—i.e., the elections.

---

[5] The provision at stake was article 61 of the Constitution.

Pierre in the Paris *Aux Ecoutes* (Ben Roth Agency), approximately September, 1962

PARIS

De Gaulle's Critics Attack in the Party Press

"By doing away with the National Assembly, the Senate and the Council of State, we could make car parks."

RITES ET COUTUMES DE LA CINQUIÈME

Jean Effel in the Paris *L'express*, January 30, 1964

— Veuillez, messieurs les journalistes, fournir vos questions à mes réponses.

A DE GAULLE PRESS CONFERENCE
"Be so good, gentlemen, as to provide questions to my answers."

Bernie in the Paris *Aux Ecoutes* (Ben Roth
Agency), approximately May 7, 1962

"—Don't forget, my dear Pompidou, that the front of the car is
only decorative! . . ."

Padry in the Paris *Aux Ecoutes* (Ben Roth
Agency), approximately November 21, 1962

"I have the impression that
the referee has already taken
sides. . . ."

— J'ai comme l'impression que l'arbitre a déjà pris parti !

A brief description of the French election system is necessary. Metropolitan France was to elect 435 deputies. The electoral law had been adopted in October, 1958, by the de Gaulle cabinet. It had chosen—after long hesitations—to abandon the modified proportional representation system of the Fourth Republic and to return to the procedure that had existed throughout most of the Third. Every district would elect one deputy, in an election to take place in two stages: after the first ballot only those candidates who had obtained an absolute majority—i.e., more than 50 percent—of the district's votes would be elected. If nobody had a majority, there would be a runoff a week after, and the candidate who had a simple plurality on this second ballot would be elected.

The advantage of this system, from de Gaulle's point of view, was that it could emphasize the importance of the candidate at the expense of the party. This, in turn, could be expected to place more stress on local than on national issues in an election, leaving the executive as the sole representative of the common good. Also, while the single-member district system would be likely to break up landslides, it would be less likely than proportional representation to lead to splintering. What actually happened in 1958, however, was that the people voted for the label, not for the individual, and the two-ballot system amplified the tide. Between ballots, candidates with poor showings withdrew in favor of those whose ideas were not too distant from theirs, a development from which the UNR profited enormously. And the UNR followed the President in practically everything. Paradoxically enough, the man who despised parties was able to govern thereafter mainly because one party had almost swept the field.

The main losers from the withdrawal system in 1958 had been the Communists (who lost all but ten of the one hundred and fifty seats they held), but the Socialists and the Radicals had also lost heavily (50 percent of their seats). Now, in 1962, many of the parliamentarians who had been eliminated from the Assembly in 1958 were trying again. This wide expectation of trouble for the Gaullists encouraged non-Gaullist candidates, so that there were almost five candidates per district. Communists, UNR candidates, Socialists, MRP-ers, Independents, Radicals, and various other representatives of the center and of the extreme right were all well represented. The idea of the *cartel des non*—that there be a single anti-Gaullist non-Communist candidate in each district—had not been carried out. On the eve of the election, France was still pretty far from a two- or even three-party system.

The Gaullist Offensive

In 1958 de Gaulle's main problem had been Algeria: he wanted, and needed, to have his hands free. His own supporters were all too often defenders of French Algeria; hence his preference for an election procedure that would not make them too preponderant and that would allow the "liberal" forces of the Fourth Republic which had accepted de Gaulle's return (Socialists, MRP, some Radicals) to be adequately represented in the Assembly. This explains why he had refused to come out for any party at all. In 1962 his main concern was the consolidation of his conception of the regime: he wanted, and needed, a parliament that would support it; hence his decision to intervene directly in the battle.

It was widely rumored that, encouraged by the referendum, de Gaulle would be determined to use against a hostile Assembly all the means with which the Constitution had provided him. Although he could not dissolve the Assembly for one year, he could either resign and get himself reelected by the people or resort to the emergency powers of article 16. Such rumors, reinforced later in the campaign by statements from prominent Gaullist candidates, seemed designed to make the more hesitant members of the opposition think twice about their future strategy. But de Gaulle was actually determined to avoid having to go so far—by winning a majority in the Assembly. Those who hoped that de Gaulle would now put an end to "an absurd war" with the old parties were disappointed and horrified when on November 7 he addressed the nation and carried the war even further.

Not only did he interpret his victory on October 28 to mean that in the future the President could always revise the Constitution through referendum. He also saw in it proof of the fact that the old parties did not represent the nation: "To confuse today the parties of yesteryear with France would be simply ridiculous." If parliament were again to divide into rival groups, "contradicting the deep aspiration expressed by the people," and "being therefore less truly representative than ever," then a "new national crisis" would result. Only as individuals, not as party representatives, could delegates serve in the government. The new vote must not "contradict the first." "Despite all local habits and fragmentary concerns," he exhorted, "may you confirm through your selection of men the choice you have made about our destiny when you voted yes."

It was a most remarkable speech. It showed, first, that de Gaulle, concerned for the "general will" of the French and convinced that this will is expressed in the procedures of "direct" democracy, considered parliament to be "truly representative" only insofar as it reflects such a will. This is exactly the opposite of Monnerville's and Reynaud's thesis. In France's parliamentary systems, the Assembly had been "truly representative" precisely because it reflected the diversity of French opinions; in de Gaulle's ideal regime, it is the chief of state who is the true representative, and parliament's legitimacy is somehow predicated on its adherence to the nation's basic choice.

Second, observers noted that de Gaulle had not at all threatened to resign should a hostile Assembly be elected. Since he interpreted the referendum as having decisively chosen between "them" and "him," since a hostile Assembly would not be "truly representative," the hopes of the opposition that he could be pushed into a corner were in vain. Backed by the only "authentic" form of popular expression, he would use all constitutional powers —and his celebration of referendums seemed to imply that he could resort again to this miraculous weapon—against an obstructionist parliament. In other words, it was they who were being told to give in, or else expect to have to get out.

Third, the speech showed that de Gaulle was trying in his way to square a circle: to intervene in the legislative elections (i.e., to behave like a U.S. President who tries to get a Congress of the same political color as himself) while preserving the ideal (or fiction) of a President who is above factions. He did not ask the French to vote for the UNR: he was not a Democrat telling the people that he needed Democrats on Capitol Hill. He told them as chief of state that the national interest required that the French elect men who approved and supported his mission. Thus the opposition was excommunicated on behalf of the common good, and from the heights of "reason of state." He was neither, as in 1946, the "national hero" incapacited from intervening in the political process by his concern for unanimity and loftiness, nor was he, as during the period of the RPF, a party leader pure and simple. He was still trying to be a national arbiter avoiding a party label, but also, he now interpreted arbitration to mean "deciding [and telling the people] who deserves to be elected."

Fourth, de Gaulle's speech made it crystal clear that he would remain the master of the electoral battleground until the end. He was turning the election into a second referendum: did the people want de Gaulle to continue to act without "partisan" interference? The "parties of yesteryear" would have to spend all their time denouncing his arrogance rather than presenting programs on specific issues. He had lifted the campaign from the level of local issues, concrete concerns, and special interests—a level on which Gaullist performance was not flawless—to the plane of "progress, development, and grandeur" vs. "ruin, impotence, obstruction, confusion," and parochialism. This was not going to make the opposition's task easy.

It certainly helped the Gaullists. They were not at all sure that UNR candidates could win a majority by themselves; but there was a good chance to obtain a working majority by attracting and endorsing candidates who, although they were not members of the party, were nevertheless sympathetic to de Gaulle or—in case they had been members of the late Assembly— who had not voted to overthrow Pompidou despite their party affiliations. To give the regime's blessing to such candidates, an "Association for the Fifth Republic" was formed under the direction of André Malraux, France's great novelist and essayist, who had been Minister of State for Cultural Affairs throughout the Fifth Republic. At its first meeting, on October 30, he gave a speech in his typical style—flashy, nervous, and eloquent. The speech was delivered, of course, over the RTF. The old parties were its main target: they had charged that the Constitution had been raped, but "in the eyes of the French, the rape of the Constitution is a *coup d'état,* not a consultation of the people."

For most of the French this Constitution is an instrument given to the President of the Republic—and quite particularly to General de Gaulle—so as to ensure France's recovery. Thus, the country does not wish this instrument to be intangible; it wishes it to be effective. It holds the referendum legitimate, for in its eyes the Constitution is at France's service, and not France at the service of the Constitution.

—a notion that would make American constitutional lawyers blanch but which corresponds only too well to France's history of constitutional instability and malleability. Malraux also answered Reynaud: "His 'France is here and not elsewhere' . . . has the fateful resonance common to great prophecies and to tragic mistakes. If in 1940, in 1958, France had been only there and not elsewhere, it might have been pretty bad for her." Modern politics requires negotiation and arbitration. Real arbitration means decision-making. Decision-making is precisely the President's sphere of action, and if he is acting for the nation, from whom should he derive his power to act ". . . if not from the nation? . . . There is no modern government without decision, no decision without legitimacy based on the nation, and no final arbitration other than that of the nation itself." This was an appeal to the old Jacobin temper of French politics—to the idea of a regime based directly on the popular will as the most perfect expression of democracy. Indeed, Malraux ended his speech by presenting the Fifth Republic as the heir of the First—the Jacobin Republic of 1792.

The Association for the Fifth Republic did not find many candidates willing to receive its support, but it did sponsor the left-wing Gaullist (UDT) candidates, a few MRP candidates who had disapproved of the motion of censure (such as Maurice Schumann, de Gaulle's wartime spokesman on the BBC, now deputy from the department of the Nord), and a number of Independents, notably those who had broken with and left their party over the issue.

The themes of the UNR's campaign were simple. On the one hand, the Gaullists reminded the voters of the errors of the past, of the Fifth Republic's achievements, of the dangers of a "revenge of the old parties," and asked them whether they wanted to see chaos again. On the other hand, they described their own concerns as essentially pragmatic, future-oriented, unideological, and concrete. They took pride in the absence of any detailed program. Such a program was good enough in the bad old days, when parties presented long platforms that they knew they could never put into action. What mattered now was, precisely, action on the various economic, social, and educational problems faced by France. The Gaullist orators listed those problems, described the reforms already accomplished under the Debré and Pompidou cabinets, and promised to go on with the job. As one student of French politics put it, "modernism was a substitute for doctrine."

Modernism marked not only the UNR's themes but also its methods. Its specialists had studied American campaign methods and applied the lessons they had learned. In a prosperous and complacent nation, militancy was low; there was little point in organizing big rallies, especially since many UNR candidates were political unknowns who had been drafted or had volunteered in order to collect Gaullist votes, who were not considered likely to win, and who sometimes did not even originate from the district into which they had been "parachuted." But there was a point to using radio debates, to calling people on the telephone, to sending out tracts, to pasting posters on walls, and—especially in the case of candidates who were already deputies or who had local responsibilities, such as Chaban-Delmas, the Speaker of the House and mayor of Bordeaux—to canvassing influential voters.

The Divided Opposition
The opposition's campaign developed slowly. Its candidates at the local level found the voters rather apathetic, except in those areas where the fate of important leaders was at stake. On the national level, access to the RTF remained limited—from November 12 to November 15 seven party leaders were given seven minutes each—but the "peripheric" stations organized debates in which only the Communists refused to take part. Those debates, and the speeches made by the candidates in the districts, soon revealed a significant break in the ranks of the opposition.

The very proliferation of candidacies showed that the *cartel des non* had been unable to turn its negative campaign against the referendum into a positive common front based on the joint program of the previous month. This time they did not enjoy the support of professional groups or intellectuals who had sided with them over the constitutional issue. Once again it was clear that, of the old parties, only the Communists and the Socialists could impose discipline on their candidates and subordinate local issues and appetites to an overall strategy. There were a number of local alliances limited to two parties which, within a department, agreed to present one candidate only in every district; but there were few alliances among all the non-Communist opponents of de Gaulle, the significant exceptions being Chaban-Delmas', Debré's, and Reynaud's districts. In a number of cases even two-party alliances failed: in the district of Arras, Mollet had to fight three opponents.

The cartel's existence was precarious, but it was shaken most rudely by a decision of Guy Mollet that gave a new twist to the campaign and was to drive the last nail into the cartel's coffin. Mollet foresaw in the trend toward a single Gaullist party a development that would probably make a return to a parliamentary regime impossible and put such pressures on the old parties that the Socialist party would either explode into factions or be forced to merge with others. It was not difficult, under such circumstances, for Mollet to convince himself that the most serious threat came no longer from what he had once called the east—i.e., the Communists—but from the Gaullists. Moreover, a pressing local concern confirmed Mollet's overall reasoning. In

1958 in his district, Mollet's MRP rival had come pretty close to his own total of votes on the second ballot; this time Mollet was threatened by a UNR candidate as well. He guessed that on the first ballot the man from the MRP would gain more votes than the Gaullist; the latter let it be known that he would withdraw in the MRP's favor should this be the case. If the Communist contestant maintained his own candidacy, Mollet would be beaten on the second ballot.

Consequently, Mollet told the voters in his district that on the first ballot they could vote for whomever they liked, but that on the second ballot the imperative was to defeat the UNR. Mollet knew that this meant asking many Socialists to withdraw in favor of Communists, but he minimized the significance this might have: he did not think that more than "ten or twelve" districts would be affected, as had been the case in 1958. (At that time, UNR candidates were elected against the Reds, thanks to such Socialist support.) Ten or twelve more Communists in the Assembly, elected with Socialist Support, did not make any real difference from the viewpoint of Communist power, but they might thwart Gaullist hopes of an "unconditional" majority. And they could help the Socialists considerably in all those districts where they would have run far ahead of the Communists, but still either far below the UNR or far below the combined vote of UNR and other moderate candidates: Mollet could save his own seat only with Communist help.

Mollet's decision, it seems, was based on a cold appreciation of the facts from the perspective of the Socialist party's survival, and his own. He had been able to see how shaky the cartel was: thus he had reason to fear that after the first ballot, if UNR candidates ran ahead, the more conservative "allies" of the Socialists would often be likely to withdraw in favor of the UNR, rather than in favor of a Socialist, despite the split over the referendum. If MRP or Independent candidates ran ahead, the UNR was likely to withdraw in their favor, in exchange for such services elsewhere. The Socialists might find themselves squeezed out of the picture.

An electoral alliance between Communists and Socialists on the second ballot was inevitably going to bring back memories of the Popular Front— the Radical-Socialist-Communist alliance of 1936. It provided the Gaullists with a new argument against the "games" of the old parties, and of the cartel. Even in the current fight against de Gaulle, the isolation of the Communists had remained a principle, indeed a condition of the cartel. Mollet tried hard to exorcise the ghost of the Popular Front, stressing that he was not advocating an outright alliance. Nevertheless, his new tactic changed the course and affected the meaning of the campaign. The Socialists were looking to their left; their more moderate allies, hard pressed by de Gaulle's threats and thunder, half tempted by the more conciliatory tone of Debré, often talked as if they were more concerned with avoiding that "irreparable division" of the country that de Gaulle had in their eyes begun to create than with winning the second round against the General. They rejected "unconditional" obedience and the theory of "reserved sectors"—in other words, they wanted a chance of influencing policy, especially foreign policy. But they did not say that they would refuse their support should de Gaulle be willing to pay a price for it. "Reconciliation" thus became an invitation as well as a request.

In the days that preceded the first ballot, it looked as if what had started as a battle between the Fifth and the Fourth (with the Communists supporting on their own the leaders of the latter) had become a struggle between right and left, with the right composed of "intransigent" Gaullists and "conditional," potential allies of the regime. At first the Gaullists did not seem to mind this twist. Even though they stuck to the far more attractive theme used by de Gaulle—renovation vs. chaos, a theme much more likely to appeal to young voters, even of left-wing inclination, than a straight right-wing, anti-Popular Front appeal based on memories and fear—the Gaullist candidates did not refrain from pointing out that Mollet was playing with fire. They hoped that the hatred of Communism would bring many hesitating voters to the UNR, as the most determined of the parties to the right of the Socialists. This was a gamble; so was Mollet's action for, as Fauvet asked in *Le Monde,* what would happen if there were many more Communist votes on the first ballot than in 1958? The Socialists would be faced with having to support their rivals in far more than ten or twelve districts, and as a result they might well get enough left-wing deputies elected to make any working majority impossible. Thus the question had changed from "Would the old parties break de Gaulle's spell?" to "Would there be a polarization of opinion favoring the two extremes of the political spectrum? Would the relentlessness with which 'renovation' had been pushed bring out in a major part of the electorate the traditional left-wing reflex of 'Republican defense' against 'personal power'?"

The Results

The elections of November 18 startled many of the observers who had predicted that General de Gaulle would be in trouble. Here are the statistics:

registered voters	27,535,019	
actual voters	18,934,733	68.75%
abstentions	8,603,286	31.25%
blank or void	601,747	3.17%

SOURCE: *L'Année Politique,* 1962.

The vote on the first ballot had many remarkable features. First, it showed a considerable increase in abstentions: 8,603,286 registered voters did not vote, i.e., 2,300,000 more than in October; the proportion of abstentions—31.25 percent—was the highest in France's legislative elections since the war. The reasons for this increase are not clear: maybe, as has been suggested, many voters were dissatisfied with all the candidates—those of an opposition too strongly tied to an unhappy past as well as the "uncondi-tional" and often uninspired supporters of the chief of state. Maybe many voters, having realized that since 1958 parliament had stopped being the center of power, simply decided that the election of an Assembly was not worth any trouble.

Second, the UNR won a smashing victory. Its candidates and those of the UDT, which had decided to merge with the UNR, collected 5,847,403 votes, i.e., 31.9 percent of the electorate, two and a quarter million more votes than on the first ballot of the 1958 elections. Deputies were elected in 96 districts on November 18, having obtained a majority; 51 of those were Gaullists or sponsored by the Gaullists. If one adds to the votes for the UNR the votes for the other candidates supported by the Association for the Fifth Republic—essentially the dissident Independents, who won 798,092 votes—one finds that the total of "Gaullist" votes in 1962 exceeded that of 1958 by almost two and a half million votes. The explanation is simple: in 1958 all the parties except the Communists claimed that they supported de Gaulle; in 1962 only the Gaullists did. As a result, those voters who put their desire to back the General above their loyalty or sympathy for a party deserted the parties for which they had voted before.

Third, all the members of the late *cartel des non* lost votes. The Independ-ents dropped from 4,502,449 to 1,742,523; the MRP from 2,273,281 to 1,635,442; the Radicals from 1,503,787 to 1,384,998; the Socialists from 3,193,786 to 2,319,662. Among the victims of the slaughter on the first ballot were Paul Reynaud, who lost almost half of the votes he had received in his district in 1958—when he had no Gaullist rival—and Mendès-France, defeated by a Gaullist Independent member of the cabinet. Students of the election results have calculated that "the UNR's gain of 14.4 percent on the first ballot over its vote in 1958 corresponds exactly to the combined per-centage loss of the Right and the MRP." Though on the one hand it ex-ceeded them "in absolute figures by about 300,000,"[6] on the other hand it is unlikely that almost all of the 1,100,000 votes lost by the Socialists and Radicals went into the abstentionists' column, and that none went over to the UNR. Thus it can be said that the UNR found its new voters primarily, but not exclusively, on the conservative side (MRP, Independents).

Fourth, the Communist vote went up very slightly: from 3,870,184 to 3,992,431. Given the increase in the number of abstentions, this meant a rise from 18.9 to 21.78 percent of the votes cast. But this gain was a small one—given the fact that the Communist party had been the only consist-ently anti-Gaullist group, and that it was the only group that ran its cam-paign not only on the theme of opposition to "personal power" but also on a platform that denounced all the social and economic inequities of the re-gime so as to attract all those who were dissatisfied. The Communists were

---

[6] Ehrmann, *op. cit.*, p. 899.

still well below their consistent vote of the Fourth Republic—which was over five million and about 25 percent of the votes.

Fifth, there was practically nothing remaining of the extreme right: its candidates—often former Gaullists who had become bitterly disillusioned by de Gaulle's Algerian policy—got less than 160,000 votes; their defeat in Paris was particularly spectacular.

The Second Ballot: Gaullists vs. Communists

As a result of those figures, the situation looked very different from what many of the opposition leaders had expected. In 203 of the 369 districts in which no deputy had yet been elected, it was the Gaullist candidate who was the leading contender, notably in 30 out of the 31 districts of Paris. Due to Communist progression and Socialist regression, the number of districts in which Communists *and* UNR candidates were ahead of the Socialists was very much higher than the "ten or twelve" predicted by Mollet. There were at least 80 such cases, and in 47 of them the Communist was the leading contender. The problem of alliances and withdrawals became acute.

The parties' reactions accentuated the trend that had become dominant on the eve of the first ballot: the cartel was dead, the battle was between left and right, and all too often this seemed to mean a battle between Communists and Gaullists. The Gaullists were almost certain to have a majority in the new Assembly: they could be defeated only if all the opposition parties agreed on a single candidate on the second ballot. This was extremely unlikely, since in so many districts it was the Communist candidate who was the leading opponent. Since many of the members of the *cartel des non* were anti-Communist first, the Gaullist tactic for the second ballot was simple. Instead of pursuing the battle of de Gaulle vs. the parties of yesteryear, the Gaullists announced, as early as November 19, that their candidates would try to build "a barrage against Communism." Talks were held between Gaullists and MRP candidates to that effect. The Gaullists hoped to get other non-Communist candidates to withdraw in their favor wherever the Gaullist was ahead, and they declared themselves ready to withdraw theirs in favor of the leading non-Communist candidates elsewhere—even if the latter had voted no on October 28. It is worth noting that de Gaulle did not speak again. Not only had he gotten what he wanted, but his intervention could have antagonized those moderates whose withdrawal the UNR was now suggesting.

The leaders of the *cartel des non* made a last effort to define a common tactic. They did not succeed because of Mollet's decision to stop the Gaullist tide and to save seats for the Socialists through his own policy of an electoral entente with the Communists. The Socialists had little chance of salvaging anything if they returned to an alliance with the remains of the *cartel des non*. In his own district Mollet would be reelected only if the MRP contender withdrew for the Gaullist, and the Communist for Mollet. Since it had become clear that the Communists might gain at least as many seats as the Socialists through an entente, the Communists pressed hard for precisely this kind of arrangement. Indeed, their tactics were in some instances quite spectacular. In Arras, a Communist leader told the Communist faithful that "not one vote ought to fail comrade Mollet."

In the last days before the second ballot, the Gaullists hammered on the theme of anti-Communism. Since the anti-Communist reflex of many members of the former opposition had operated, the Gaullists were now certain to have a majority in the Assembly. What remained in doubt was how stable this majority would be. This depended on the number of "Popular Front" alliances aimed at defeating Gaullist candidates and on the willingness of Socialist and Radical voters to switch their votes to Communist candidates in those districts where a Socialist withdrawal in favor of a Communist had been decided. On November 23 Pompidou was once again interviewed on television. He said he had been pleased but not surprised by the consistency of French voters, and went on to denounce the Communists' tactic:

> The Communist party cannot hope to get its candidates elected in most districts. . . . Consequently what it needs and seeks is to find men thanks to whom it could somehow infiltrate the Assembly massively, albeit obliquely. These men—it will turn them today into its prisoners, tomorrow into its accomplices. For once one is elected with Communist votes, one is no longer one's own master.

Mollet, in a round table organized by Radio Europe I on the same day, replied angrily that his main objective was to prevent a party that had obtained only 32 percent of the votes cast from getting a majority of the seats. True, there now was a risk of thirty or forty Communist deputies, not twelve—but they would not play any role in France's political life, whereas the thirty or forty UNR deputies who could otherwise be elected would be "capable of providing that unconditional majority that might destroy French democracy."

During the debate, Mollet's former associates from the cartel carefully avoided polemicizing with him, but they lamented both the "unconditionality" of the winning party and the Communist peril. They repeated that they were "ready to dialogue" with the UNR, and Chaban-Delmas approved. Deserted by their former Socialist ally, dwarfed by a Gaullist group that would not need their services in the new Assembly, having no choice but to back Gaullist candidates in many districts where the alternative would be the election of a Communist, the moderate opposition leaders were in an unhappy fix. This was particularly true of the Independents and MRP, for a number of Radical candidates, despite Maurice Faure's anti-Communism, followed Mollet's example: they withdrew in favor of better placed Communist contestants in return for Communist support where Radicals were ahead, so as to stop the Gaullists.

On the eve of the second ballot, the situation in metropolitan France was as follows. There were 369 districts in which the competition continued. In 227 of these only two candidates remained: in 180 cases, a Gaullist backed by the withdrawing moderates faced a single candidate of the left (94 Communists, 60 Socialists, 25 Radicals, 1 PSU)—i.e., a straight return to the "left-right" cleavage characteristic of the interwar Third Republic. In 36 districts, a champion of the "yes" vote faced a single candidate of the "no" camp; in 2 of those cases, the Socialists and Communists went so far as to support defenders of French Algeria against UNR candidates. In 11 cases, the contest opposed a Communist and an anti-Communist (Socialist or UNR) backed by all non-Communist parties: this is all that was left of the pattern which had prevailed in 1958. In 128 districts, there were 3 candidates: in 82 of those, a Communist faced both a Gaullist and (usually) an Independent, Radical, or MRP candidate.

	FIRST BALLOT			SECOND BALLOT			
	VOTES	PER-CENTAGE OF TOTAL	SEATS	VOTES	PER-CENTAGE OF TOTAL	SEATS	TOTAL SEATS
Communists	3,992,431	21.78	9	3,243,041	21.31	32	41
Other Extreme Left	449,743	2.45		183,844	1.2	2	2
Socialists	2,319,662	12.65	1	2,304,330	15.2	64	65
Radicals	679,812	3.7 ⎫		635,712	4.2 ⎫		
Other Center Left	705,186	3.85 ⎭	8	432,389	2.8 ⎭	34	42
MRP	1,635,452	8.92	14	806,908	5.3	22	36
Independents	1,742,523	9.5	6	1,177,152	7.8	23	29
Extreme Right	159,682	0.87					
UNR	5,847,403	31.9	46	6,165,929	40.51	183	229
Gaullist Independents	798,092	4.36	12	241,853	1.6	8	20

SOURCE: *L'Année Politique, 1962.*

The vote of November 25 produced the following results. First, the Gaullist vote went up: it amounted to 6,407,782 of the total, almost a million and a half more than on the first ballot in these 369 districts. Second, votes of the "traditional left"—Communists, Socialists, and Radicals—increased in percentage slightly by comparison with the first ballot; the main beneficiaries were the Socialists, who got 15.2 percent of the votes cast (by comparison with 12.5 percent on the first ballot), and who gained 277,490 votes in those districts whereas the Communists, PSU, and Radicals lost about 460,000. Obviously some left-wing voters had deserted to the UNR. Third, the Independent and MRP vote went down drastically; together they lost almost

750,000 votes. In other words, the UNR continued to swallow votes at their expense. Fourth, in the case of "Popular Front" alliances, Communist and Socialist voters followed on the whole their parties' instructions: Mollet was elected, thanks to the Communists' votes. Radical voters proved somewhat less docile.

Fifth, with respect to seats in the Assembly, the UNR-UDT obtained 229 altogether—64 more than in 1958 in metropolitan France, more than any party had ever had in a French Assembly, and only 12 less than the absolute majority; but 20 dissident Indépendents elected as allies of the UNR provided the necessary complement. Of the 225 new deputies who entered the House, 121 were Gaullists. The Communists won 41 seats (31 more than in 1958), the Socialists 65 (24 more), the Radicals 42 (1 more): thus the "Popular Front" type of alliance had proved beneficial to the parties of the left—and especially to the Socialists. Whereas the UNR won 103 of its "duels" with Communists (backed, in most of those cases, by the Socialists), it won only 23 of its 58 duels with Socialists (supported, in all those cases, by the Communists). Almost all the seats won by non-Communist candidates, thanks to Communist withdrawals, were in the southern half of France, and 35 out of those 52 were Socialists. Most of the Communist victories came not as the result of duels with the UNR, but in "triangular" battles or against candidates other than the UNR's. Particularly spectacular, however, was the victory of the Radical contender, backed by the Socialists and Communists, against Michel Debré. All of the 31 seats of Paris went to the UNR (an addition of 14); but in the suburbs the Communists got 12 seats (a gain of 7), the UNR only 10 (a loss of 4). The great losers in the Assembly as well as in the electorate were the moderates, torn between their opposition to de Gaulle and their anti-Communism. The MRP lost 20 seats (down to 36), the Independents no less than 78 (down to 28). Motte and Simonnet, among others, lost their seats.

A few important conclusions can be derived from the election. First, in giving the Gaullists so impressive a vote, and de Gaulle a majority in the Assembly, the electorate heeded de Gaulle's call and turned the elections, as he wanted, into a second referendum. A look at the map of the Gaullist vote shows that it is to a large extent similar to the map of the "yes" vote: the three blocs of western, northern, and eastern France are there, whereas the areas of Gaullist weakness are those of the south and center. Just as with the referendum, there is no obvious connection between the level of economic prosperity and the vote. Western France is economically underprivileged and had been the scene of antigovernmental demonstrations by angry farmers, yet it voted for de Gaulle. On the other hand, the Communist vote rose in some very prosperous areas. The reasons for the Gaullist vote were simple: many UNR deputies were elected despite their lack of political experience or of previous contact with their districts, just because they were "the General's men." What they promised was on the one hand support for de Gaulle,

The Referendum of October, 1962

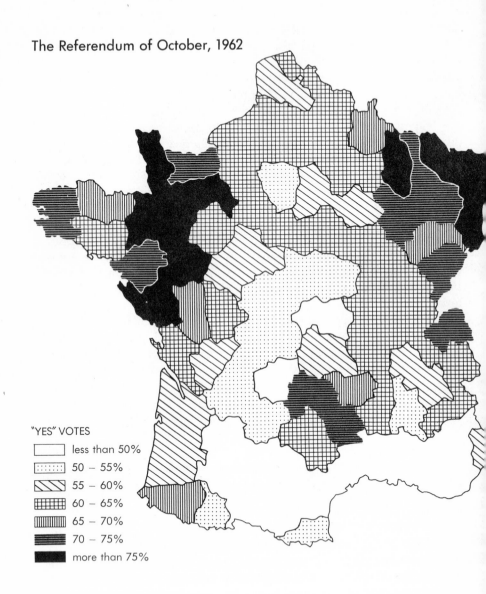

"YES" VOTES

▭	less than 50%
▦	50 – 55%
▨	55 – 60%
▦	60 – 65%
▥	65 – 70%
▬	70 – 75%
■	more than 75%

SOURCE: *Les Élections Législatives de 1962* (Imprimerie Nationale, Paris, 1963). Drawn by Harry Scott.

The Elections of November, 1962

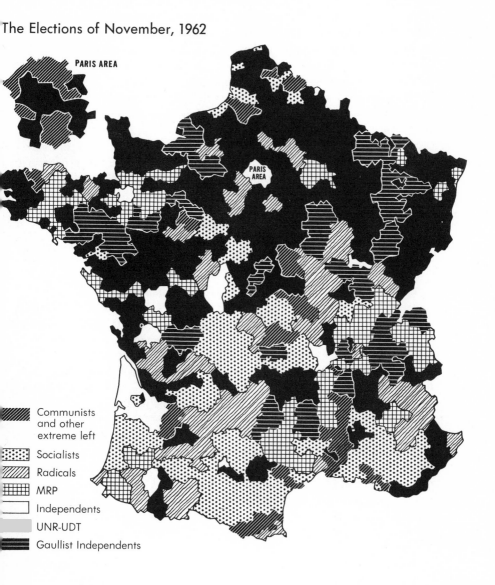

PARIS AREA

PARIS AREA

Communists
and other
extreme left

Socialists

Radicals

MRP

Independents

UNR-UDT

Gaullist Independents

SOURCE: *Les Élections Législatives de 1962* (Imprimerie Nationale, Paris, 1963).
Drawn by Harry Scott.

on the other the defense of local interests—and being the General's men they had a better chance of acting as effective spokesmen for their districts than non-Gaullists.

This effect provided an admirable coincidence of de Gaulle's conception with the voters' wishes. De Gaulle requested support from parliament, and he also wanted the deputies to leave big policy matters to him and to his cabinet: it was enough for them to look after local ones. The voters wanted stability and a channel for the expression of local grievances (pragmatism in the framework of strong government); thus they turned away from those men who represented a discredited past and increasingly irrelevant ideologies and toward those who spoke of the future without presenting a set of dogmas. In the Gaullist Republic, most of the work in defense of special interests was being carried out, not through parliament, but through economic associations of the pressure-group type that cooperate, or struggle, directly with the executive, by-passing parliament. The voters had become used to those new channels and saw no need to restore parliament's bygone importance by endorsing the champions of the traditional representative system. It made more sense to vote for a party that was not likely to rouse parliament from its sleep.

Second, however, the vote for the Gaullists was not as impressive as the vote for de Gaulle: not every "yes" was turned into support for a Gaullist-sponsored candidate. This was particularly noticeable in northern France, in Brittany, and in central France, where the figure of Gaullist votes was significantly lower than the national average percentage of "yes" votes that were turned into Gaullist votes on November 18. (That national average was 51 percent on the first ballot.) In those areas, many voters who had supported the General in October despite the "parties of yesteryear" remained faithful to those parties—Communists and Socialists in the north, Independents and MRP in Brittany and in the center.

What turned the Gaullist "wave" into a parliamentary majority was—as paradoxically as in 1958—the very electoral law that had been supposed to weaken parties. Proportional representation would have given only about one hundred and fifty deputies to the Gaullists, and as many as one hundred to the Communists; a multi-member district system with majority vote would have obliged the Gaullists on the second ballot to accept many non-Gaullists on their local slates of candidates in order to avoid being overtaken by "Popular Front" slates.

Third, the election of 1962 consolidated the transformation of the French political landscape that had startled observers in 1958. From 1958 to 1962, true enough, the traditional left (Communists, Socialists, and Radicals) kept the same percentage of the total vote (43 percent): thus it could be argued that the rise in the Gaullist vote represented only a reshuffling of votes within the right. However, such an analysis does not go far enough. On the one hand, in 1956 the left had collected 56 percent of the vote: it suffered huge losses from 1956 to 1958 and the sudden switch during the 1962 campaign (from a "yes-no" to a "left-right" division) did not help the left recoup its losses. On the other hand, the fact that within the right the UNR had gradually weakened the MRP and—between 1958 and 1962—crushed the Independents meant that the new right was profoundly different from the old one.

The change in the right shows that the conservative electorate had become disenchanted with its previous representatives, who were too deeply committed to a parliamentary system that had proved inefficient and that had left "the people absent." The once-powerful Independents were notables with solid local positions and a deep attachment to the traditional values of a predominantly rural society; the new representatives were essentially pragmatic "modernists," with fleeting local links, relative independence from the notables, and a genuine concern for the economic and social aspects of an increasingly industrial and "planned" society. The old Independents and the socially moderate Radicals stood for both a system of government and a society that were obsolete. The forces that had profited from postwar social changes—business, the new middle classes of technicians and employees, the more efficient farmers—were more attracted by the UNR than by either the old-time conservatives or the somewhat unexciting MRP, too deeply involved in the fiasco of the Fourth Republic. In this respect, to present the victory of the UNR and the slight increase in the Communist vote as progress for the "extremes" is misleading, for there was nothing "extreme" about the UNR, either in its platform or in its electorate. It is a huge center-right party, comparable to the Radical party in the last period of the Third Republic after its passage from the role of militant opposition to that of a "managing" party of government.

Fourth, this transformation of the political landscape has not affected the left nearly as deeply as the right. Because the left is essentially the collector of discontent, the parties of the left have been able to capitalize on inequities and to turn protest against the regime itself without any need to revamp their own structures or doctrines. The biggest political force on the left remains the Communist party. It has been weakened by de Gaulle but not visibly undermined; the loss of seats in parliament is no indication of its real power, since it results only from juggling the electoral law and can be remedied at least partly by opportune alliances, as in 1962. Its bulk and presence—in 1962–64 as well as in the Resistance days of 1942–44— serve to immobilize the Socialist party, just as car lights fascinate and immobilize a rabbit.

Conclusion: Toward a New Political System?

The crisis of the fall of 1962 was a turning point in the history of the French political system. On the surface, it provides us with a spectacular demonstration of de Gaulle's political skill and methods. He got what he wanted when he wanted it, through shock tactics that frightened the timid and the scrupulous, enraged his targets, but delivered the goods, thus providing him not only with the reform he requested but also—for the first time—with a majority entirely composed of his own followers. But the meaning of the crisis goes deeper.

The first phase of the Fifth Republic could be seen as an attempt at achieving a kind of synthesis between the two types of French regimes of the past: representative regimes in which the representatives occupied the center of the stage and made effective, strong, and stable government impossible, and "savior" regimes in which a Great Man provided such government at the expense of the representatives. The Constitution of 1958 tried both to maintain the main feature of France's previous representative systems—i.e., parliamentarism—and to institutionalize strong government in the dual form of a solid cabinet and a powerful President. In practice, by 1962 the Gaullist regime had come close to the "savior" pole—insofar as the function of the representatives had been steadily reduced and the role of the President (rather than the cabinet) increased. But the procedure of selection of the President and the continuing divisions of French parties made it possible (and led de Gaulle to fear) that after the General the regime would veer back to the representative pole. The reform of 1962 was an attempt at blowing up the road back to the Fourth Republic by making sure that the dominant organ would be the presidency.

De Gaulle's version of the ideal political system is definitely close to the "savior" extreme; it is hostile to, or suspicious of, traditional representative channels. Convinced that French parties (in contrast, for instance, to British and American ones) are essentially selfish and splintering factions, he wants a regime in which the nation would be represented by one man endowed with the power to act. De Gaulle's conception focuses on the President. It will be his task to cooperate with parliament, but should parliament prove unwilling to support him, he must be given, and must exercise, the means of governing despite its opposition. In order to play such a role, he must be "the man of the nation," "the only one to hold and to delegate the authority of the state." This means that he cannot behave as merely the leader of a party, and that the cabinet must be his organ, not just "the product of a combination of groups." He must govern—with the parties' support if he has it, despite the parties if not: he can use either new elections or a referendum or both in order to overcome their resistance. This was exactly what he did in 1962. His behavior then was a preview of what he had in mind, his success a model of what he wishes.

It is a dramatic conception. But it poses serious problems, for it requires, in effect, a succession of de Gaulles. Another President, even being elected by the people, may not be as imperious and impervious a gambler; he may not have either the energy and authority to use the weapons the Constitution gives him in order to force parliament to behave, or the skill and prestige to get the people—through referendums and new elections—to support him against a hostile parliament, even if he uses those weapons. In other words, the new Constitution makes parliamentary predominance much more unlikely, but it does not of itself ensure presidential supremacy.

Nor does the new Constitution ensure stability. Indeed, it may lead to violent conflicts. The German Constitution of the Weimar Republic—which also provided both for a popularly elected President and for a cabinet responsible to parliament—is a sinister precedent: one extreme alternative could be a kind of *coup d'état* by the President, using his emergency powers to maintain himself against parliament. The dual executive may turn out to be the Achilles' heel of the system. In de Gaulle's version there is no duality, for the Premier is subordinated to the President. But a parliament hostile to the President could make his life miserable by harassing or destroying his Premiers, and a parliament dominated by a majority opposed to him could impose its own Premier, i.e., try to detach the Premier from his present position as appendage of the chief of state and turn him into the President's rival. The existence of the Premier—the last remnant of parliamentarism—introduces into the system a permanent temptation for parliamentarian "games, poisons, and delights" and a ferment of insecurity.

Thus for the regime to function smoothly, there will have to be *not* the situation de Gaulle seems to envisage—i.e., a President as lion-tamer facing cowed lions—*but* a transformation of the party system which will make executive-legislative conflicts the exception rather than the norm. If the party system remains unreformed, even de Gaulle's new system may prove inadequate. The irony of the situation lies in the fact that with a reformed party system—for instance, a reduction to only two major parties—there would be stability and effective government even with a parliamentary Constitution— even with the Constitution of 1958, or even with that of the Fourth Republic! Michel Debré, on November 23, wisely told a press conference that should the French political system at last be able to provide majorities in parliament, the problem of institutions would become secondary.

Now, what makes the events of the fall of 1962 so interesting is, first, that they demonstrated the truth of Debré's proposition: it is because de Gaulle won a majority in parliament that he has been able to govern since 1962 without massive resort to the panoply of whips and lashes the Constitution gives to the lion-tamer, i.e., in a relaxed constitutional atmosphere, as if he were a British Premier assured of his party's support in the House of Commons. Thus he enjoys, in his foreign policy, a freedom from domestic restraints that no other Western leader knows and that he exploits to the hilt. Second, those events are important for another reason as well: given the fact that until now the French party system has not been rejuvenated, de Gaulle's political operation tends, on the one hand, to strengthen the President's hand until such a change has come into effect and, on the other, to put maximum pressure on the parties to reform. He himself may well be convinced that French parties will not improve anyhow (hence the need for a "man of the nation" above them); but, as Debré has said, whatever de Gaulle's actual motives and beliefs may be, the *result* of his actions could be to transform the party scene. As we saw earlier, the Constitution of 1958, and subsequent practice, had had little effect on it. This is no longer the case.

The events of 1962 administered two shocks to the old parties. First, the constitutional change made it clear that in the future French political life would be focused *not* on the legislative elections but on the presidential one: the change thus tends to force the parties out of their sleep and their nostalgia by making the conquest of the presidency rather than the restoration of parliament their necessary objective. This change in target entails a need for alliances, coalitions, mergers. In particular, it weakens the Communist party in the long run, for no Communist has a chance of being elected President. Thus Communist *voters* can be expected to vote for non-Communist candidates in order not to waste their votes; knowing this, such candidates will have no particular incentive to make deals with or concessions to the Communist *party*. Second, the French electorate in November, 1962, acted to a large extent as if a presidential system existed already—i.e., as if the referendum had amounted to the election of de Gaulle by universal suffrage; thus the voters sent to the Assembly a majority of the same "color" as the President. This second shock, administered by the voters themselves, was even more stinging than the constitutional reform, for it dashed the hopes the old parties might still have harbored of turning parliament into a fortress of resistance against, and perhaps a base for a future reversal of, the new presidential system. The very obstinacy of the old parties, their apparent refusal to change between 1958 and 1962, the purely negative tone of their campaign in September–October, 1962, proved their undoing. In a way, they committed suicide in order not to die.

But if the events of 1962 were important, were they decisive enough to provide the streamlined political system desired by Debré? The two shocks have indeed put pressure on the old parties, but is the intensity of this pressure sufficient? On the one hand, the establishment of a presidential regime does not suffice to create a two-party system: in many Latin American countries, the popularly elected President has to cope with a fragmented and often hostile parliament. On the other hand, the behavior of the electorate in November, 1962, although encouraging, is not decisive: after all, only half of the Frenchmen who voted yes in October were consistent in their November vote. Also, when faced with a UNR landslide, the non-Communist "parties of yesteryear" did not choose to coalesce, thus foreshadowing a sensible "regrouping" of the French party scene: the *cartel des non* split, with the Socialists and many Radicals looking for electoral salvation in the direction of the Communists. In other words, it was a traditional reflex which took over, not a calculation turned toward the future, for the least one can say is that a lasting alliance or merger of the three "left-wing" parties is hardly either a likely prospect for the future or an encouraging one. There are too many deep differences between the Communists and the other two groups for such an alliance to be solid, and the Communist party is too obviously the strongest of the three for any such grouping to be healthy.

Thus if it is true that the ultimate success of de Gaulle's reform depends on the transformation of the party system, all that can be said at present is that the events of the fall of 1962 provided both highly favorable *and* disturbing factors. The favorable ones we have pointed out. The disturbing ones are inextricably linked with the very nature of the regime and the style of the operation; they are all serious and likely to delay a reorganization that is made difficult anyhow by the parties' resilience, divisions, animosities, and divergent interests. Yet none of the disturbing factors is necessarily fatal. First, the party that has become dominant is not an ordinary party. It is thoroughly dependent on de Gaulle (who paradoxically refuses to be its leader), and it is a mass of executants rather than a force that participates in decision-making; consequently its capacity to survive as a major force after de Gaulle is in doubt. Debré has expressed the hope that its very weight and size would oblige all the other parties to change their ways; but as long as they can hope that it will melt after de Gaulle, this will not necessarily be the case—unless de Gaulle remains in office for very many more years. This is, of course, not impossible. The longer the regime lasts, the more the UNR, whose cohesion has been impressive, has a stake in its own survival.

Second, the very vigor and determination with which de Gaulle's war against the old parties has been waged have, in the short run, made the "regrouping" of parties more difficult by reviving left-wing reflexes that delay such a change. De Gaulle's tactics helped the Communists break out of their quarantine. They also shoved the Socialists away from those elements of the opposition to de Gaulle that may have been both too weak electorally and too hesitant to protect the Socialist party from the Gaullist landslide, but with which a "regrouping" may, in the long run, have been most sensible. The Socialists (as in 1943–44–45) have preferred to save their autonomy and identity through a purely electoral alliance with the Communists. This spares them at present the need for an agonizing reappraisal of their plight. It also strengthens the purely negative grip the Communists have over French political life, thus offsetting for the time being the blow that the creation of a presidential system administers to Communism. A "regrouping" limited to the MRP, Independents, and those Radicals not inclined to imitate the Socialists may prove to be both too limited and too difficult. In other words, a complete transformation of the French political scene requires that there appear on the left a personality capable of revolutionizing the picture, just as de Gaulle has redesigned it on the right. This means, in particular, finding a way of "lifting the Communist mortgage" by getting the party's voters away from the party. Given the *immobilism* of Mollet, it may be that such a personality will have to be imposed from the outside, just as de Gaulle was. The current attempt by a variety of nonpartisan clubs and union leaders to launch the candidacy of a rather unorthodox Socialist, Gaston Defferre, for the presidency of the Republic constitutes precisely such an effort. For, while a man of the left, he refuses to negotiate deals with either the Communists or even his own party, so as not to tie his hands—in a manner that reminds one of de Gaulle.

Third, de Gaulle's own methods may not have served the cause of constitutional stability. In order to bolster France's constitutional system, he had to adopt a highly debatable procedure for revision. Also, he sticks to a conception of the presidency that may prove unworkable after him. Many people sympathetic to his overall constitutional design nevertheless regret that it places parliament in a permanently inferior position and gives the President alone the power to resort to referendums. Consequently, the legitimacy of the new constitutional system is far from assured. In a country in which the old ideological issues are fading, the debate on institutions may well continue. But it is possible to hope that this will be a debate on details: that the principle of a popularly based presidency is here to stay and that the traditional form of French parliamentarism is a thing of the past.

The fate of the new system depends ultimately on the behavior of the parties: the new system in the long run should oblige them to change, even if little change develops as long as de Gaulle—so widely seen as unbeatable —remains around and dominates the scene.

Selected Bibliography

The collection of *Le Monde* for the year of 1962 is the best source of information. Very useful also is *L'Année Politique 1962,* Presses Universitaires de France, Paris, 1963, with a preface by Edgar Faure; in addition to its summary of the year's events, it reproduces many important documents. The Fondation Nationale des Sciences Politiques has published two mimeographed volumes of speeches and debates, *La Campagne électorale Oct.–Nov. 1962.*

The subject matter in this chapter has also been analyzed in the following books and articles:

ANDREWS, WILLIAM G. "Evreux 1962: The Referendum and Elections in a Norman Constituency," *Political Studies,* vol. XI, no. 3, October, 1963, pp. 308–26.

EHRMANN, HENRY W. "Direct Democracy in France," *American Political Science Review,* vol. LVII, no. 4, December, 1963, pp. 883–901.

GOGUEL, FRANÇOIS. L'Electorat gaulliste," *Nouvelle Frontière,* no. 5, January, 1964, pp. 25–31.

GOLDEY, DAVID B. "The French Referendum and Elections of 1962: The National Campaigns," *Political Studies,* vol. XI, no. 3, October, 1963, pp. 287–307.

HOFFMANN, STANLEY. "Stability and Succession in France," *Journal of International Affairs,* vol. XVIII, no. 1, 1964, pp. 86–103.

MACRIDIS, ROY C., and BROWN, BERNARD E. *Supplement to the De Gaulle Republic,* Dorsey Press, Homewood, Ill., 1963.
RÉMOND, RENÉ. "L'Enigme de l'UNR," *Esprit,* February, 1963, pp. 307–19.
Revue Française de Science Politique, vol. XIII, no. 2, June, 1963, "La Vie politique sous la Vᵉ République": articles by François Goguel, A. L., René Rémond, and Claude Neuschwander.
WILLIAMS, PHILIP. "The French Referendum and Elections of Oct.–Nov. 1962," *Parliamentary Affairs,* vol. XVI, no. 2, pp. 165–173.

Study Questions

1. Were there any alternatives to de Gaulle's course of action? If so, what were they?

2. Why did de Gaulle feel that a presidential system is more stable than a parliamentary one? How far is the success of de Gaulle's presidential system really dependent on maintaining control of parliament through a dominant party?

3. What changes did de Gaulle create in the French party system by virtue of his insistence on the direct election of the President? Given the factors that cause French voters to choose party identifications, what kinds of regroupings would you expect?

4. Did the use of a referendum to make such a significant decision strengthen or weaken the French political system?

5. Have the various French parties behaved during this crisis (a) as they had previously behaved in France's parliamentary regimes, (b) as parties ordinarily behave in other parliamentary regimes, (c) as parties in a presidential system tend to behave?

3

A Free Press in a Democratic State?

The Spiegel Case

Otto Kirchheimer
Constantine Menges

On October 27, 1963, a strange kind of national birthday party was held in Germany. Radio, television, and the press joined the star performer, ex-Minister of Defense Franz Josef Strauss, in presenting their stories on the first anniversary of the *Spiegel* affair. Only the federal prosecutor was missing from the gala reunion—rightly so, because the other participants had all made their contributions in the exciting autumn and winter days that followed the government's attempt to smash the mirror which had so often cast back unflattering reflections. Only the legal brethren—judges and prosecutors—were laggards, still working overtime and hoping to have their contribution ready by the second anniversary.

On the evening of Friday, October 26, 1962, black vans filled with a special commando unit of the Federal Criminal Police converged on Hamburg's central press office building. Within minutes, the police occupied the offices of the *Spiegel* ("Mirror"), Germany's most outspoken weekly newsmagazine, began impounding documents, cleared all the rooms, and took two editors into custody. At the same time, other police units were searching the *Spiegel*'s Bonn offices and had spread a dragnet for Rudolf Augstein, the *Spiegel*'s publisher, and Conrad Ahlers, its military affairs editor. At about 4 the following morning, in far-off Spain, Ahlers and his wife were yanked out of bed by the Spanish police and thrown into prison at the request of the German military attaché.

The reason for these nocturnal police raids was tersely stated in an official announcement:

> On the grounds of having published information dealing with important defense questions in such a manner as to threaten the security and freedom of the German people, the business quarters of the newsmagazine the *Spiegel* in Hamburg and Bonn have been searched at the order of the investigating judge of the Federal Court.[1]

Specifically the charge against the *Spiegel* was *treason,* through intentional publication of classified military information.

What was so unusual about these events? In the thirteen years of the Federal Republic's existence, never before had anything so dramatic and extraordinary occurred. Disloyalty had remained the province of rather placid, only occasionally energetic, and sporadically subversive Communists operating from outside bases or of minor, rightist, crackpot groups. The political system could be characterized as one of sluggish competition between well-behaved parties acting primarily in response to the demands and pressures of well-organized interest groups. As prosperity increased, the population took only a modicum of interest in the day-to-day activities of these parties, so that politics, as in many other industrial Western countries, increasingly became the affair of the professional politician and his interest-group colleagues. In Germany, state authority came to be symbolized by the Chancellor and senior citizen (Adenauer) who combined the qualities of a somewhat cynical professional politician with the traditional civic virtues of steadfastness, discipline, and national purpose. The impression of orderliness was enhanced by the usual German reliance on the rigid functioning of administrative routine. The government bureaucracy performed smoothly, even though its reputation for incorruptibility had been somewhat tarnished.

Since this system now had functioned for thirteen years without any but minor changes in the Christian Democratic Union, the ruling party, and without any major domestic political upheavals, the CDU had developed some of the confidence and proprietary attitudes that come with long tenure. The domestic political confrontations that occurred at four-year intervals were increasingly devoid of substantive dispute, and their outcome served to confirm the existing political line with some slight variations. Foes and critics would contend that politics in the Federal Republic was merely a reflection of economic well-being and the cold war context.

How would such a system function in the event of an internal political

---

[1] Press and Information Office of the Federal Republic of Germany, *Bulletin des Presse und Informationsamtes der Bundesregierung,* Bonn, November 6, 1962.

crisis? How would the various political actors make use of the democratic possibilities in defending their position or attacking their adversaries? Would the public be content to remain passive and let the professionals decide matters in good back-room fashion? Or would it be drawn in, and if so how?

We shall now turn to the two main protagonists in Germany's political drama: Franz Josef Strauss and the *Spiegel*.

In 1946 the military government lifted the year-long ban on political parties in Bavaria, and former First Lieutenant and *Landrat* (rural county administrator) F. J. Strauss rushed to join the Christian Social Union (CSU) —successor to the Weimar Republic's Bavarian People's party. As is usual when long-suppressed parties attempt to reestablish themselves, a struggle for power broke out between the former leaders, who were older and more conservative, and the would-be leaders, who were younger and more pragmatic. Strauss cast his formidable energy and oratorical skill on the side of the rebels, and their success was reflected in his job advancement within the state government and his increased political stature within the party.

Strauss worked ceaselessly for the party's success in the first state elections, campaigning in every corner of Bavaria; and after the CSU's comfortable victory, he continued his political travels around Bavaria, this time with the intention of bettering his position within the party. Given the provincial milieu of Bavaria and the easy, unsophisticated nature of most of his colleagues, it is not surprising that the dynamic and adaptable Strauss was among the handful in the party who easily reached positions of leadership. Less than three years after joining the party, Strauss's political base in Bavaria was secure: he was chosen secretary general of the CSU, the semi-autonomous Bavarian counterpart and hitherto permanent coalition partner of the reigning CDU, and shortly afterward, in 1949, was made chairman of the CSU faction in the Federal Republic's first national parliament.

Strauss first gained national attention in 1952 during a fierce parliamentary debate, when he used his knowledge of defense policy issues and facts— garnered as chairman of the parliament's Military Affairs Committee—to rescue Chancellor Konrad Adenauer from the onslaught of the Social Democrats, whose party (the SPD) has a ninety-year history as an ideological spokesman for the German worker. Despite the immediate rumors that Strauss would be named the Federal Republic's first Minister of Defense, Adenauer appointed Strauss minister without portfolio to his second cabinet in 1953, and in 1954 chose him to head the newly created Ministry for Atomic Affairs. For two years Strauss displayed his formidable capacity for absorbing and utilizing complex technical information. Then, in October 1956, Strauss's hopes were fulfilled when Adenauer appointed him Minister of Defense.

In the four preceding years the Social Democrats had been unceasingly opposed to the government's intention to rearm, with Strauss having to content himself with promoting the official defense policy from the sidelines. As parliamentary spokesman, Strauss had judged correctly that the widespread domestic and international implications of German military policies would assure him a prominent voice in German and European politics. With skill and energy he exploited his new position to the full and quickly established his ascendancy in the CDU-CSU, both as uncontested military spokesman and as runner-up for national leadership. In numerous public speeches and appearances, he gave the government's general anti-Communist and pro-Western policy a sharper and more militant profile. Quite naturally, his zeal in baiting the Social Democrats and in mocking their stand won him many friends and many enemies as well. But the Bavarians were very proud of their native son, and when the job fell vacant in March, 1961, the CSU elected him chairman, a position that assured him control over his fief and through it over the vote of the CSU faction that constituted an indispensable part of the government bloc.

The Spiegel

Not alone among the minister's enemies was the newsmagazine the *Spiegel,* but after 1960 it was to be counted as the most formidable of his foes.

The importance of the press as a means of shaping public discussion in Germany today is a result of several important postwar trends in European political behavior. Most important of these is the general decline of parliamentary conflict in the wake of the consensus on the welfare functions of the state and the consequent removal from the political arena of many issues that had formerly been bitterly contested. Moreover, especially in the case of divided Germany, the cold war has "internationalized" many political issues and removed them as subjects of domestic political debate and contention. Concurrently, the major political parties, which before the war primarily concerned themselves with ideology and the promotion of abstract goals, have become far more interested in maintaining stability and in fulfilling the mandates of the assorted interest groups that support them. The entire postwar history of Germany's SPD tells the story of ideology's decline and, especially since 1959, of the adoption of pragmatic programs designed to win the support of diverse social groups.

Under these conditions the communications media, if independent and resourceful, are left with golden opportunities for the exploration of controversial issues. The German newspapers, however, appear bent more on commercial success than on involvement in political controversy. Lacking a muckraking tradition and content to accept official versions of events, the typical German newspaper tends to offer the reader long-winded articles that build a maximum of interpretation on a minimum of facts.

In sharp contrast to this blandness, the *Spiegel* has since 1946 specialized in penetrating, fact-filled, and at times jarring exposés of hypocrisy and malfeasance in government, business, political parties, and most other sectors of the German polity. Rather than waiting for news handouts or for things to "happen," the *Spiegel*, with its own full-time research staff, library, and extensive archives, has been able to do its own investigations of current events and special topics. The *Spiegel's* boldness in criticism and its often startling accuracy in the detailed information it divulges have led many disgruntled or concerned persons to bring issues and information to the attention of the *Spiegel* editors—even more than sometimes occurs in the case of American political columnists, who seem to have innumerable "inside" sources. While government officials may have given little attention to parliamentary doings, there always has been considerable curiosity and at times anxiety about what the "Mirror" would next reveal.

The *Spiegel's* commercial success, as indicated by the increase in circulation from approximately 200,000 in 1949 to 483,000 the week before the start of the affair in 1962, owes as much to its style as to its substance. Mixing essential, irrelevant, and at times slightly lascivious information, the *Spiegel* writes stories that appeal not just to politically interested and influential readers but also to those who like a peek into the intimate affairs and foibles of the powerful. The latter are given the illusion of full participation in the events described, while the former are furnished with factually provocative material for further discussion, in particular through well-planned interviews. These interviews, quite unlike the parliamentary question periods, force government notables to give coherent explanations of policies and motivations.

Following the SPD's 1959 shift toward a so-called embracement strategy aiming at agreement with the CDU where possible as a prelude to being admitted to the government in a CDU-SPD coalition, it seemed to many that the *Spiegel* was practically the only voice of opposition and criticism in West Germany. Beginning in the spring of 1961, the course of the *Spiegel's* campaigns against Strauss's conduct of his office, and later against his views on defense policy, strongly reinforced the opinion of many observers, both inside and outside West Germany, that the *Spiegel* was essential to the survival of effective opposition and criticism in Germany. These campaigns are also the prelude to the *Spiegel* affair.

The Spiegel *Probes Strauss's Affairs*

Although neutral and even somewhat friendly to the new Defense Minister in 1956, the *Spiegel* was to become increasingly critical of Strauss's policies. More important, it came to keep an unrelenting vigil over what it considered his unbridled desire for power and his insensitivity to the informal requirements of a democratic political context—personal and rhetorical restraint. By March, 1961, when the CSU elected Strauss its leader, the *Spiegel* commented darkly:

Three weeks ago, F. J. Strauss at the age of 45 took the next to last step to the chancellorship. . . . The Federal Republic, its back to the wall, has to make a decision on Strauss, either accepting him or shaking him off. Without the agreement of the CSU—under the present division of seats in the parliament . . . it is impossible to choose a chancellor.[2]

In his five years as Defense Minister, Strauss became increasingly controversial and, naturally, the subject of many disparaging comments, cartoons, and jokes. Though fiery-tongued himself, the thin-skinned Strauss often used the technique of initiating libel suits against critics—a technique that he and other German politicians had found beneficially intimidating. Strauss was successful in preventing the further dissemination of the above-quoted *Spiegel* article, but two months later, on May 31, 1961, the *Spiegel* dropped a bombshell on its "friend" that no lawsuit could muffle.

The Fibag Affair

In the May 31, 1961, *Spiegel,* an article titled "Hans and Franz" charged Strauss with serious abuse of his official position. According to the *Spiegel,* Hans Kapfinger, owner of a politically important Bavarian newspaper and intimate friend of Strauss, had joined with a would-be architect of six months' university training to form a company (Fibag) in the hope of securing a 75–million–dollar U.S. army housing construction contract. The *Spiegel* said that Kapfinger signed an agreement promising to "use all his influence in order to promote this project" for which he would receive thirty thousand dollars. The *Spiegel* further alleged that Strauss then wrote the U.S. Secretary of Defense a "to whom it may concern" letter recommending the Fibag Company for the contract and, after an interval, wrote a second, personal letter, directly and emphatically recommending the Fibag Company. Completing its accusations, the *Spiegel* quoted an alleged letter from Strauss to his Bavarian friend Kapfinger: "I don't think we should push the Americans too much, since I know from past experience it leads to negative reactions." Public reaction to these accusations of influence peddling—behavior that is not common in Germany—was predictably partisan, perhaps even more so since the national elections were but six months off.

On June 15 the SPD parliamentary group sent Minister Strauss a detailed questionnaire about the *Spiegel*'s accusations. After four weeks, Strauss returned a two-page reply in which he avowed that he had "no official connection with any project or enterprise of Dr. Kapfinger" and that "the Minister of Defense . . . knows nothing about any project in which Dr. Kapfinger has a business interest." Clearly, either the *Spiegel* or Strauss was abusing the truth.

But the elections and, more important, the crisis initiated by the building

---

[2] Erich Kuby et al., *Franz Josef Strauss: Ein Typus Unserer Zeit* (Verlag Kurt Desch, Munich, 1963), p. 206.

of the Berlin wall obscured the Fibag matter, despite the *Spiegel's* efforts to keep the issue alive in 1961. Six months later, in February, 1962, Strauss resorted to his favorite branch of the government, the judiciary, and initiated a libel suit against the *Spiegel* in order to "clear his name" in the Fibag matter. He quietly dropped it a year later. The *Spiegel* countered Strauss's much-publicized legal offensive by a special "Fibag Issue," which presented photostats of all the correspondence in which Strauss and the Fibag people had engaged, complete with numerous notations in Strauss's own handwriting. This and other impressive evidence was coupled with a loud question, "Why were the numerous public denials and Strauss's false reply to parliament being allowed to stand unchallenged?"

Gerhard Jahn, the legal secretary of the SPD parliamentary faction, urged his party colleagues to demand a parliamentary investigating committee. According to article 44 of the Basic Law (the constitution that the Federal Republic adopted at its founding in 1949), any 25 percent of the *Bundestag* may request a committee of investigation. Recalling their experience with ten previous committees, however, the SPD leaders were reluctant to try again. Everything in the German parliament is handled by proportional representation of the parties, with the result that in the investigating committees the minority proposes while the majority, which until then had always controlled the chairmanship, disposes. Instead of attempting to establish the facts impartially, the majority attempts to avoid political damage to its party colleagues in the government. In the United States, Congress frequently unites in opposition to the executive branch and investigation can be controlled by a single chairman who is a party maverick. In Germany there is no such chance for a political inquiry. The prevailing spirit was well expressed by the CDU chairman of the judiciary committee: "We don't believe in scoring any points for the opponent."

Nevertheless, the SPD did request an investigation, which took place in April. In June the majority presented a report concluding: "It cannot be said that Defense Minister Strauss's behavior was improperly motivated . . . his main purpose was to assist the American allies by expediting the construction project." To complete the whitewash, the CDU sponsored a parliamentary resolution that would have completely cleared Strauss had not the FDP (Free Democratic party) members balked. The resolution failed to pass, leaving the Fibag question open. Determined to obtain complete vindication, the CDU set October 25, 1962, as the date for another attempt at parliamentary absolution.

The Barth Affair

The spring of 1962 was a busy time for Strauss, thanks to the *Spiegel*. In May, following the Fibag hearings, another *Spiegel* accusation led to Strauss's appearance before parliament's Defense Committee. This time, the *Spiegel* alleged that Strauss had abused the rights of an air force officer. As told by the *Spiegel,* Strauss had demoted Wing Commander Barth after two of his pilots had accidentally flown their jets across the East German border to Berlin. Using the legal procedures established for the specific purpose of giving armed forces personnel access to regular administrative remedies, Barth appealed Strauss's decision before the Armed Forces Section of the Federal Disciplinary Court. The court called six generals, including the air force commander, as witnesses. But despite its urgent requests, Strauss's personal representative, State Secretary Volkmar Hopf, insisted on the minister's order that no armed forces officer would be permitted to testify in this case. Strauss did not stop there. When the disciplinary court came to a decision favorable to Barth, Strauss released the decision five months later, only after he learned that the *Spiegel* was preparing an exposé.[3]

Three days after the *Spiegel* story appeared, Strauss testified in secret session before the Defense Committee, claiming that the "security of the nation" and "consideration for NATO" were among the reasons he had forbidden the officers to testify. Strauss selected excerpts from the decision of the court in such a way that even the SPD committee members were persuaded to join the CDU and FDP in voting that his behavior had been "completely correct."

But this was not the end of the matter. Gerhard Jahn, who shortly before had insisted on the Fibag investigation, found that in five instances the excerpts Strauss had read from the court's opinion had reversed the original meaning to favor his position. The *Spiegel* obtained (in a manner we shall discuss later) a copy of the then still classified transcript of Strauss's testimony and called attention to his action by printing excerpts from the testimony and the also classified text of the court's opinion. But nothing came of these revelations. The CDU-CSU's majority seemed to make Strauss immune to parliamentary censure.

A month before the case broke, the *Spiegel* again opened a campaign against Strauss's private doings. This time he was accused of abusing his official position by awarding defense contracts to personal and family intimates.

The Defense Debate

But the many unresolved questions the Fibag and Barth affairs raised caused Strauss's political position within the country and the CDU to deteriorate at the beginning of summer in 1962. Recognizing this fact, Strauss had announced that during the summer he would decide whether or not to resign as Defense Minister in order to campaign for the job of Bavarian Minister President in that state's fall election. As if to help him decide to leave Bonn,

---

[3] Barth's wife had decided that the only place help could be found was the *Spiegel* and had taken her appeal to the editors.

in June the *Spiegel* printed the first of several detailed, sharply critical analyses of Strauss's defense policy. The last article of the series appeared in October, after Strauss had decided to stay on as Defense Minister, and this article was the proximate cause for the government's arrest of the *Spiegel* editors on treason charges.

The 1962 defense debate in which the *Spiegel* so energetically intervened was only the latest episode in the ten-year-long national debate over defense policy—a debate that had several distinct phases. From 1950 to 1955 the main issue was whether or not Germany should rearm and become a member of a Western defense alliance. Chancellor Adenauer and the CDU felt that only through close political and military cooperation with western Europe and the United States could a defeated and disgraced Germany regain its position in the Atlantic community and in time secure unification at an acceptable political cost. In diametric opposition, the SPD, and for a time the FDP, joined many sectors of the German press—including the *Spiegel*—in calling for an "Eastern policy" of contact with the Soviet bloc and disengagement from the cold war. Consistent with this policy, the SPD opposed Germany's entrance into the European Coal and Steel Community and the Common Market, as well as NATO. When Germany joined NATO in May, 1955, the SPD shifted its attention to the kind of army Germany should have. It strongly opposed a large, conscript army for Germany. As a military reason for this position, the SPD said that large armies were unnecessary in an age of nuclear weapons. Here the SPD was in agreement with the military doctrine underlying the "new look" strategy of the Eisenhower administration, whereby the United States intended to deter Soviet provocations by threats of nuclear war while the local military balance in Europe would be maintained by increasing NATO's tactical nuclear weapon capability rather than its troop strength. But at the same time the SPD violently opposed the stationing of any nuclear weapons on German soil and especially NATO's plans to provide the *Bundeswehr* with the training and equipment to use tactical atomic weapons, arguing that this would make Germany the most likely battlefield in an atomic war.

In 1956 Chancellor Adenauer and the CDU initially opposed the American reliance on nuclear weapons, but after brief resistance the German government abandoned this preference for a conventional-force strategy and accepted the NATO tactical nuclear weapons doctrine. Strauss personally had always favored atomic weapons. Beginning in March, 1958, the SPD's opposition to NATO and nuclear weapons waned, and in 1960 the party endorsed the American doctrine of nuclear defense.

Several months later, however, a new President with different military views took office in the United States and immediately began efforts to alter NATO's policies for defending Europe. The Kennedy administration wished to preclude the spread of nuclear weapons and therefore rescinded the previous administration's offer to sell medium-range Polaris missiles to the NATO countries—a policy that Defense Minister Strauss had warmly welcomed. In order to meet the European demands for a dependable strategic force and to prevent other countries from following the example of France in building an independent nuclear force, the Kennedy administration offered to provide equipment for a jointly manned NATO fleet of missile-launching ships. This policy change ended for the moment any possibility of Germany obtaining direct control of strategic delivery vehicles, though there had never been any thought of ending the U.S. monopoly of control over the atomic warheads.

Another important policy change was the American intention to give increased emphasis to NATO conventional military power and to scrap the notion that tactical nuclear weapons could compensate for the alleged manpower superiority of the Communist countries. In 1961 the U.S.S.R.'s possession of field nuclear weapons raised fears that any crossing of the nuclear threshold in a local battle situation would increase the likelihood of expansion to all-out thermonuclear war. Strauss opposed this strategic reasoning. He was, he said, more concerned about preventing than about limiting battles that would be fought on German soil.

In March, 1962, Strauss, through his press chief, publicly and virulently attacked the American strategists who had formulated the new NATO policy. This provoked severe reaction in Washington, which in turn forced an ostensible reversal of Strauss's position, as evidenced by the announcement that the Defense Ministry was instituting a "reeducation course for the *Bundeswehr* to deemphasize the need for nuclear weapons." At the May, 1962, NATO conference of Defense Ministers, Strauss even endorsed the American strategy.

So far the year-long defense debate had been carried on between opposing factions within the German Defense Ministry and between Strauss and the new U.S. strategists in NATO military and political councils. The SPD applauded the new NATO emphasis on conventional weapons and urged that "West German defense policies be in harmony with the resolutions of NATO." But, in sharp distinction to the 1952–60 period, the SPD did not choose to make defense policy a major or even an important political issue.

It was left to the *Spiegel* to initiate an informed political debate of Strauss's defense plans by publishing in June, 1962, an article titled "Stronger than 1939." Essentially the *Spiegel* charged that Strauss's public acceptance of NATO-U.S. defense views in May was an attempt to deceive the American government and the German people. Actually, the *Spiegel* contended, Strauss was still more interested in atomic weapons than in increasing ground troops in fulfillment of NATO-force goals. In order to have some potential for an independent strategic force, Strauss intended to (1) remodel the F-104G jet fighter for use as a supersonic plane capable of delivering nuclear bombs against the U.S.S.R. and (2) save from funds allotted for ground troops in case a future opportunity should occur to buy medium- or long-range missiles or to support the French nuclear arms program in return for a share in the military results. This atomic policy, said the *Spiegel,* was being rammed through by Strauss against the violent protests of army generals who felt it to be both dangerous and ineffective in meeting Germany's defense needs. As in the earlier but similar American defense policy debate, which had led Army Chief of Staff Maxwell Taylor to resign in protest, the army generals argued strongly for conventional as well as atomic capabilities, while the air force and naval officers were disposed to rely on nuclear weapons.

Most of the *Spiegel's* accusations were new to the general public; and while the very well informed knew the direction Strauss's policy was taking, the article probably was written with inside information. Yet there was no immediate government reaction, although a law professor, shortly after being appointed the first general in the *Bundeswehr* reserve, wrote in a small-town newspaper:

> What is said here [in the *Spiegel*] under the guise of an objective report in the way of truths, half-truths, and lies about the internal functioning of the *Bundeswehr,* is more than mere indiscretion. In a time when the existence of the state and the freedom of us all are at stake, this borders more on conscious treason.[4]

The *Spiegel* was quickly able to obtain a court injunction against the further spreading of this treason charge.

In July, 1962, the replacement of NATO Supreme Commander Lauris Norstad was followed in the United States by the appointment of General Maxwell Taylor as Chairman of the United States Joint Chiefs of Staff. Norstad had been trusted by the German government; Taylor was widely known as the architect of the conventional defense doctrine. This change in military leadership was the signal for Strauss to renew public efforts to oppose the new NATO strategy. Apparently Adenauer had been won over to Strauss's defense policy, because the CDU now publicly supported this position in an official party statement:

> We don't agree with all of General Taylor's opinions . . . because this Taylor wants in the event of a Soviet conventional attack on Europe . . . to withhold atomic firepower [and] leave Europe to the undertermined fate of a conventional war.[5]

The SPD said nothing, and the *Spiegel* continued its criticism of Strauss's defense policy until the October 10 publication of its feature story on NATO's maneuvers in the fall of 1962, which took its title from that of the maneuvers, "Fallex-62."

---

[4] J. Seifert, "Die Spiegel Affäre," in Kuby, *op. cit.,* p. 239.
[5] *Spiegel,* vol. 16, no. 32 (August 8, 1962), p. 13.

The Fallex Article

The principal author of the *Spiegel*'s articles on defense policy was Conrad Ahlers, who had been public information officer in the Defense Ministry but had resigned when Strauss took the post—despite Strauss's invitation to stay on. Ahlers had an expert acquaintance with German defense matters and many knowledgeable friends in and out of the Defense Ministry. In preparing the Fallex article, he had taken his draft manuscript for comment and advice to a number of these friends, including several generals, a CDU parliamentary deputy, and Helmut Schmidt, one of the SPD's military experts and adviser on defense policy, who felt that at a number of points the article appeared to include classified information. Ahlers then asked Colonel Wicht of the Federal Intelligence Agency (roughly equivalent to the CIA) for an opinion on the sensitivity of a number of items he submitted and was given unofficial "clearance" on all but one item, which was deleted from the published article. Prior to publishing the Fallex article, the *Spiegel* made efforts to secure an interview with informed and responsible officers in the Defense Ministry in the hope of discussing the contents, but these efforts were unsuccessful.

In the light of the government's violent reaction to its publication, the most surprising aspect of the Fallex article was its lack of any novel themes or world-shaking information. The *Spiegel*'s aim was to continue to present the arguments against Strauss's defense policy and to document these with detailed evidence. Its principal objections were the same as in previous articles: (1) Strauss was not taking the steps needed to fill NATO's conventional-force goals and (2) Strauss was saving funds in order to procure medium-range missiles and in the meantime was converting jet fighters for use as a small nuclear retaliatory force.

The article began with a discussion of the fall maneuvers. In its best "you are there" style, the *Spiegel* related in detail the terrible consequences for NATO and especially Germany of a Soviet attack in central Europe. In effect, the *Spiegel* contended that the maneuver's results conclusively demonstrated that Strauss's policy of reliance on tactical atomic weapons left too little manpower to conduct a successful defense of the German frontier. And, what is more, the *Spiegel* informed the German people for the first time that NATO headquarters had given Strauss's army the lowest ranking possible in NATO, "conditionally fit for defense." Following this blast, the main elements underlying the evolution of NATO policy for the defense of Europe were discussed with emphasis on the conventional forces–atomic weapons debate. The last section discussed the *Spiegel*'s view of the inside workings of the Defense Ministry. Here, as in the previously discussed article "Stronger than 1939," Strauss's deeds were shown to contrast with his public statements of support for NATO's policy.

After the *Spiegel* crisis had broken, Hanson Baldwin, military analyst of the New York *Times,* described the Fallex article in these terms:

To well-informed Americans, the article appears to carry little information that was not generally known to the Russians or other observers . . . .[6]

The *Spiegel* tried to underpin this overall impression by preparing in May, 1963, a paragraph-by-paragraph analysis of Fallex sources, showing that most of the information had been prepublished somewhere.

But Ahlers' clearance endeavors were obviously made for some good reasons. He knew that he was writing on the basis of much inside information and was concerned that he might accidentally reveal state secrets. In fact, the article did offer new information, some of which was irrelevant but much of which was central to the *Spiegel*'s policy disagreements with Strauss. The irrelevant but possibly classified information was probably slipped into the article as part of the *Spiegel*'s usual "inside dopester" approach, and their military significance may well have been incomprehensible to the general reader.

Nevertheless, information not previously known to the German public and buttressing the *Spiegel*'s case against the Defense Minister was given about developments inside the Defense Ministry. Here the *Spiegel* concentrated on providing evidence for its contention that Strauss had an unhealthy and dangerous love for atomic weapons.

Preemptive Strike Doctrine

We have already mentioned that Strauss intended to use converted jet fighters as a small nuclear retaliatory force. Now the *Spiegel* alleged that some elements in the air force favored Germany's adopting a preemptive strike doctrine to deter particular Soviet provocations. This would mean that if a Soviet attack were believed imminent, the German air force would rush to attack Soviet bases first. Since high performance aircraft need long runways, it isn't possible for them to survive an enemy's missile attack and then retaliate. So it is logical that air force officers often favor the doctrine of "hit them as soon as you think they're coming."

Obviously this strategy makes an opponent extremely nervous—should he fear that his enemies think he is going to attack, he is *forced* to do so first. In the days when the United States and the Soviet Union depended primarily on their vulnerable bombers, this reciprocal fear of surprise attack was considered most likely to be the cause of World War III.

The *Spiegel* did not say that this doctrine had become official German policy, but it did point out that Strauss and elements in the air force were advocating such a policy. While this inside information was known in Washington and probably in Moscow, it was carefully kept not only from the German public at large but also from wider governmental circles. Fears of the consequences that the adoption of such a strategy might bring were one of the major reasons for the opposition of army officers, including Colonel Alfred Martin, to Strauss's policy.

---

[6] New York *Times,* November 23, 1962.

Calculations of Alternative Force Structures and Costs

The other major items of important and previously unknown information were cost estimates made by Defense and Finance Ministry experts. After listing the publicly known NATO-force requirements, the *Spiegel* contended that Strauss had a choice of three options:

1. a force meeting all of NATO's conventional plus all of Strauss's atomic requirements, requiring 750,000 men and an annual budget of DM 30 billion—"3 to 4 billion alone for the German portion of the European atomic force";

2. "an armed force of 580,000 men; cost including missiles, DM 23 billion; without missiles, 20 billion"; or

3. "an armed force of 500,000 men; cost including missiles, DM 20 billion."

According to the *Spiegel,* the army officers favored the 580,000 men and no missiles choice—since Germany could then meet its NATO obligations. But Strauss chose the third alternative, so that he could have his missiles, and then talked Chancellor Adenauer into agreeing with his plan.

These revelations certainly harmed Strauss's position, but did they undermine that of Germany? Their implications for Germany's national security will be discussed in the legal analysis after an examination of the events that followed the article's publication.

Preparation

Exactly what happened between the publication of the Fallex article and the eventual arrest of the *Spiegel* editors is not yet entirely clear, but through the use of the government's replies to SPD questionnaires, the SPD's report on the *Spiegel* affair, the government's own report, and the statements of the responsible officials to the parliament and press, it has become possible to trace the significant steps in the preparation and execution of the government's offensive against the *Spiegel's* alleged traitors.

The obvious first question is: Who lit the fuse on this explosive matter? While the answer is not definitely known, the evidence suggests that on October 8 and 9 an official in the Federal Attorney's office expressed suspicion of the Fallex article. Thereupon, the Federal Attorney's office telephoned the Ministry of Defense and requested its advice on whether state secrets had been betrayed by the article. Who in the Defense Ministry received and then approved this request is not clear. In any case, orders were given for Dr. Wunder, a lawyer in the Defense Ministry, to prepare with the assistance of Colonel Hopffgarten, his superior, a comprehensive assessment of the article. By October 13 Wunder had visited Federal Attorney Kuhn and informed him that "numerous and in some cases highly important military secrets" had been revealed in the article. On October 16 Strauss, together with State Secretary Hopf—a career civil servant and the highest ranking official in the Ministry of Defense—was briefed on the contents of the report. Two days later the report was finished, and on October 19 it was given by Dr. Wunder to the Federal Attorney.

The role of the Defense Ministry, and of Strauss in particular, is of critical importance in assessing the extent to which the government's actions against the *Spiegel* were inspired by legal or political considerations. One point to consider is the Federal Attorney's willingness to be guided by the Defense Ministry's view of the case. Neither the lawyers of the Defense Ministry nor the representatives of the Federal Attorney made any effort to assemble the data necessary to ascertain to what degree the material of the story had appeared in other German or foreign publications.

On October 20 Hopf met with the Federal Attorney and discussed with him the future course of proceedings, including the ministry's interest in ferreting out the informants of the *Spiegel.* How far the original initiative for extending the search into *Spiegel* documents and files of previous periods came from Hopf or from the Federal Attorney, who at any rate had to carry through the legal arrangements, rests somewhat controversial.

Although the Federal Attorney's office is directly subordinate to the Ministry of Justice, the report on the *Spiegel* article had been requested and received by the Federal Attorney's office wholly on its own authority. Not until October 18 was the Ministry of Justice sent the information that an investigation had been begun, and for some reason this did not reach the ministry until October 22. The Ministry of Justice was first brought into the matter on October 24 through a briefing given at the Defense Ministry by State Secretary Hopf to his counterpart State Secretary Walter Strauss. Defense Minister Strauss then told State Secretary Strauss that on the order of the Chancellor the Minister of Justice was not to be informed because of the need for secrecy. Minister of Justice Stammberger, who learned about the activities of his subordinates only through the news reports of the *Spiegel* raids on October 26, said that the Defense Minister "had these preparations in his hands to the last detail."

The Chancellor's role in the preparations became the subject of national and party debate in the coalition crisis which followed the *Spiegel* raid. In parliament Chancellor Adenauer had contended that he knew nothing until the last minute, but it is now known that Strauss briefed Adenauer in detail on October 18, 22, and 23. Since Strauss later retracted his statement that the Chancellor had ordered the circumvention of the Minister of Justice, and also admitted that the Chancellor had never given particular instructions, it seems safe to assume that the Chancellor had been an attentive listener to what the Minister of Defense reported but had taken a wait-and-see attitude, giving no more encouragement than required by the delicate situation.

The final preparations were begun on October 22, when Hopf briefed the Minister of the Interior and informed him of the imminent need for the services of the security group of the Federal Criminal Police. The next day, October 23, the investigating judge at the Federal Court issued warrants for the arrest of *Spiegel* publisher Rudolf Augstein and editor Conrad Ahlers on the grounds of serious suspicion of having betrayed state secrets through the publication of the Fallex article. At the same time he ordered the search of the person, home, and other quarters of the accused in addition to "the various offices and archives of the *Spiegel* in Hamburg and Bonn."

On the same day, officials of the security police and Federal Attorney's office took up strategic positions in Bonn and Hamburg—all was now prepared. No satisfactory official explanation has yet been offered for the three-day delay in carrying out the arrest and search orders.[7]

Night and Fog

The Beginning

It is also unclear why the *Spiegel* offensive was launched at night. This perhaps more than any other feature of the bizarre proceedings brought back chilling memories of Gestapo times. The government claims that the erroneous arrest of a *Spiegel* employee believed to be publisher Augstein forced immediate action before the employee, freed about 7 P.M. on October 26, could alert the *Spiegel* to hide or destroy incriminating evidence. But there is some suspicion that night was chosen intentionally, perhaps because it was believed the *Spiegel*'s offices would be conveniently empty over the weekend, or possibly because the German papers do not publish over the weekend, so there would be no press reaction until the following Monday. The search order against Augstein and applicable to all *Spiegel* property was explicitly declared valid for the night also.

Another questionable aspect of the procedure concerned the notification of the state governments that the federal police were about to act. Whenever federal authorities infringe on the police power of the individual German states they must give advance notice to the state governments. In this case, the security groups did not inform the state police that "executive measures" were imminent until after the first arrest. The state governments were notified for the first time at 8 P.M., simultaneously with the departure of the security group's commando units for the *Spiegel's* offices. Even so, the state authorities in North Rhine Westphalia and, after some initial hesitation, the SPD government of Hamburg rendered administrative and personnel assistance.

---

[7] The Federal Attorney's official version of the arrest, search, and seizure proceedings is now contained in his submission to the Federal Constitutional Court, 1004 E(933–849/63), annex g, December 20, 1963.

As one state official later said, "I thought it was the usual Communist party affair." Later on, the state authorities would protest both the late notification and the irregularity of the search and seizure proceedings.

The Night

In Bonn the security group went to *Spiegel* editor Hans Dieter Jaene's house at about 9 P.M. and accompanied him back to the *Spiegel* offices, where a representative of the Federal Attorney read the search and seizure orders. The officials then began to search and collect documents for several hours, continuing the following day. Jaene himself was kept overnight but was released the following day, since no warrant had been issued for his arrest.

The Hamburg security group was assigned the more complicated task of finding, arresting, and searching the homes of Augstein and Ahlers and two other *Spiegel* editors, Johannes K. Engel and Claus Jacobi. They were also charged with "occupying" the large *Spiegel* headquarters building. During the night of October 26–27, the private residences of these four *Spiegel* editors were thoroughly searched, and numerous private papers, diaries, and notebooks were confiscated.

The security group was surprised to find the *Spiegel*'s offices buzzing with activity on a Friday night. Work was in progress on the next issue. In order to facilitate their search of the *Spiegel*'s files, the police demanded that work cease and the editorial offices be cleared. The editor in charge refused, and, after much discussion, the Federal Attorney's office "permitted" a team of ten persons to remain and continue the work on the new *Spiegel*. But a policeman was assigned to maintain constant supervision of each of these people, and they could obtain access to documents, files, and so forth, only after presenting a written request to the police official in charge. No use of the telephone or teletype was allowed; thus all opportunities for outside contact were cut off. The *Spiegel* later charged that the Federal Attorney, in taking the galleys of the forthcoming issue, examining them for "evidence" concerning the Fallex article, and then having them released by the investigating judge, was in fact precensoring the *Spiegel*—an activity forbidden by German law.

The Initial Arrests

Of the four men sought on the night of the twenty-sixth, arrest warrants had been issued for only two. The other two, Jacobi and Engel, were captured at the *Spiegel* headquarters by the security group. Rudolf Augstein, for whom a warrant had been issued, heard of the raid the next morning and promptly drove to the nearest police headquarters. But shortly after midnight of October 26–27, the police discovered, much to their surprise, that Konrad Ahlers, the second man for whom a warrant had been issued, was vacationing in Spain.

The Ahlers Arrest

The police discussed the situation with the "assisting" Defense Ministry representatives, who in turn called State Secretary Hopf in Bonn for further orders. Hopf replied that the Ahlers arrest had to be made immediately. When the security group head protested that he did not have the authority or means to do this, Hopf is said to have replied, "If you can't do it, the Defense Ministry has its own methods."[8]

Just before 1 A.M. Defense Minister Strauss called the embassy in Madrid and spoke with the chancellor of the embassy. He asked whether Ahlers was in Spain. When informed that he was, Strauss told the embassy official to have Colonel Oster, the military attaché, return the call, and that he was not to talk about it to anyone in the embassy. Strauss went on to say, "This is an order. At the moment I'm speaking in the name of the Chancellor and the Foreign Minister."[9] When Colonel Oster returned the call a few minutes later, Strauss told him that security measures were being taken against the *Spiegel* and that Ahlers was a very high priority suspect. He further informed him that Ahlers was believed to be on the way from Spain to Tangiers and that, given the severe crisis between the Soviet Union and the United States (the Cuban missile crisis), Ahlers' arrest was of the greatest importance for the security of the Federal Republic and NATO. A warrant for Ahlers' arrest, Strauss added, had been issued and was on the way. In the meantime, Oster should take all possible steps to persuade the Spanish police to "secure" Ahlers.

Very shortly after this phone call, State Secretary Hopf spoke with the representative of the Ministry of Justice about possible means of arresting German citizens in foreign countries, and learned that in the case of both Ahlers and Heinz Schmelz, an editor at the moment traveling in Budapest, extradition was not legally possible. Forty-five minutes later the Federal Attorney and the representative of the Justice Ministry agreed that Interpol was not legally available to them and that it would not be a good idea to issue wanted notices.

Meanwhile, Colonel Oster and two members of the Madrid legation were contacting the Spanish police. The Madrid police called Malaga and asked that Ahlers be "secured." At 5 A.M. Colonel Oster called Minister Strauss and told him that Ahlers was in custody.

The Search and Seizure Operations

The search and seizure operations connected with the *Spiegel* raid were unique not only because they were begun at night but also because of the wide range of materials which the police read through and confiscated—both in the homes of *Spiegel* personnel and in its offices. Partial "occupation" of the *Spiegel*'s offices lasted four weeks, until November 26, during which time

[8] Kuby, *op. cit.*, p. 263.
[9] *Ibid.*, p. 264.

search operations were continued and the work of the *Spiegel*'s employees was seriously impeded. All possible types of written matter were examined by the task force of police officials.

It has been noted here that the search warrants were issued without specifying in any way what concrete evidence was sought. In a later legal protest, the *Spiegel*'s lawyers contended that the search and seizure operations were in fact a fishing expedition for all and any type of incriminating information rather than being related to a particular article.

Only at the insistence of the *Spiegel* personnel present during the search operations did the police officials furnish a list of the material that was being confiscated and removed from the premises. These lists show that numerous documents having no relation whatsoever to defense policy matters were taken along. For almost a year much of this material remained in government hands, with the bulk of the material first being returned in the summer of 1963.

Further Arrests

Informed of the search of the homes and offices, the Federal Attorney's office immediately began to request additional arrest warrants. On October 27, the day following the raid, arrest warrants and search orders were issued for *Spiegel* editors Jacobi (already under detention), for publishing the Fallex article, and Hans Schmelz, for cooperating in the writing of the article. Schmelz was visiting Hungary at the time, and after refusing offers of political asylum, he immediately returned to Germany and was taken into custody.

On November 2 publishing director Hans Becker was also arrested for his part in publishing the article and for acting as one of the contact men with Colonel Wicht, who was arrested two days later.

Not until November 28 did the Federal Attorney obtain the leads that enabled the government to arrest the *Spiegel*'s high-ranking military informant, Colonel Martin. Later, looking back at the month's events, the federal prosecutor saw this as one of the two major misfortunes that severely damaged the government's case before the public. Had they been able to catch Colonel Martin along with their kettle of journalists during that hectic weekend, the action would not have taken on its appearance of being solely persecution of a periodical that the government loathed. This compounded the bad impression made by the unorthodox methods used to arrest Ahlers—methods for which the prosecutors were not directly responsible.

The evidence that led to Martin's arrest shows that Paul Conrad, a Bonn lobbyist, had initially put Colonel Martin in touch with his lawyer, Josef Augstein, who in turn introduced Martin to *Spiegel* editors. Conrad was arrested December 2 and lawyer Augstein on December 4, on the grounds of suspicion of aiding in the dissemination of state secrets.

All in all, twelve persons were now involved in the *Spiegel* affair. Of these, *Spiegel* editors Engel and Jaene were held for one day and then released.

Three others were placed under investigation arrest for varying periods of time: editor-in-chief Jacobi, 18 days; Becker, 34 days; and Colonel. Wicht, 49 days. To their number should be added the name of Hamburg Interior Senator Helmut Schmidt, who was not arrested but against whom preliminary proceedings were initiated in February, 1963, ostensibly for having helped Ahlers to write the article. (The Federal Attorney did not ask, however, for a judicial examination of these four cases, nor has a nolle prosequi —a request to dismiss the inquiry—so far been entered on their behalf.) The cases of the remaining six individuals, who had likewise spent considerable time under investigation arrest, began to be transferred to examining magistrates in December, 1962: Rudolf Augstein, the *Spiegel*'s publisher, 103 days' detention; *Spiegel* editor Hans Schmelz, 81 days; Conrad Ahlers, 56 days; lawyer Augstein, 6 days; Paul Conrad, 12 days; and Colonel Martin, 30 days.

The Political Impact

The initial reaction to the dramatic events of October 26 and the dawn of October 27 can be summed up as surprise, shock, and curiosity. For all, the question was, "What did the *Spiegel* do?" although even in the earliest hours some also wondered, "Who did what to the *Spiegel?*"

The official announcement of the treason charge that weekend by no means told the press or the people what they really wanted to know. What puzzled and disturbed many citizens, journalists, and politicians were the following salient questions: Why did the search and seizure of *Spiegel* materials and personnel occur in the dead of night? Which government ministries initiated and carried out the action against the *Spiegel?* Why was not the Minister of Justice informed? In particular, what was Strauss's role—did he use the Fallex article as a pretext to eliminate the mirror that cast back such unflattering images? Who ordered the Spanish police to "secure" a German citizen vacationing on its territory?

On Monday, October 29, the federal government held a press conference which satisfied nobody and roused many. Press representatives of the various ministries were on hand. But occasional confusion and repeated evasion left the major questions unanswered, or half-answered. In reply to one journalist's query as to how any journalist could be sure that he wouldn't also be accused of high treason, the speaker for the federal press office replied, "I could say that we all have occupational hazards."

In the first three days press reaction with few exceptions had been hesitant, though the great majority of papers expressed shock at the night arrests. But as the government's reactions aroused suspicions, the press took more clear-cut stands and divided into three groups. A minority of papers applauded:

. . . there is only one thing to debate here, the suspicion of high treason. The legal authorities believe that the *Spiegel* collects state secrets as others collect stamps or beer coasters. That's why they clamped down, and without first sending a calling card.[10]

The overwhelming majority of papers, including those favorable to the government, sharply questioned the methods of the arrests and the contradictory government statements, especially regarding the Ahlers matter. Newspapers and citizens wondered aloud whether this was "a political punitive expedition" against the *Spiegel*. But little was written about the basic question of state secrets and freedom of the press.

A number of leading pro-SPD newspapers almost immediately condemned the "police action" as an alarming sign of the frailty of the new German democracy. The Frankfurt *Rundschau* expressed the anxiety which increasing numbers of persons felt:

When the doorbell rings in the early morning, we can no longer have the comfortable feeling that it must be the milkman. . . . When somebody knocks at the door at midnight, we can no longer be certain that at the worst it's a telegram or a drunken neighbor at the wrong door. We have to suppose that it might be the political police that looks for traitors in the night.[11]

On Tuesday, October 30, the students of Frankfurt University staged a mass demonstration. This led the way, and the next day students at five other universities joined in the public protest. Quite a number of professors signed petitions to the Chancellor and the parliament expressing dissatisfaction, disappointment, and alarm at the manner in which the government had acted against the *Spiegel* and at the failure of the government to inform the public more candidly.

Strauss, whom the protesters suspected was behind what had happened, spent the week denying his involvement. Some sample comments: October 30, "I may say that neither I personally nor the direction of this ministry had anything to do with the initiation of this action." November 3, "No, it is no revenge on my part. I have nothing to do with the matter, in the true sense of the word, nothing to do." To prevent the FDP from leaving the government coalition and toppling the government, two civil servants, State Secretary Strauss of the Justice Ministry and State Secretary Hopf of the Defense Ministry, were blamed for keeping the FDP Minister of Justice uninformed and were removed from their positions on November 4. Hopf went "on vacation" and State Secretary Strauss's transfer to a plush job in the Court of the European Community, promised him before the crisis, was

[10] From the West Berlin *Zeitung* as quoted in the *Spiegel*, vol. 16, no. 46 (November 14, 1962), pp. 34-37.
[11] From the Frankfurt *Rundschau*, October 29, 1962.

speeded up. But this easy political solution did not answer the salient questions. Since the protests were not stimulating the government to reveal the facts voluntarily, the call became insistent for the opposition party to take up the matter in parliament. As the leading Bavarian newspaper put it, "That parliament has not done anything in the ten days since October 26 is surprising. . . ."[12]

But was it really surprising? The CDU had long branded the SPD "soft on communism" if not secretly pro-Communist. Although some individual SPD leaders immediately denounced the "police action," the party leadership withheld public comment to avoid any possibility of appearing to defend traitors to the German fatherland. And their failure to catch Strauss in the Fibag matter made them even more dubious than before about the value of parliamentary inquiry. But the public protests and confusion of the government gradually gave the SPD courage. On November 5 the parliamentary group presented a "small questionnaire" to the government. The SPD, however, firmly stated that its inquiry would not deal with the basic legal and constitutional questions, since these were for the courts to decide.

On the same day, another government press conference stirred up matters further when the official representative used strong language to chastise the press and the *Spiegel:* "The government does not intend to stand by passively while the press puts the German judicial system in the defendant's chair," and, "This is the worst case of suspicion of treason that has yet occurred in the Federal Republic."

Despite the intense criticism by the national and foreign press, the public protests, and the growing ebb of confidence in the government, no clear and satisfactory explanations could be obtained from individual or official government sources. Attention turned to the parliament—would the government give revealing answers to the opposition's questions? In three days a political storm blew up.

Partial Unveiling

On November 7, when parliament finally assembled, the SPD made use of the one-hour question period at the beginning of each session, a device introduced only two years previously, to initiate and continue the three-day *Spiegel* debate. Making clear its opposition to treason when it really occurs, the SPD said it was "concerned singly and solely with the methods employed [in the *Spiegel* matter]." The initial question was simple: Who instructed the Spanish police to arrest the *Spiegel* editor Ahlers in Malaga?" A long and complex reply by the Minister of the Interior was typical of the replies often given in the ensuing days, when many words were used to say little. The minister did not say who instructed the Spanish police.

Then Chancellor Adenauer trained his oratorical guns on the *Spiegel* and

---

[12] From the Munich *Süddentsche Zeitung,* November 5, 1962.

the SPD. So far as the SPD was concerned, Adenauer expressed bewilderment that they felt the need to question the government, and even delivered a veiled threat: ". . . just await the results of further inquiry. Then you will be sorry you asked these questions."[13]

After praising the Federal Attorney's office and the federal police for their zeal, the Chancellor gave his judgment of the *Spiegel* case:

> . . . we have an abyss of treason in the country. . . . When a magazine with a circulation of 500,000 systematically practices high treason in order to earn money [enraged cries of "Pfui!" and whistles from the SPD]. . . .[14]

This type of outburst by the Chancellor aroused not only the parliamentarians, but also the press and public at large. As a major newspaper stated: "Who is suspected of treason is . . . in the eyes of the Chancellor, already judged and sentenced . . . this must stop."

The second-day sessions began with the same SPD question. Progress was made insofar as Strauss admitted that "the Defense Ministry" telephoned Oster in Spain. To the question *"Who* telephoned?" there came long, evasive replies. And then the next questioner broke continuity, and the minister escaped.

But on November 9 the question that had been the focus of German attention for two weeks was answered. In reply to the persistent direct question "Did the Defense Minister himself telephone, or if not, who else?" Strauss finally brought himself to answer: "Since Oster said, 'I recognize only the minister's voice,' I was connected with him and discussed the situation [shouts of 'Aha!' from the SPD]."[15]

But Strauss was not ready for a complete unmasking. In reply to a question as to whether he had participated in any conferences for the preparation of the arrests between October 16 and 28, he replied:

> In the time from the sixteenth to the twenty-sixth of October . . . I took part in no conferences. But of course, I was informed by the members of my staff that the matter was pending. I didn't know more. I didn't know what was coming, when it was coming, and against whom, and so forth.[16]

Following Strauss's heated and often repeated denials of complicity in the arrest of Ahlers, and three days in which the government ministers repeated and added to their complex and conflicting stories, these partial admissions caused a general furor. Now even the large number of people who out of antipathy for the *Spiegel* and trust in the government had preferred to be-

---

[13] *Verhandlungen des Deutschen Bundestages (Bundestagsprotokolle)*, 4. Wahlperiode, Stenographischer Bericht, Bonn, Session 45, November 7, 1962, p. 1982.

[14] *Ibid.*

[15] *Ibid.*, Session 47, November 9, 1962, p. 2078.

[16] *Ibid.*, p. 2084.

lieve the authorities felt that the government had systematically deceived them. Although few of the SPD's eighteen questions were even dealt with, much less answered, Strauss's admission was enough to trigger a government crisis.

The events of those November days demonstrate the difference between the form and the substance of parliamentary government in its German context. The executive seemed to question in word and deed the right of parliament and the public to inquire into its activities. And far from considering itself bound to tell the truth to the representative of the sovereign people, the government seemed content to play a cat-and-mouse game of deception.

Parliament itself, even in such a major crisis, did not act with unity and cohesion vis-à-vis the government, but rather the party bond was the most powerful, and the parliamentarians of the largest party remained in their customary alliance with the ministers of the executive.

Coalition Crisis

Many politicians felt uncertain about the consequences of the *Spiegel* raids and, now, these events in parliament, and they looked at the elections in Hesse and Bavaria for indications of popular reaction. The first, coming within three days of the *Bundestag* debates, brought the SPD a 3 percent gain and the CDU a 3 percent loss. On account of both the immediacy of the elections and a generally favorable reaction to the SPD's administration and policies, it was difficult to guess how much the *Spiegel* affair had affected the result. But in any case the SPD national leadership was encouraged enough to demand Strauss's dismissal from the government. The FDP followed their lead. Dramatizing their opposition to Strauss, the five FDP ministers pulled the rug out from under the coalition by simultaneously resigning from the government.

The Bonn coalition managers now waited for the outcome of the November 25 Bavarian elections. But if they were waiting for definite cues they were somewhat disillusioned. While the CSU suffered a 2 percent decline and the SPD gained by 5 percent, the CSU kept its majority. It seemed that parts of the more sophisticated urban population had lost patience with a party guided by Strauss, but the countryside vote was a declaration of loyalty to him.

In the attempts to rebuild a cabinet there now entered a number of interrelated issues. Did the present situation offer Strauss's foes—and they were numerous in the ranks of the CDU as well as in the SPD and FDP—an opportunity to get rid of him? Would Adenauer once more be able to paste together a government either by keeping or by scuttling Strauss? Would the minor coalition party, the FDP, have a possibility of continuing to govern with the CDU if it insisted too much on the resignation of the man who had made their Minister of Justice, Stammberger, look ridiculous? Or would such insistence work to favor those in the CDU and SPD who wanted to use this opportunity to make a fundamental change in German politics by inaugurating an SPD-CDU coalition that would eliminate the pivotal positions of the FDP and of Strauss, through his hold over the CSU?

For some time it almost looked as if the *Spiegel* affair would enter history as the catalyst of a new phase in German domestic politics. But mistrust and dislike of Adenauer was still too strong in the SPD to permit its leadership to agree quickly enough to the CDU's conditions for coalition, especially in regard to changes in the electoral law that probably would have eliminated the FDP as a national party. In the last analysis Adenauer and the CDU leadership did not deem the gains that might come from stifling the *Spiegel* and the *Spiegel* inquiry significant enough to throw overboard ten years of anti-SPD political practices.

But the collapse of the SPD's chances helped Strauss as little as the frantic repetition of his attempts of 1961 to eliminate Adenauer in favor of Erhard. Then he had seen Adenauer's retirement as a step in his own succession to the chancellorship; now he saw Adenauer as the scapegoat who might save his own national reputation and his job. But again Adenauer proved the more skillful—this time helped along by the FDP's adamant opposition to Strauss and the halfhearted support Strauss got from his CDU colleagues. For in December, 1962, Strauss had to leave his government job, but his continued hold over the CSU and his seat in parliament kept him at least a nuisance factor, if not more, in national politics.

The Expanding Affair

The repasting of the coalition created a new situation. If the SPD had entered the government, the political part of the *Spiegel* story, by common—perhaps tacit—consent, would have ended then and there. The politicians would probably have been glad to leave it to the interplay between public opinion and the judiciary to decide how to dispose of the still-glowing ashes of the once brightly burning edifice of "treason."

Though the SPD's directing spirits were chagrined that they could not use the *Spiegel* crisis to join the government, they continued to cling to the major tenet of their "embracement strategy"—don't antagonize the CDU unnecessarily. Thus, although Chairman Ollenhauer called for a "fair determination of the *Spiegel* issues," in practice the party kept the matter warm but added no fuel. Neither a full-scale committee of inquiry nor further parliamentary debates were demanded. Instead, the SPD selected a strategy that put the government officials into endless dispiriting attempts to harmonize their contradictory accounts of the preparation and execution of the *Spiegel* offensive. The SPD's tactic was to shoot a continuous stream of questionnaires at the government (which is legally obligated to answer written ques-

Die Pressefreiheit wird gesichert

Freedom of the press is being secured.

The Press Views the Spiegel Affair

„Ob es auffällt, wenn wir ihm die Spiegelakten jetzt schon mitgeben?"

"Will anyone notice if we give the *Spiegel* file to the junk man *now*?"

Wigg Siegl in the Munich *Simplicissimus*, September 7, 1963

Josef Sauer in the Munich *Simplicissimus*, December 1, 1962

„Nicht ärjern, Caudillo! Dat deutsche Volk dankt Ihnen für demokratische Amtshilfe in kritischer Stunde."

"Don't fuss, Caudillo! The German people thank you for your democratic administrative assistance in a critical hour."

Mussil in the Frankfurter *Rundschau,* January 2, 1963

„Grüß Gott!"

"Howdy!"

tions submitted by a parliamentary group) and to wonder aloud when the official government report, requested by Chancellor Adenauer on November 13, would be released. Adenauer had ordered the Defense, Justice, Foreign, and the Interior Ministers to prepare complete accounts of their involvement in the wake of the national and international embarrassment caused by the government's having been caught in lies and evasions.

Finally, when the long-awaited report came out on February 4, 1963, it did little to improve the government's position. It tacitly admitted that the answers of Interior Minister Höcherl and Defense Minister Strauss before the *Bundestag* had been less than candid, and it contained in addition tantalizing discrepancies both between the Foreign and Defense Ministry stories in regard to Ahlers' arrest, and between the Justice and Defense Ministry stories as to the occurrences during the search and seizure operations. Perhaps the most astounding feature of the report—frequently commented upon later on in the legal discussion—was the attempt to cover up the irregularities of Ahlers' arrest as "administrative assistance." Even the staunch pro-CDU paper *Rheinischer Merkur* characterized this part as reading "like a bad detective story."

Public reaction to the inconsistencies and gaps of the government's *Spiegel* report was generally unfavorable, with one of the most authoritative German papers commenting: "It is the Chancellor himself upon whom the contradictions in the report cast the longest shadow."[17] Making political hay of this reaction, the SPD announced that since the government wasn't disposed to frankness, it would prepare its own report.

For the CDU this was a most unwelcome prospect, especially in view of two forthcoming political contests, the February 20 Berlin assembly elections and the March 20 Rhineland Palatinate state elections. The CDU therefore made explicit a threat that perhaps had been hinted at cryptically by Adenauer in the November *Bundestag* debate (see pp. 1982D, 1994B) and at varying times by other CDU politicians. It concerned two SPD members of parliament, deputy chairman of the Defense Committee Merten and the SPD group's legal secretary, Gerhard Jahn, who were alleged to have given *Spiegel* editor Schmelz the two classified secret documents found when his offices were searched in the October raids. In this way the CDU hoped to link the SPD to the "treasonous" *Spiegel,* because Schmelz was not only the man who helped Ahlers write the Fallex article, but was also a member of the SPD party's defense policy advisory group. The CDU had still more ammunition to use in playing upon the SPD's fear of being cast in the role of helper of "Communist traitors." They knew that the Federal Attorney had found out that Ahlers had shown a preliminary draft of the allegedly treasonous article to Helmut Schmidt, one of Hamburg's SPD senators and an authority on defense policy. There is some evidence that the CDU quietly

[17] From the Munich *Süddentsche Zeitung,* February 5, 1963.

threatened that any SPD report would be followed by a revelation of these potentially damaging facts.

Nevertheless, the SPD went ahead and released its report on March 11. Using only official government documents, the report, with a touch of understatement, concluded:

1. There remained eight important issues of fact that the government had not yet clarified.

2. In five instances the government had abused legal or constitutional guarantees.

3. No fewer than fifteen untruthful statements were made: five by Minister of Interior Höcherl, one by Chancellor Adenauer, and nine by Minister Strauss.

Nine lies were told to the parliament, three appeared in the official report, and three were told by Strauss to fellow government officials before or during the *Spiegel* arrests.

Aside from a few pinpricks in parliament, this report was the last major parliamentary action centered on the *Spiegel*. From now on, the bulk of the *Spiegel* case shifts to the judiciary, with the new FDP Minister of Justice expressing what is probably a widely held opinion about the expected outcome by calling what in November had been an "abyss of treason" a "minor case."

The Parliament's Defense Committee and SPD Security Leaks

It was precisely this prevalent expectation that there would be no clear-cut court victory to justify the "great offensive" begun in mid-October that made the CDU nervous about the long-term political consequences. Why not, therefore, shift the emphasis from the apparently ambiguous problem of treason by an opposition press to the more clear-cut situation at hand— security leaks by SPD members of parliament? It was in this spirit that the CDU now dragged the Jahn-Merten-Schmelz affair into the public arena. Jahn immediately admitted that he had given Schmelz a copy of the then classified (but since published) army court opinion on the Barth hearing. A second classified document, which contained the records of the committee's hearings on a series of air force accidents, was also apparently leaked by another SPD member of the Defense Committee.

Criminal accusations against members of parliament can be legally investigated only after parliament has decided to suspend immunity at the petition of the public prosecutor. Within a brief time after the CDU made the accusations against the SPD parliamentary deputies, the federal prosecutor asked that their immunity be lifted, and the CDU rushed to bully the SPD with this possibility. For obvious political reasons a legal complaint of "false imprisonment" (because of the means used by Strauss to secure Ahlers' return from Spain) took months, not days, to traverse the legal apparatus in North Rhine Westphalia. As a result, the SPD could not yet make an effective counterthreat to have Strauss's immunity lifted if the CDU moved to do this to SPD members. So the SPD went on the warpath against the government with questionnaires about various past unclarified affairs. Apparently the SPD threatened parliamentary investigation of possible political pressures in the handling of the lawsuit against Strauss, which seemed to guarantee the CDU an inside track for information as to what evidence the Federal Attorney collected and also to make the legal machinery move quickly for the CDU but sluggishly for the SPD.

Perhaps this strategy worked, for the CDU decided not to press for a vote on removing the immunity of Jahn and Merten, and the issue was postponed over the summer until the fall, 1963, session. After long discussions by parliament and the public concerning the prerequisites of lifting immunity, and after the failure of various attempts to arrange compensation deals, the parliament, to general surprise, voted to lift the immunity of *both* the SPD deputies *and* former Defense Minister Strauss. Therefore, depending on the decision of the public prosecutor, the cases could now be brought before the courts.

Aside from interest in these new developments, echoes of the original *Spiegel* affair were, by December, 1963, mainly restricted to SPD and CDU altercations over the slow movement of the *Spiegel* defendants' cases through the legal system.

German Criminal Procedure and the Spiegel

After the events of October, 1962, how did the case enter its legal phase? An answer requires a brief review of the German criminal procedure applicable to our case. Since the government's charge was "treason," jurisdiction to try the *Spiegel* case falls under the original (as opposed to the appellate) jurisdiction of the Federal Court.[18] The action in such cases starts either when the Federal Attorney's office investigates complaints filed by an outsider or when the Federal Attorney's office itself initiates an inquiry.[19] It is the job of the Federal Attorney's office to determine whether or not public charges should be preferred, for, in contrast to the ideal of a duel between prosecution and defense, which underlies Anglo-American procedure, the German prosecutor is supposed to weigh both the incriminating and the exonerating elements.[20] It may be asked whether it is ever possible to weigh both aspects equitably. At any rate, the early press conference statements of the Federal Attorney's office in this case looked more like those of an American prosecutor than of a self-effacing and objective German civil servant.

---

[18] Law on Court Administration (GVG) (abbreviated in German from *Gerichtsverfassungsgesetz*) par. 134.

[19] GVG 142, Code of Criminal Procedure (StPO) (abbreviated in German from *Strafprozessordnung*) par. 160.

[20] StPO par. 160.

Once an inquiry is launched, the Federal Attorney can take various pre-liminary steps on his own. He or, at his behest, the police may hear witnesses who are willing to appear voluntarily. In law, the police are regarded as an auxiliary of the prosecution. In practice, however, as the distribution of roles in this case amply shows, the police force is a coordinated office following its own predispositions and interests as long as the legal officers are disposed to give it cover. The prosecutor may, as he did in the *Spiegel* case, ask for an opinion from other federal offices. For some actions—such as search or seizure, preliminary apprehension of a suspect, or the taking of a witness' oath—he would need the authorization of investigating judges, in this case formally appointed by the president of the Federal Court.[21] Here an investi-gating judge from Karlsruhe, the seat of the Federal Court and the Federal Attorney's office, was taken along to Hamburg to sign the necessary papers. This action serves the preliminary purpose of finding out whether enough evidence exists to justify further proceedings. If the prosecutor then decides to continue rather than to dismiss the inquiry (nol-pros), he sends the case to an examining magistrate.[22] Designation of an examining magistrate is mandatory in all cases that come under the jurisdiction of the Federal Court.

This thoroughness is explained not only by the importance of these cases but also by an often criticized traditional German legislative policy: no regu-lar appeals are admitted in cases coming under the original jurisdiction of the Federal Court. Nonetheless, the setting up of a separate Constitutional Court in 1951 has had the effect of giving parties access to an additional jurisdiction, and the *Spiegel* defendants quickly availed themselves of this opportunity. By asserting the violation of a constitutional principle (in our case represented by article 5, section 1, freedom of the press; article 13, in-violability of domicile; article 14, property guarantees and general *Rechts-staat* principles), the jurisdiction of the Constitutional Court can be invoked either immediately via injunction[23] or after the exhaustion of other legal remedies.[24]

Although there is no parallel to the open conflict that often characterizes relations between federal and state courts in the American system, a certain amount of tension exists between the Federal Court and the Constitutional Court. This tension results not only from the superior position of the separate type of jurisdiction exercised by the Constitutional Court, which rests on the Bonn Basic Law, but also from the fact that its members are drawn from different groups—i.e., judges, administrators, and former politicians—rather than being recruited almost exclusively from those having judicial ca-reers in the regular law courts. Though the Constitutional Court exercises its power of judicial control with restraint, there has never been any doubt

---

21 StPO par. 168a.
22 StPO par. 186.
23 BVG Constitutional Court Law par. 32.
24 BVG Constitutional Court Law par. 90, sec. 2.

about its final authority over the vast and still expanding field of constitutional jurisprudence.

The examining magistrate appointed by the president of the Federal Court (in the *Spiegel* case, three examining magistrates assigned for the six defendants) examines the witnesses, takes depositions from the defendants, confronts them with the witnesses, and, if necessary, appoints an expert of his own,[25] as was eventually done in this case. Once the work of the magistrates is terminated, they will send the file back to the federal prosecutor for his decision whether to prosecute or not. He has authority to proceed first against one or another of the defendants—e.g., against Colonel Martin—in order to learn from the Court's reasoning how it reacts to the evidence and, more important in this case, what legal theories it sees fit to adopt.

If the Federal Attorney decides to prosecute, he formulates an indictment reciting the facts in the case, cites the applicable laws, and enumerates the witnesses at hand. The initial emphasis in a German trial, in contrast to American practice, is on the recital of the facts rather than on the selection of the exact legal category in which the case fits. In fact, the trial court, with due notice to the defendant, may change the legal category of the case during the trial.[26] In contrast to American grand jury proceedings, the filing of the indictment does not guarantee that the case is automatically put on the court's docket. The third criminal section, which consists of five judges[27] who handle such original jurisdiction cases, examines the file to decide whether the facts and evidence so far available are sufficient to warrant a trial. If the judges concur with the Federal Attorney, they render a decision to that effect;[28] otherwise they nol-pros the case. There is no redress possible against either decision. Thus, many steps must be taken before a case such as the *Spiegel* case is brought to trial.

It is not entirely clear whether the Minister of Justice, the official who is responsible to parliament for the administration of justice in government, has any say in the decisions as to indictment before the Federal Court. While there was close, even too close, collaboration between the office of the federal prosecutor, the Minister of the Interior, and the Minister of Defense in the preparatory stages of the *Spiegel* action, the Minister of Justice and his staff played, as we have seen, a surprisingly modest role in the initiating proceedings. Here lies a problem transcending the particularities of the individual case. German legal theorists and practitioners have spent much time and energy in expounding the legality principle as spelled out in paragraph 152, section 2, of the StPO. In principle this provision requires that, except for a few designated exceptions, all offenses should be prosecuted. Some commentators assert that this principle excludes any interference of the political

---

[25] StPO par. 75.
[26] StPO art. 265.
[27] GVG par. 139, sec. 2.
[28] StPO par. 207, GVG par. 134.

authorities in the initiation of criminal proceedings, in spite of some quite different language inserted in paragraph 147 of GVG. Because this issue is unresolved, there is lacking in Germany the clear-cut and explicit under- standing (maintained in most other European countries) that political prose- cutions contain enough discretionary elements to warrant association of the Ministry of Justice in the more important stages of policy formation. The result is that the Federal Attorney, if he is so inclined, can use the protective shield of the legality principle to keep decisions of far-reaching political im- portance within the exclusive confines of his office and free from major par- ticipation by the Ministry of Justice, a type of decentralization that endows the professional bureaucracy with a highly sensitive role for which it may not always be fully prepared.

At what stage the defense lawyers will be able to see the government's in- vestigative file is another interesting problem illustrated in the *Spiegel* con- troversy. In the United States, unless the trial court allows defense lawyers to see their client's or some witness' statement to the police or F.B.I., the de- fense sees nothing of the government's case prior to trial. In Germany, the defense has access to the file at least when the examining magistrate has fin- ished his job, and sometimes before. The court allowed the *Spiegel* lawyers access to a few documents earlier, in line with the provision allowing for such facilities if they do not hamper the inquiry.[29] After some defense arguments with the prosecutor, the third criminal section of the Federal Court, acting under a new president (appointed in spring, 1963), allowed the *Spiegel* lawyers to take home a copy of the classified opinion of the Defense Minis- try's legal expert that was originally requested by the Federal Attorney's ex- pert.

Since the file includes every item of the case, from the first police investi- gation to the final decision to have a trial, it is a major aid in planning trial strategy, e.g., making interlocutory motions—complaints against order of ar- rest, of search and seizure, etc.—and thus it is of vital importance that the lawyers have early and full access to it. We have already seen that the de- fense was successful in getting permission to take home the classified "expert opinion" from the file. They were less successful with various motions brought before the Federal Court during November, 1962, complaining about the extravagant amount of search and seizure, and then filed as a peti- tion for injunction before the Constitutional Court on the charge that spe- cific constitutional guarantees had been violated. In spite of many raised eyebrows in the oral hearings before the Constitutional Court, and some searching questions that explored the remote relation between some seized documents and the objectives of the search, the Constitutional Court finally refused to enjoin the orders of the investigating judge. This refusal was based largely on the fact that methods smacking of precensorship and impeding the

---

[29] StPO par. 147.2.

further conduct of the *Spiegel* business had been abandoned by that time. Enlarged motions resting on similar complaints were filed in the summer of 1963 before both the Federal Court and the Constitutional Court; these were turned down by the Federal Court in November, 1963, while the constitutional complaints are still pending at this writing.

Once the trial date is set, the file is studied carefully by the five trial judges, especially the presiding officer and the rapporteur, who is likely to draft the reasonings. They had better be well prepared because, unlike U.S. judges, they are not umpires watching over the rules in the duel between defense and prosecution but officials who have the duty to do everything possible to ferret out the truth. Thus, the presiding judge is the real master of the proceedings, questioning the defendants and the witnesses while the prosecution and the defense chime in only with his permission or question after he is done.

Basic Issues in the Spiegel Case

1. Extradition of Persons

The *Spiegel* proceedings raise issues of both procedural and substantive law. Some of the procedural problems have, since the outset, either become moot, leaving behind a trail of suspicion and excitement, or found preliminary solutions; others are still pending, mainly in the Constitutional Court. The substantive problems have so far not advanced beyond the desks and mind of the Federal Attorney and the examining magistrates, but meanwhile they are being thoroughly discussed in professional circles and among the public at large.

The first among the procedural problems concerns the attempt of Minister Strauss to get hold of Conrad Ahlers via extradition proceedings. If Strauss were serious in his underhanded suggestions that Ahlers might try to escape, he could have suggested that the German Foreign Office obtain Ahlers' expulsion from Spain. But there was no legal way to ask for extradition on a charge of treason in conformity with the 1878 German-Spanish extradition treaty or to take preliminary steps to secure Ahlers' arrest within the framework of the Interpol organization. The extradition specialist of the federal Ministry of Justice and other officials had made it quite clear to the Ministry of Defense that political offenses were not within the purview of the treaty. In addition, in spite of recently reiterated statements of Strauss about the legal duty of one German government branch to extend a helping hand to another branch, nobody had asked him to phone the German military attaché in Madrid to prevail on him to secure the arrest of Ahlers. Such a request is specifically reserved to diplomatic intercourse by article 8 in the extradition treaty. The fact that he added in the phone conversation the allegation of corruption was a clever device to come within the terms of the extradition treaty, but it did not provide a mantle of legality to an illicit action completely outside his bailiwick. Actually his phone call was both completely unnecessary—Ahlers proved more than eager to face his accusers and stand by his collaborators—and also counterproductive. It was one of those extraordinary steps that increased general mistrust and disquiet over the cavalier treatment of both law and truth by Interior Minister Höcherl and Defense Minister Strauss when they were questioned in the *Bundestag* sessions on November 7–9.

2. Search and Seizure

It is not likely that the search and seizure problem raised by preliminary motion will play a major role in the Federal Court, if the main *Spiegel* case ever comes to trial, for the simple reason that the prosecution can dispense with any of the documents it originally seized, most of which have meanwhile been returned by the examining magistrates to the *Spiegel*. It does not need them. Since both Ahlers and Martin have testified before the judges, neither the authorship of the articles nor the person who gave the information is in doubt. They have admitted in detail both authorship and the extent of the information purveyed. Nevertheless, the *Spiegel* has pursued its preliminary complaints, not only in the hope that a favorable decision may create a predisposition by the Federal Court to dismiss the whole criminal case, but also in an attempt to protect the press in general against future "censorship" attacks by criminal prosecution.

In this case the prosecution searched the *Spiegel* files for three weeks before they discovered what they were really interested in: the link with Colonel Martin. To what extent German procedure allows such "fishing expeditions," searches for any material to substantiate suspicions rather than for specific pieces of evidence, is easier to discuss in theory than for defendants to test in practice. Before the use of such methods can be held to affect the rights of specific defendants, German procedure requires proof that the outcome of the trial as a whole rested on the government's search. This is hard to prove. The defense, therefore, in its procedural motions from the outset concentrated its guns on showing that the *Spiegel* action was not "merely" illegal but was *unconstitutional*. It contends that the press medium itself has special status, not just that of individual working newspapermen who are granted some privileges when called upon as witness. Their contention is supported by the case of a publishing-house accountant who was to be imprisoned for contempt of court because he was unwilling to testify on whether a member of the local police force had been paid for giving certain information. The Constitutional Court in 1962 required the trial court to do more than quote the Code of Criminal Procedure section allowing such a contempt-of-court arrest, and the judges instructed the lower court to weigh the requirements of a free press against those of criminal prosecution.[30] On this analogy, one might say that suspicion of treason by publication would not justify the all-embracing search and seizure procedures permissible in cases where those suspected were accused of having been espionage agents. The Court might be willing to look at the variety of allegations proffered by the *Spiegel* as an interconnected whole that pierced constitutional guarantees for the free and uninterrupted functioning of the media—to wit: waiting with the execution of the search, seizure, and arrest warrants till the weekend; inspecting and frequently carting off a great number of files containing information politically interesting to the government but entirely unconnected with the affair; detaining *Spiegel* personnel in Hamburg and Bonn without arrest warrants, though afterward releasing them without initiating further proceedings; etc. Whether the Constitutional Court should single out the procedural problems of media protection for immediate treatment or treat them as substantive problems involving the balancing of the public's right to information against the requirements of state protection is still another point of speculation. Emphasizing the latter aspect would allow the Constitutional Court to wait until the prosecution and Federal Court had worked out their own responses to these problems, much as the United States Supreme Court usually prefers to have trials held in lower courts rather than decide constitutional issues on preliminary motions. Of course, if the Federal Court should reject all the pending parts of the incidental motions, the Constitutional Court might not be able to avoid taking a position on the limits of search and seizure in cases affecting the media of communication. But even a favorable decision, while important as a precedent and a great moral victory for the *Spiegel,* will not affect the substance of the *Spiegel* case, as we have already noted.

3. The German Notion of Treason

The *Spiegel* affair is only the second case of its kind in the Federal Republic applying the notion of treason by publication. (A number of other preliminary inquiries begun by the Federal Attorney's office were nol-prossed.) In the other case, the appeal court in Hamm, on January 15, 1963, convicted a journalist on a Bielefeld paper who was responsible for the local news of the Detmold district, sentencing him to three months in prison. He had reported plans for new rocket installations that had been discussed in a closed meeting of military, state, county, and municipal officials in an article that expressed local fears as to the possible effect of such installations on the local tourist trade. In the opinion of the court and its military expert such facts opened to a potential foe a range of information that should have been kept secret in the interest of national defense. The court's opinion held that the act of the defendant in making these facts pub-

---

[30] Decision of December 18, 1962, reprinted in *Neue Juristische Wochenschrift,* vol. 16, January 24, 1963, p. 147.

lic was a negligent endangering of the security of the realm.[31] A constitutional complaint has been lodged against this final judgment, and the same member of the Constitutional Court to whom the *Spiegel* complaints have been assigned has been appointed rapporteur in this case also.

The theme of treason by publication is not new in Germany. Part of the excitement over the *Spiegel* case derives from its very historical connotations. The older generation considers this a resumption of the nefarious practices of the Weimar days, symbolizing an attempt by the defense and judicial establishments jointly to suppress criticism of official policy. Though the present legislation was passed in 1951, its two major props are indeed the ones that served for treason-by-publication trials in the Weimar era. First, the crucial element is not the official classification of the document but whether the facts, objects, specific knowledge, or news published relate to things that should be kept secret from a foreign power in the interest of the Federal Republic.[32] Second, it is treason if such state secrets are made accessible to anyone not entitled to receive them or if their circulation among the public endangers the welfare of the Federal Republic.[33] Thus, German law puts on the same level both secret trafficking with foreign powers and throwing open knowledge to the public at large. Now it is perfectly possible, as German commentators have pointed out, that publishing classified material would give potential foes access to information which otherwise they might not have come to know. But there is a vast difference between prying loose from the government information that it wants to keep from its people and what is commonly called "communicating with the enemy of the realm." It is the element of deadly surprise to the state, based on a misplaced trust that information is still secret, that is totally absent in the case of public communication. For this reason statutory enactments in many countries differentiate between the unauthorized publication of classified material and the intent of delivering such material to a foe. Thus, for example, the British Official Secrets Act of 1911 calls the former a misdemeanor punishable with a maximum of two years and the latter a felony liable to net its perpetrator, as it did in the Klaus Fuchs case, fourteen years in prison.

How treating political foes as traitors became part of the politics of the Weimar Republic is worth recalling. The long line of cases started in 1922, with a penal servitude term of eleven years for the publication of diplomatic documents of the World War I period that reflected unfavorably on German official policy, and led steadily to the eighteen-month prison sentence given in 1931 to Carl V. Ossietzky, later a Nobel Peace Prize winner, for publishing a report that the Ministry of Transport had illegally diverted funds for subsidizing the building of military aircraft banned under the Versailles Treaty. In such cases, expert opinion that the publication jeopardized

---

[31] Par. 100 c(1) of the Penal Code.
[32] Par. 99 (1) of the Penal Code.
[33] *Ibid.*, (2).

national security was furnished by the very section head of the Defense Ministry who had originally initiated the proceedings. As far back as 1927 Gustav Radbruch, a leading authority on criminal law and legal philosophy, said of such practices: "The penalizing of treason becomes more and more a professional risk for a journalist, militating in the ranks of the opposition. Under such circumstances punishment loses more and more its character of moral reproach, previously attached to it."

But while one might argue that this is all past history, though uncomfortably parallel, other aspects of the *Spiegel* case gave rise to more contemporary fears. There may still be people with a more or less pronounced National Socialist past in the ranks of both the police and the judicial establishment, and although it is doubtful whether their present behavior would mirror their NS past, their appearance in such sensitive and strategic jobs might still seriously weaken popular confidence in the impartiality of the proceedings. This is why the police commissioner directing the Hamburg *Spiegel* action had to be suspended immediately when allegations of an NS record, later on officially refuted, were put forward. Also the presiding officer of the third criminal section of the Court, in line to handle the *Spiegel* case, transferred to another job within the Court in spring, 1963, after some public discussion of various stages of his record. With the near universal reintegration of NS civil servants into the government apparatus there is never any guarantee that the record of any of these people might not suddenly reveal unsavory spots—possibly brought to light by East German agencies interested in discrediting the Federal Republic. While this problem is of diminishing importance simply because of the passage of time, it is still liable to pop up intermittently, and is an indication of the insecurity of a judicial establishment that has profited from the absence of sharply drawn domestic battle lines but has not invariably displayed a noticeably acute perception of the political realities of the time.

Those who will eventually have to make decisions in the prosecutor's office and on the Federal Court bench have before them, as we noted, the two *Spiegel* articles, the memos preceding these articles, and testimony on other information furnished to author Ahlers by Colonel Martin. Should any part of this material have been kept from the public altogether under the present terms of German treason legislation? A distinction suggests itself between the various types of material utilized by Ahlers:

It has never been doubted that a great part of the material worked up by Ahlers was simply the fruit of his long preoccupation with military affairs before and after he joined the *Spiegel* staff. This includes his prolonged discussions with all sorts of official and unofficial military specialists and his efforts to piece this knowledge together into a coherent analysis of German military plans and preparations, with the whole result obviously penetrated by his own particular views. Let us assume for a moment that no classified information entered the picture. The prosecution still would not be forced to give up the pursuit of a conviction. There would remain a theory emanating from the Federal Court that has been invoked against espionage agents: the so-called mosaic theory. This says that anyone who, with treasonous intent, pieces together unconnected odds and ends of unclassified material to solve a jigsaw puzzle about state secrets falls under the treason provision.[34] It is by no means clear that this kind of punishment for using one's intelligence would be transferred by the Federal Court from the field of catching agents of foreign powers to that of catching wayward journalists. *Mens rea,* the individual's possession of a legally sufficient awareness of the wrong done, might be a bit more difficult to establish.

But what if the prosecution is able to prove that Colonel Martin did rather more than carry on purely theoretical discussions with Ahlers? In this respect the prosecution might do better than in its initial clumsy bribery allegation, which revealed the narrow limitations of its political horizon. It had asserted that life experience would point to the fact that such intimate knowledge as shown in the Fallex article could be gained only via bribery in the ranks of the Defense Ministry—a hypothesis that had entered the original search warrant but was later completely abandoned. Yet the prosecution might well be able to show that, as a means to carry on the fight against the then prevailing military planning, Martin had given Ahlers some more novel concrete data. Would these factors be sufficient to bring him under the purview of the German treason provisions?

4. Freedom of the Press
Some learned German authors, among them Federal Court judges, have approached the problem by taking the Chancellor's constitutional prerogative to lay down the lines of governmental policy as their starting point. Consequently they assert that the yardstick of what should be kept secret and what may be freely discussed among the public should derive from official government policy, as long as the policy—shades of the Ossietzky case—stays within the framework of the law. But how far can the government then go in its attempt to exclude material from public discussion? What would the role of the expert be in the determination of the need for secrecy? Could he, as the prosecution's first expert from the Defense Ministry apparently did, argue such matters without knowledge of the available literature and publications in the field? Could he fill the role of a real expert in the traditional sense of the word, working as he did as a civilian employee of the defense establishment, predominantly interested in stopping the flow of communication between an insider and the *Spiegel* group? Would the examining magistrates find experts measuring up to the requirement of objectivity, even if they too could not dispense with official connections because of the kind of knowledge and type of material concerned? According to criteria now

[34] *Bundesgericht, Entscheidungen in Strafsachen,* vol. 7, p. 234, and vol. 15, p. 17.

generally accepted, the new expert, General Gerber, selected in 1963 by the examining magistrates from a list of three submitted by the prosecution, will first have to offer some opinion on the extent to which the Fallex material and possibly the memos preceding it contained information hitherto unknown outside official quarters. Then, he will have to analyze the consequences arising from the fact that foreign governments may thus have received, from the Fallex blend of inferences, conclusions, and asides, information possibly hitherto unknown to them.

While our analysis of the Fallex article showed that the *Spiegel* was in essence giving a further push to what by then were old themes in the defense debate and although the *Spiegel* had demonstrated that the overwhelming proportion of the facts had already been published, the experts might still pose the following questions:

1. Was it damaging for the Federal Republic and NATO that the *Spiegel* made an issue of Strauss's decision to give priority to his atomic ambitions rather than to NATO's conventional force requirements?

2. How valuable to the U.S.S.R. might be the *Spiegel*'s revelation of the three alternative force structures and costs that the defense experts had prepared for Strauss? (The answer to this question would be influenced by the fact that Strauss himself had revealed one of the calculations.)

3. Is the revelation that some elements in the air force and on the general staff seriously considered the desirability of a preemptive strike doctrine likely to have been of important help to the opponent, even though this document has not become official German policy and even though there is strong evidence that the very well informed—though not necessarily German—public know about these trends?

4. How likely is it that an unfriendly power would take seriously any information printed in a magazine such as the *Spiegel,* at least until official German government sources indicated—by an accusation of treason, for example—that it was not a product of imagination and might contain real secrets? After all it is one of the oldest intelligence maneuvers to slip supposed "secrets" to overt publications in order to confuse or mislead an opponent. Thus it might have been the prosecution rather than the *Spiegel* that alerted a potential foe to the existence of this worthwhile and hitherto inaccessible information.

Even if experts are able to make concise enough statements on all these points, the final determination rests with the judges. In the final analysis the evaluation of the objective facts in the case involves an ultimate question of constitutional interpretation: the respective priorities between the protection of military information and the demands of article 5 of the Basic Law guaranteeing freedom of the press. If the Federal Court should refuse to take up these questions or should answer them in the negative, they would certainly be presented to the Constitutional Court via a complaint by the defendants.

As early as 1954 the Constitutional Court had held that the protection of freedom of opinion provided an institutional guarantee of the press "as the carrier and distributor in the opinion-forming process."[35] This basic right of the press stems from the procurement of information to the spreading of news and the creation of opinions.[36] Disregarding side issues, the court will have to decide whether the German people's right to such information transcends the potential benefit of the information to a foe. In other words, whose education was more advanced by the Fallex publication: the German public's at home or the potential foe's abroad? Or, to put the issue on a slightly different basis: was the Defense Ministry mainly concerned with the effect of the publication in the offices of Soviet intelligence or with the effect that widespread publicity might have as a domestic obstacle to public acceptance of the defense strategies that at the moment loomed large in the military planning?

The plight of journalists in this situation can be seen by asking whether Ahlers could have learned what inside details to omit without harm to his information mission. Let us assume that the questions he submitted to various official and unofficial experts really concerned all foreseeable security angles of his piece. Since Germany does not have anything akin to the British D notice system, which puts the journalist on the alert about what the authorities would like to have kept from public knowledge, Ahlers could have no warning about crossing the line into "treason territory." Whatever the original intention of Minister Strauss and the prosecution, and whatever the political value of the treason charge hurled by Chancellor Adenauer in the *Bundestag* session, the very fact that Ahlers made attempts to get clearance suggests that the treason provision of paragraph 100 of the Penal Code is inapplicable. What remains is a minor charge taken from paragraph 100 c(1), which also presupposes that the welfare of the state has been endangered, but as a result of negligence rather than treasonous intent. And even then there remains a question whether the Basic Law does not make the information mission of the press supersede the element of negligence in endangering state security.

5. Control of Leaks by Government Officials

The prosecution may be quite aware of the pitfalls involved in Ahlers' and publisher Augstein's prosecution and therefore prefer to concentrate on Martin; but if it wants to score a significant victory, it must try to convict Ahlers and possibly Augstein. For this reason, the prosecution cannot be satisfied to put just Martin in the dock for the unauthorized leaking of office "secrets." Martin might have parted with office "secrets," and the court

---

[35] *Entscheidungen des Bundesverfassungsgerichts,* vol. 4, p. 96.
[36] *Ibid.,* vol. 10, p. 118.

might be willing to believe that Minister Strauss has a justified public interest in keeping deliberations of his office from the public eye. But this would probably not help catch any of the *Spiegel* group. While the purveyor of office "secrets" may be pursued,[37] the journalist receiving them, unless he gets them in a crooked way, has only done his professional duty.

Consequently, the prosecution would have to insist that the information that Martin passed on to Ahlers contained state secrets valuable to a foe rather than office "secrets" possibly valuable to the public. While Martin would contend that he had no dishonorable intention, his defense position would be more vulnerable than that of Ahlers. The constitutional protection of freedom of the press would scarcely arise in his case.

At any rate revealing state secrets may be more serious from the viewpoint of potential consequences than just parting with office "secrets"— information about matters the organization would like to keep from competitors or from the public at large. Negligence in handling the first may conceivably hurt the country. Negligence in handling the second may hurt one's organization, but in the process the country might benefit. In neither case, however, is that intent to harm the country commonly called treason involved.

The Spiegel and German Democracy

On the strictly legal and administrative level the *Spiegel* affair teaches a number of things: the use of treason charges against persons who unintentionally endanger the state's security, or who confide office "secrets" to snooping journalists, is fraught with danger for civil liberties in the West German republic. Perhaps the German legislature will now overrule the bureaucrats and professors who specifically omitted from the penal code reform a proposal for a clear-cut separation of treason from trespassing on state secrets in publications, endorsing the old treason concept as "resting on an old German legal tradition." Perhaps traditions such as this are too expensive to be conserved. But as important as reform of the penal code is the setting of an authority which, for the benefit of the sprawling and competing bureaucratic interests, would define concrete subjects that journalists might be expected to treat as out of bounds. Of course, such an authority would need to have enough prestige with the journalistic community to make its rulings stick.

The Public's Reaction to the Spiegel Case

Undoubtedly there was considerable public dissatisfaction with the *methods* used by the government. In a sample survey of 1877 persons 52 percent were not in agreement with the official handling of the proceedings, with 26 percent having no opinion and only 22 percent having no objections. In re-

---

[37] Par. 353 (b and c) of the Penal Code.

ply to a question on what was most disturbing about the case, 25 percent pointed to the evasive tactics of the government, 15 percent named Ahlers' arrest in Spain, and another 15 percent the activities of Strauss, while 14 percent were disturbed by the shroud of night and 10 percent gave a variety of other reasons, leaving 21 percent with no opinion.[38] To some extent, at least, this disapproval of government methods is reinforced by a different poll which probed reaction to Strauss's elimination from the cabinet. (See accompanying table.) No fewer than 42 percent of those asked approved, with only 17 percent on Strauss's side, although a surprising 41 percent were undecided. Partisanship played an important role: the SPD figures were 68 percent for elimination, 9 percent for Strauss, and 23 percent undecided, although even in his own party the anti- and pro-Strauss opinions balance at 29 percent and 30 percent, with 41 percent undecided. The most clear-cut anti-Strauss occupation group was the civil servants, with 52 percent against him, 20 percent for him, and only 28 percent undecided—suggesting that the "correctness syndrome," traditionally to the fore in the minds of officialdom, was more important than the substantive aspects of the case or Strauss's policies.

On the underlying substantive question of the public's right to information about defense policy, a clear 57 percent of the 1877 sample held that the press should inform the public about national defense issues. Only 10 percent were uncertain, and 33 percent felt that the defense policy was not a concern of all citizens. But when asked whether it would be proper to publish "previously unknown military information" 43 percent answered no, 30 percent said yes, and 27 percent were uncertain, suggesting that some of the public is unclear about the depth to which the press should be allowed to dig, and why. Interestingly enough, opinion within the SPD was almost evenly split, with 41 percent calling publication treason and 40 percent not.

The fact that 62 percent of the total were willing to let the journalist who published even secret information go scot free and concentrated their disapproval on the informant shows how unclear and basically unsettled these matters remain in the mind of the public. This confusion of views on the public's right to be informed perhaps underlay the public's tendency to suspend judgment on the treason issue until the courts decided. A poll showed that 42 percent were waiting for the judges to decide while only 27 percent —nearly evenly divided—had already made up their minds on whether or not the *Spiegel* was guilty of treason. (Twenty-one percent had no opinion.)

The Impact on the Spiegel *and on Strauss*
On balance, the *Spiegel* affair had no major impact on permanent circulation. Immediately after the raids, circulation shot up from an average of 480,000 per week to a temporary high of 665,000. But the 12 percent an-

---

[38] *"Spiegel* Affäre und Offentliche Meinung," public opinion survey of January, 1963, by Dr. Wolfgang Hartenstein and Dr. Klaus Liepelt, Institut für Angewandte Socialwissenschaft, Bad Godesberg, Germany.

QUESTION: As you may have heard, Defense Minister Strauss left the
federal government. Did you welcome or regret his departure?

His departure was

	welcomed by (%)	not welcomed by (%)	no definite opinion (%)	total (%)
TOTAL QUESTIONED	42	17	41	100
Party preference				
SPD	68	9	23	100
CDU/CSU	29	30	41	100
FDP	66	15	19	100
Other parties	70	11	19	100
No response	31	10	50	100
Men	52	20	28	100
Women	35	14	51	100
States				
Schleswig-Holstein Hamburg	51	11	38	100
Niedersachsen, Bremen	45	15	40	100
Nordrhein-Westfalen	43	15	42	100
Hessen	34	16	50	100
Bayern	35	22	43	100
Baden-Württemberg	52	19	29	100
Rheinland-Pfalz, Saar	34	17	49	100
Occupations				
Worker, farm worker	46	13	41	100
Salaried employees	48	19	33	100
Civil servants	52	20	28	100
Independent occupations	43	17	40	100
Farmers	17	23	60	100
Pensioners	34	16	50	100
Religion				
Protestants	47	13	40	100
Catholics	35	21	44	100
Others (no religion or no response)	53	17	30	100

SOURCE: EMNID Public Opinion Poll Data, No. 13, March 28, 1963. By permission
of EMNID-Institute.

nual growth pattern normal for the *Spiegel* since 1960 returned soon after,
so that by the spring of 1963 *Spiegel* circulation was growing at neither more
nor less than this previous rate. On the advertising side the story at first looked
less rosy. Perhaps not wishing to tarnish their brand names, a number of
business-opinion leaders like Bosch and Hoechst Chemicals made use of

their right to cancel contracts. But with the *Spiegel*'s increased circulation indicating its continued public, in the latter part of 1963 advertising returned. By now the *Spiegel* affair is written on the credit side of the accounts.

More difficult to judge are the affair's consequences for the magazine's editorial policy. Without question the *Spiegel* has become more cautious in its handling of government scandals and related issues, even at times going so far as to deliberately let itself be scooped by its Hamburg confrere the *Zeit*. It is not clear whether the change indicates only a transient temperance lasting until the possibly very remote day the court decides its case, or whether it is due to deeper causes deriving from the possibly new political requirements of the post-Adenauer era.

We can be rather certain that the *Spiegel* will continue as a German institution. As for Strauss, it is only a little less certain that he will do likewise. This may seem surprising to those who expect that when ministers are discovered to have seriously abused their official positions their political usefulness has come to an end. Strauss, though facing a multitude of Bavarian enemies, including political competitors and the Catholic church, preserved his local power position through his re-election as chairman of the CSU in August, 1963. Again standing on political *terra firma,* Strauss now actively sponsored a multitude of disjointed causes, ranging from a type of anti-communism more strident than that of his competitors to the special claims of war veterans. All of the causes were calculated to increase the political difficulties of those who had failed to support him staunchly in his struggles to retain the Defense Ministry job and to provide him with a national political following. They all serve to prepare his full-fledged political comeback at the opportune moment—to be determined by changes in the objective political situation as much as by his own and his competitors' political skill.

Conclusions

What further political repercussions the case may have will depend essentially on the action of the courts. Even if the classified opinion of the new military expert were couched in unambiguous terms, the federal prosecutor would still be fairly free to select among the persons and types of indictments. It is still harder to forecast the action of the Federal Court. Will the Court restrict itself to proceeding in one way or another against Colonel Martin alone as a scapegoat, thus underscoring the need for bureaucratic cohesion and intraoffice loyalty? Will it thus seek to avoid a head-on clash with the *Spiegel,* a clash that would result in a concrete definition of intersecting spheres of freedom of the press and national security?

Accepting this indeterminate state of affairs, we can still learn much of the workings of German politics. We are still left free to consider whether or not the seeming shocks of the *Spiegel* earthquake have caused any political structures to topple or to be redesigned.

Perhaps the two clearest lessons of the *Spiegel* case are, first, that it isn't easy to find out what a government has really done if it wishes to conceal its true actions and, second, that the communications media have an indispensable function in controlling the government. Whether it is orienting the public at large to the most important problems of defense strategy, or whether it is laying bare administrative malfeasance, the independent journalistic outsider must substitute for the politician who is abandoning such taxing pursuits. Consequently, the public confrontation with administrative power—its supervision and, if necessary, its domestication—resembles a duel between press and governmental office, with the opposition party restricting itself to a role reminiscent of the chorus in a Greek tragedy—underlining in cautious and measured tones the results safely acquired by others.

Nevertheless, it is quite evident that even a political opposition which is timid and lacking in initiative is better than none. Only a political party could have taken the *Spiegel* issues to the parliamentary arena and attempted to badger the government ministers into answering the questions that the press had raised. If the party had not done this, Strauss would probably never have been caught in his lies. If the government had not destroyed its credibility by being caught in numerous bald lies to parliament, it is doubtful whether the balance of public opinion would ever have swung decisively against it in this affair.

But these lies would not have sufficed to evict Strauss from office. In contrast to the U.S. tradition of legislative-executive conflict, the German parliament does not act as a cohesive unit against the government. As we have seen in the Fibag and Barth affairs, this condition severely limits the control function of parliament. On this occasion, Strauss was eliminated only because the FDP—a necessary part of the government coalition—could not otherwise have recouped the prestige it lost as a result of Strauss's treatment of their party colleague, the Minister of Justice.

The *Spiegel* case also suggests that when an ambitious political figure is able to harness pliable civil servants to his purpose, the possibilities for cutting the corners off administrative and legal guarantees are substantial. However, important as is the fact that Strauss was able to wield some measure of critical influence over several distinct federal bureaucracies, it is significant that he was never able to jump all jurisdictional hurdles. When it slowly became clear which authorities had either refused to participate or had remained outside the operation, this knowledge became the point of departure for protests against the methods employed.

From the viewpoint of the German politician, the *Spiegel* affair formed another link in the endless chain of strategies that an individual uses to improve his bargaining position or to deter the attacks of others. To that extent the *Spiegel* affair and its corollaries were not outside the routine of professional German politics with its increasing emphasis on incremental tactical advantages to be gained from fleeting constellations of events.

Changes

But some things are different since the affair. What is new is that the distance between official politics and the general public did not necessarily lead to a blind acceptance of what the political apparatus offered. Recollections of Germany's recent political history made the government's heavy-handedness immediately objectionable to substantial numbers of people, even though many had no decided opinion on the substantive aspects of the case. In the still waters of German domestic politics one concern, the extent and impact of which has so far never been precisely gauged, became clear and visible. This is a concern for the strict observance of correct and proper procedure.

While the majority had no particular knowledge of or interest in the fine line between security and liberty, the defenders of even the most wayward press profited from the suspicions aroused by the government's blunders. By this "backstage" method the conflict between security and freedom of the press, which in Germany has traditionally been prejudged by considerable reliance on the government's point of view, was now introduced as subject matter on which opinions should only be formed, after long deliberation, by completely neutral observers. Even if part of the judiciary still tends to think along traditional lines, the new situation arising from the public outcry has itself helped to change the role of the judiciary by demonstrating the dangers of what might be termed subliminal identification with the executive. It is in this new, popularly created balance between government and the aggressive presentation of deviating viewpoints that the importance of the case has come to light, long before it has formally been brought to judgment.

"When the state's security is at stake, why worry about a little unconstitutionality?" The dictum of the Minister of the Interior when he attempted, eleven months after the *Spiegel* raids, to cover up the unconstitutional use of Allied wire-tapping facilities suggests a continuing rift between an ingrained executive predilection for convenience and the requirements of constitutional government. In this light the *Spiegel* affair appears as an important but not decisive battle in the continuing fight for German public liberties.

There is a general assumption that nearly all political attitudes and actions are caused by, or can be correlated with, social, economic, or personal interests. Yet the *Spiegel* case highlighted a new issue that could not be immediately argued with the help of the usual symbols of political-social cleavage. Of special importance was the inability of the government to attach its banner of treason vs. loyalty to the *Spiegel* so firmly that it could then rely on the automatic support normally available for any anti-Communist measure.

Instead, more or less spontaneous realignment of opinion over the issue of freedom of expression and inquiry vs. complacent trust in the correctness of government action took place. This was especially visible in the nearly unanimous critical attitude of the frequently Establishment-oriented press.

If it is an accident of history that a person such as Strauss rises from Bavarian politico to serious contender for the leadership of Germany, the sequence of events that led to his first political fall seem all the more the result of a particular confluence of events which cannot be explained as the necessary culmination or effect of any discernible social, economic, or political trends in Germany.

In the same way it is clear that were it not for some real accidents of history, the raids on the *Spiegel* would probably not have aroused public or press reaction.

If, for example, the government had been able to arrest Colonel Martin, the military informant, at the same time as they swooped down upon the *Spiegel* editors, the initial government case would have looked much better even though the underlying substantive issue was the same. Or if the raids had not been carried out during the night, if Ahlers had not been in Spain and had not had to be unceremoniously and illegally captured, if dramatic nighttime searches of private homes had not occurred, or even if the government had known how to lie better, the attempt to crush the *Spiegel* might well have been successful and had the passive support of a duped public. For even if the memory of the individual's helplessness before the Nazi secret police has left an acute sensitivity to government invasion of private rights, there is still a woefully underdeveloped sense of public liberty in Germany. And given what we now know about what went on behind the scenes, it seems certain that if the government and Strauss had successfully repressed the *Spiegel,* the quality and character of public discussion and inquiry and, in time, of individual liberty would have drastically deteriorated.

But the particular events of the *Spiegel* affair focused attention on the latent anxiety of the German people and for the first time provided a pure case of state power vs. individual liberty. Without overestimating its operational impact, one can safely say that the extended and dramatic confrontation between the government and those who demanded an account of its actions may provide symbols and experience out of which a tradition of opposition to any government's authoritarian tendency might develop.

POSTSCRIPT

Just before the second anniversary of the affair the Federal Attorney submitted a seventy-three page indictment to the Federal Court. It levies charges against Colonel Martin, editor Ahlers, and publisher Rudolf Augstein. Among other offenses the indictment accuses Martin of treason (par. 100 [1] of the Penal Code) for having furnished to the *Spiegel* information that had not been made public previously and that should have been kept secret in the interest of national defense. It indicts Ahlers and Augstein for having procured and published part of such secret information (par. 100 [2]).

As the text of the indictment is considered secret, we do not know which of the information given to the *Spiegel* by Martin is considered to have been treasonable and which divulging of office "secrets" only. The cases of two of the defendants, lawyer Josef Augstein and lobbyist Paul Conrad, have been nol-prossed. No decision has been rendered so far in regard to the other defendants.

While the third criminal section of the Federal Court is studying the indictment and the files of the *Spiegel,* lawyers for the defendants have not been inactive. They have taken issue with the equally secret opinion of the prosecution's second military expert, General Gerber, who, being a mere brigadier general with a field command, is considered not to have enough familiarity with the complicated problems raised by the case. They have also complained that the new Secretary of State of the Ministry of the Armed Forces—Hopf, his predecessor has been transferred to the presidency of the Federal Court of Accounts—under one or the other flimsy pretext has rejected additional experts named by the defense.

There have occurred, in addition, some rather startling incidental happenings that pinpoint the quixotic nature of the case. The former Federal Attorney, Max Güde, since 1961 a prestigious CDU member of the *Bundestag* and its Legal Committee, has suggested that if a trial becomes necessary it should not take place before the September, 1965, *Bundestag* elections. Still more startling than Güde's all too public calculations of the trial's possible effect on next autumn's election was the fact that in November, 1964, the *Spiegel* was able to procure a contribution from the pen of an anonymous "Judex"; entitled "Are we facing another Ossietzky case?" it sharply criticized the unsastisfactory state of German treason legislation and ended with suggestions as to how the Federal Court might reason to avoid unjust convictions. After initial denials, "Judex" turned out to be the very selfsame presiding Judge Jagusch, who, in the spring of 1963 had suddenly transferred from the third senate—which was about to handle the *Spiegel* case—to another section of the Federal Court. After his authorship became known, he quickly asked to be put on the retired list.

The fact that Franz Josef Strauss has so far dodged the judicial summons in the preliminary inquiry concerning the abduction of Ahlers in Spain has not prevented him from quickly regaining his former status as the Federal Republic's most successful politician. The Federal Minister of Justice has made the necessary formal demand initiating the prosecution of Gerhard Jahn—the progenitor of parliamentary inquiries into Strauss's methods and practices—for divulging office "secrets" to the *Spiegel* crew (par. 353 (b and c) of the Penal Code). Will Jahn have a chance to meet his colleague Franz Josef Strauss on the crowded stage of the Bonn District Court? Will the courts take Güde's hint? In this event Colonel Martin, the closest approximation to an *anima candida* ("pure soul!") among the dramatis personae, might well be left to hold the bag.

December, 1964

Selected Bibliography

Books

BERGNER, GERT. *Rudolf Augstein und die "Spiegel" Affäre*, Stoedtner Verlag, Berlin, 1964.

ENZENSBERGER, HANS MAGNUS. *Einzelheiten*, Suhrkamp Verlag, Frankfurt, 1962.

ESCHENBURG, THEODOR. *Die Affäre, eine Analyse*, Die Zeit, Hamburg, 1962.

KUBY, ERICH, et al. *Franz Josef Strauss: Ein Typus unserer Zeit*, Verlag Kurt Desch, Munich, 1963.

LÖFFLER, MARTIN. *Der Verfassungs-Auftrag der Presse: Modellfall "Spiegel,"* Verlag C. F. Müller, Karlsruhe, 1963.

OSGOOD, ROBERT. *NATO: The Entangling Alliance*, U. of Chicago Press, Chicago, 1962.

RUGE, GERD, ed. *Landesverrat und Pressefreiheit, ein Protokoll*, Kiepenheuer und Witsch, Cologne, 1963.

General Articles

BAILEY, GEORGE. "The 'Spiegel' Affair: A Distorting Mirror," *Reporter*, December 6, 1962, pp. 29–32.

HAFFNER, SEBASTIAN. "The End of the Affair," *Encounter*, vol. 20, no. 3, March, 1963, pp. 62–67.

HEINRICH, HANS. "Deutsche Politik," *Gewerkschaftliche Monatshefte*, vol. 14, May, 1963, pp. 301–5.

HENTIG, HARTMUT V. "Verräterischer Verratsbegriff—Der Verrat und die gemeinsame Sache," *Merkur*, vol. 17, no. 1, January, 1963, pp. 103–4.

Legal Articles

ARNDT, ADOLF. "Das Staatsgeheimnis als Rechtsbegriff und als Beweisfrage," *Neue Juristische Wochenschrift*, vol. 16, May 14, 1963, pp. 465–69.

GUEDE, MAX. "Die Geheimsphaere des Staates und die Pressefreiheit," lecture of the then Federal Attorney before the Association of German Journalists on April 15, 1959.

HANOVER, HEINRICH. "Der loyale Landesverrat," *Werkhefte*, 1963, p. 53.

HEINEMANN, GUSTAV. "Der publizistische Landesverrat," *Neue Juristische Wochenschrift*, vol. 16, January 10, 1963, pp. 4–8.

JAGUSCH, HEINRICH. "Pressefreiheit, Redaktionsgeheimnis, Bekanntmachung von Staatsgeheimnissen," *Neue Juristische Wochenschrift*, vol. 16, January 31, 1963, pp. 177–83.

KUECHENHOFF, ERICH. "Landesverrat, Oppositionsfreiheit und Verfassungsverrat," *Die Neue Gesellschaft*, 1963, pp. 124–27.

MAIHOFER, WERNER. "Pressefreiheit und Landesverrat," parts I and II, in *Blaetter für Deutsche und Internationale Politik*, vol. 8, nos. 1 and 2, 1963.

RIDDER, HELMUT, and HEINITZ, ERNST. "Staatsgeheimnis und Pressefreiheit," two lectures before the 3. Bundestagung der Arbeitsgemeinschaft sozialdemokratischer Juristen in Berlin on May 25, 1963.

STREE, WALTER. "Zur Problematik des publizistischen Landesverrats," *Juristenzeitung*, vol. 12, nos. 17 and 18, September 13, 1963, pp. 527–32.

WILLMS, GUENTER. "Der Sachverstaendige im Landesverratsprozess," *Neue Juristische Wochenschrift*, vol. 16, January 31, 1963, pp. 190–91.

WILLMS, GUENTER. "Landesverrat durch die Presse," *Deutsche Richterzeitung*, vol. 47, January, 1963, pp. 14–16.

WOESSNER, HORST. "Das Mosaikgeheimnis im strafrechtlichen Staatsschutz," *Neue Juristische Wochenschrift*, vol. 17, October 8, 1964, pp. 1877–80.

Government Publications

The government spoke through its ministers in parliament, through its daily German language press bulletin, or through its weekly press bulletin. One comprehensive report was issued in February, 1963, and published in the German language bulletin; this was, however, an attempt to justify the government's actions rather than to objectively examine the case. See the following:

Press and Information Office of the Federal Republic of Germany, *Bulletin of the Press and Information Office* (weekly, English language).

————, *Bulletin des Presse und Informationsamtes der Bundesregierung*, October 24, 1962, *et seq.*

————, "Spiegel Bericht des Bundesministers der Justiz an den Bundeskanzler der Bundesrepublik Deutschland," *Bulletin des Presse und Informationsamtes der Bundesregierung*, no. 23, February 5, 1963, pp. 195–204.

Discussions in Parliament

The three-day *Spiegel* debate and discussion can be located in the German equivalent of the Congressional Record:

Verhandlungen des Deutschen Bundestages (Bundestagsprotokolle), 4. Wahlperiode, Stenographischer Bericht, Bonn, Sessions 45, 46, and 47, November 7, 8, and 9, 1962, pp. 1949B–63B, 1981D–2010D, 2013A–25D, 2075B–90A.

The main debate on reforms and needed changes in the state protection section of the penal code, March 28, 1963, appears in the following:

Bundestagsprotokolle, Session 70, pp. 3180D–3217D.

Publication of the Social Democratic Party (SPD)

Fraktion der SPD im Deutschen Bundestag, *Bericht der Sozialdemokraten über die Behandlung der "Spiegel" Affäre durch die Bundesregierung*, Neue Vorwärts Verlag, Bonn, 1963.

Publications of the Spiegel
a. Pertinent issues of the *Spiegel* in vols. 15–18 (1961–1964).
b. Privately printed and circulated by the publishers of the *Spiegel:*
Verfassungsbeschwerde, 1 BvR 586/62, Hamburg, 1963.

HÖHNE, HEINZ, and SPIERING, ROBERT. *Belege zur Titelgeschichte Foertsch,* annex to 1 BvR 586/62, Hamburg, 1963.

Schriftsatz des Bundesministers der Justiz an den Ersten Senat des Bundesverfassungsgerichts Karlsruhe, 1004 E(933–849/63), December 20, 1963.

Acknowledgements

We are indebted to Dr. Wolfgang Hartenstein and Dr. Klaus Liepelt of the Institut für Angewandte Socialwissenschaft in Bad Godesberg, Germany, for permission to use their public opinion survey of January, 1963, *"Spiegel* Affäre und Offentliche Meinung,"* and to S. H. Drescher and P. v. Wrangell of EMNID-Institute for permission to use their surveys. We are also indebted to the Spiegel Verlag for the utilization of its archives. We are grateful to Professor Dr. Horst Ehmke, Freiburg, for the opportunity to peruse the briefs addressed to the Bundesverfassungsgericht.

Study Questions

1. In the *Spiegel* affair several social interests came into collision—armed forces military security, the role of the press in informing the public, and the public's right to know government policy in order to judge it. How does any society assign relative weight to these competing values?

2. It is often said that the principal defense of civil liberties in the American political system lies in the courts, and in Britain in the parliamentary question-period process. As you read the *Spiegel* affair, where do you think this role lies in the German system?

3. How do you think the functions of political parties in Germany will affect the outcome of the *Spiegel* affair?

4. One way to view the action of the administration in the *Spiegel* case is to say that once Strauss committed himself to action against the magazine, the administration's support of him was natural and inevitable. To what extent do you think that the German legal system, press, and interest-group patterns made it easier for this to happen than it would have been in Britain or France?

5. Putting the case into the American setting, how would you expect the main actors—journalists, politicians, army officers, and prosecutors—to have acted differently? Would you say that "It just couldn't happen here"?

4

THE COMMON MARKET

Farmers and Foreign Policy

An Agricultural Agreement for Europe

Michael G. Duerr

The lights never went out the night of January 13, 1962, at the Palais de Justice in Brussels, Belgium. In fact, the old crystal chandeliers had blazed with electric lights almost continuously since December 29, when the Council of Ministers of the European Common Market had assembled for a last attempt to come up with a common agricultural policy.

Then, at 5:30 in the morning of January 14, as the sun still lay beneath the horizon, French Foreign Minister Maurice Couve de Murville picked up his pen and initialed an agreement in front of him. So did representatives of the governments of the Federal Republic of Germany, the Italian Republic, the Kingdoms of Belgium and the Netherlands, and the Grand Duchy of Luxembourg. The basic decision had been made for establishing the common agricultural policy that was the keystone of the European Common Market.

As delegates, staff specialists, and secretaries split into small groups and bundled out into the icy twilight in search of bed or breakfast, newspaper correspondents scribbled the last sentences in their stories and hurried to telephone or cable their offices. Next day their dispatches were front-page news stories all over Europe and were carried under bold headlines in Buenos Aires and Montreal, in Tokyo and Sydney. With good reason, the agreement attracted worldwide attention.

This common agricultural policy of the European Economic Community would affect the pocketbooks of about twenty million farmers in the Common Market's six member countries. Its impact would reach far beyond the boundaries of "the Six" to Australian sheep farmers, Arkansas chicken growers, and agriculturalists everywhere. Beyond that, events in 1961 had endowed this agreement with even wider significance. Observers all over the world agreed that the common agricultural policy was the crucial test case for the European Common Market. Failure might end the vitality of the Common Market. Success would open the way to moving ahead on other fronts. Furthermore, the agreement reached on that chilly January morning revived a movement with historic antecedents that reached back to the Roman Empire—the movement toward a united Europe.

The European Movement

The urge to unite had been recurrent in Europe, but the hard fact was that unity had never been fully achieved. For that matter, it had rarely been tried by peaceful means. Now, seventeen years after the end of World War II, any effort at union still faced major obstacles. The countries to be linked were of different ethnic stock, had distinct cultural backgrounds, spoke separate languages, and had a history of bloodshed, hatred, and warfare stretching back more than a thousand years. Furthermore, all were advanced, complex economies with industrial and agricultural bases that had long been nurtured behind protective tariff barriers. Their rivalries and self-sufficiency had produced a climate for conflict. The essential conditions for peace and growth were cooperation and interdependence.

At the end of World War II circumstances made European unity attractive enough to spur major efforts. Five years of war had torn apart old national economies. It was doubtful that political nationalism could achieve a a return to the power, prestige, and prosperity of prewar days. As the postwar era began, it was clear that the real centers of power had polarized elsewhere. To the west, the United States enjoyed world power through its great wealth and nuclear monopoly. To the east, the Soviet Union had become the greatest force on the massive Eurasian continent.

Between these two superpowers lay a shattered western Europe, its cities devastated by bombs and shells, its people wearied and wounded, its countryside exhausted by levies. Britain, at least, had not been occupied by hostile troops, and it kept some of its influence in the Western world. On the Continent, however, only France was accorded any deference in the councils of the West, and that was largely ceremonial.

This, then, was the atmosphere of economic and political uncertainty in which the movement toward European unity was born anew. Its early leaders, dubbed the "Good Europeans," which was then shortened to the "Europeans," included men from every country and nearly every political persuasion. Foremost among them was a politically independent French businessman, Jean Monnet. Others ranged from the conservative Konrad Adenauer of Germany to the socialist Paul Henri Spaak of Belgium. Notably absent were the Communists.

Pressure from Overseas

Aside from the hard core of "Europeans," many others agreed that a new degree of cooperation would be necessary to rebuild Europe. The Marshall Plan urged them in this direction. United States aid was made conditional upon cooperation among the European nations in allocating funds and in coordinating their economic development and reconstruction programs. Accordingly, in 1947 the Organization for European Economic Cooperation was formed.

A different kind of pressure came from the East with the Communist takeover of Czechoslovakia in March, 1948. But even more feared perhaps than further Soviet expansion to the west was a return of German militarism. In the early approaches to European unity Germany was considered an enemy not a partner, and the North Atlantic Treaty in 1949 sidestepped the issue of rearming Germany. As German economic recovery progressed, however, the rearmament issue became increasingly difficult to avoid. Those concerned about European unity proposed, therefore, that the German armed forces be woven into a European Defense Community that would be subordinate to a supranational council representing all member countries. Although the United States favored the scheme, it never became popular in Great Britain and France, and in 1954 the European Defense Community proposal finally died on the floor of the French National Assembly. Europe was not yet ready for a supranational army.

Nevertheless, economic necessity was stimulating creative moves toward cooperation and coordinated action. The secret of initial success was to concentrate on a specific, limited objective.

A Breakthrough in Steel

Meanwhile, the European movement had been progressing on the economic front. Robert Schuman of France had proposed that the coal and steel industries of Europe be integrated through a supranational High Authority, and in 1952 France, Germany, Italy, and the Benelux countries adopted the proposal. The essence of this European Coal and Steel Community was free trade among the Six, with the High Authority supervising coal and steel investments, prices, wages, freight rates—even social conditions in each member country.

It is hard to imagine a better pilot industry for economic integration than steel. Costly plants and equipment put a premium on investment planning and give the large operator a distinct competitive advantage. Under the High Authority's guiding hand European steel prospered. Production increased by nearly half in five years. Trade in iron and steel nearly tripled.[1] Yet the demand for steel was so great that free trade produced few hardships. Even the ECSC's sacrificial lamb—the small and highly protected Italian steel industry—surprised experts by recording the fastest rate of growth in the Community. By 1957 the steel industry had convincingly demonstrated the economic benefits of supranationalism and free trade among the Six.

But a grimmer message was emerging from the coal sector. The European coal industry was, in 1952, as sluggish an industry as steel was dynamic. Many coal mines had been worked intensively for a hundred years and operating costs were becoming exorbitant. Postwar Europe was switching to oil for its energy, yet many regions had built their whole economies around the mines. The High Authority's program, therefore, included plans for gradually closing unprofitable mines and helping unemployed miners to move, learn new skills, and start their lives afresh in places where new industries were growing and labor was scarce.

Although this program was perfectly logical, it ran into a maze of difficulties. Unemployed miners did not want to uproot their families and move; they wanted to keep on digging coal. And the national governments, responsive to the wishes of this group of voters, were reluctant to shut down the mines in the face of their vocal opposition. Thus the High Authority's imaginative coal program drew much praise but accomplished little.

The Birth of the EEC

The ECSC's success in the steel sector encouraged a further experiment in economic integration. In May, 1955, representatives of the Six met in Messina, Sicily, to discuss the possibility of extending the supranationality principle throughout the economic life of Europe. Great Britain declined an invitation to join. After eight days, the Messina delegates appointed a committee headed by Spaak to draft a program; a year later the committee filed a one hundred and fifty page report. The Spaak report contained a blueprint for a European Common Market, which was based on the principles of the Coal and Steel Community but extended to all industry. It provided for the elimination of all tariff and quota restrictions among member states and for the establishment of common barriers to outside trade. It also provided for "harmonization" of nearly all national policies that could impart an advantage to the industry or agriculture of one country over another—income

---

[1] *Eighth General Report on the Activities of the Community* (European Coal and Steel Community, High Authority, Luxembourg, 1960), pp. 424, 429.

taxes, government subsidies, antitrust laws, transportation regulations, restrictions on the movement of capital and labor.

When the representatives of the Six again sat down together in Rome, in March, 1957, it took them less than three weeks to hammer out a treaty that embodied most of the principles of the Spaak report and committed the Six to the creation of a European Economic Community. Undoubtedly the two lessons of the Coal and Steel Community—that economic integration can work very well in a robust industry, but that its chances for success in a sick one are not assured—had come home to the leaders of the European movement. The first lesson contributed to the speed and apparent ease with which the Rome Treaty establishing a European Economic Community was initialed by the Six and ratified by the six parliaments soon after. The second pointed an advance warning finger at the sector of Europe's economy that would cause the most trouble—agriculture.

A European Government on Paper

The delegates who gathered in Rome in March, 1957, found that the removal of industrial tariffs was among the least of their problems. Free trade promised tangible benefits—wider markets for producers, lower prices for consumers, economic growth, and a rising standard of living. Although there was some opposition to dimantling tariffs in France and Italy, where they had been highest, it soon became clear that these objections could be met through concessions and escape clauses that would not prove disastrous. More difficult would be the problems of harmonizing national laws and forging common policies, and of establishing some supranational authority to make and enforce the rules necessary to weld the economies of the Six.

To this end, the Six designed a sort of European government on paper and set forth a fairly elaborate timetable calling for the gradual accomplishment of the various tasks of economic integration over a twelve-year period. Tariffs on industrial products would be reduced 10 percent at a time until they reached zero. Tariffs on industrial products from outside the Community would be adjusted in three steps until they reached a level roughly equal to the average tariff of the member states. Restrictive "quotas" on imports from other members would be relaxed each year until the end of the transition period, when they would be removed entirely. For parts of the economic integration scheme which did not lend themselves to rigid scheduling—such as patent law or agricultural policy—the transition period was divided into three stages, with definite objectives for each stage. By the end of the third stage, economic integration was to be fully achieved.

The national governments were unwilling to turn over the control of such a sweeping evolution to a supranational authority, as they had in the limited case of the Coal and Steel Community. Too many of their own responsibilities were tied up in the package. Therefore, they created a supranational Commission to formulate common policies and administer their execution, but retained for themselves the right to approve or disapprove all such policy. During the first stage of the transition period practically all policies written by the Commission would have to be approved unanimously by a Council of Ministers representing the six national governments. During the second stage many of the Commission's decisions would have the effect of law if approved by a "qualified majority" of the member states. More decisions would be accepted after such majority approval in the third stage, and at the end of the transition period nearly all of the Community's policy would be decided by majority vote.

The most striking characteristic of the Common Market "government" is its dependence on a balance of national interests. The Council of Ministers is the center of power and makes the major policy decisions—both legislative and executive in character—for the Common Market. But the six ministers of the Council are responsible first to their own national governments. They are, in fact, important cabinet ministers in their own governments, devoting nearly all their time to their national offices and meeting only periodically to vote on Common Market legislation.

Since the ministers hold office at the pleasure of their national electorates, it is no surprise that they tend to view Common Market business in the light of its domestic political consequences when deciding how they will vote. Particularly during Stage One, therefore, it is imperative that important Common Market legislation somehow be made palatable to the voters of all six member states. Theoretically, a key block of voters from Luxembourg could put enough pressure on their minister to stymie Common Market progress completely.

Actually, of course, this is unlikely. The Rome Treaty was ratified only because each of the Six felt that it was gaining more than it was giving up. A balance of national interests implies that each minister can count more voters in his country who favor the whole Common Market idea than voters who oppose any specific Common Market proposal. To the smaller countries the EEC brought such dramatic expansion of markets and such sweeping opportunities for economic growth and enhanced political influence, that a minister who obstructed its progress probably would have lost more votes than he gained.

In the larger countries, however, the issue was not so clear-cut. The idea of a new Europe, stronger than the sum of its parts, had appeal in France; but the National Assembly would not have agreed to expose French industry to German competition if France had not been promised development aid for its African colonies and access to the German agricultural market. Similarly, Italy gave up its high tariffs in exchange for aid in developing its depressed south; and Germany agreed to open its frontiers to French farm products and to underwrite more than its share of the various Community development funds in exchange for access to industrial markets in France and Italy as well as reinstatement in the Western family of nations.

Most of the EEC's supranational authority rests with the Commission, a nine-man body whose personnel is selected jointly by the member governments for four-year terms and which acts collectively in making decisions. It sits permanently in Brussels and is charged with acting in a spirit of independence and for the benefit of the Community as a whole. In practice it works through a number of committees. The Commission administers the Common Market, works out detailed policies for implementing the Rome Treaty, and supervises the execution of policies approved by the Council of Ministers. It acts independently in regard to technical matters on which decisions have been reached and initiates proposals in the Council after they have been discussed by the Economic and Social Committee of the European Parliament (if it is so required).[2] Thus the Commission serves in part as a permanent executive and in part an administration dependent on the Council of Ministers.

How can the Commission function with no legislative power under its control and no political party or parties supporting it? How can it function with an insignificant budget, no treasury, and no patronage to dispense? Yet the Commission does operate under these conditions, and it is no small testimonial that it has been able to exert as much influence as it has from such a small power base.

In the first place the Commission has a strong moral influence. It also draws some real power from two unusual sources. First, its right to draft and submit policy proposals to the Council permits the Commission to assemble package deals, which maintain the balance of national interests while advancing those of the Community. Second, its status as the only day-to-day administrator of the Common Market permits the Commission to maintain a large and expert staff in Brussels which can confer constantly with pressure groups and political parties from all six member countries.

This unique combination allows the Commission to attempt the subtlest power plays in all European politics. Starting with a sophisticated appraisal of the domestic political situation in each country, the Commission is sometimes able—after months of staff work and careful drafting—to present its proposals to the Council in a form that is hard to reject.

The European Parliamentary Assembly, a 142-man body appointed from the parliaments of the member states, has no legislative power though it can debate and recommend. Thus it plays a relatively small, though vocal, role in the Common Market's governing process. Significantly, it may censure the Commission by a two-thirds vote, which would oblige the Commission to resign. The Assembly has no direct power over the Council of Ministers.

---

[2] A. R. Campbell and D. C. Thompson, *Common Market Law* (Stevens, London, 1962), p. 90.

INSTITUTIONS OF THE EUROPEAN COMMUNITIES

SUPERVISION

European Parliamentary Assembly
142 members selected by
national parliaments

Court of Justice
7 judges and 2 advocates general

EUROPEAN COAL AND STEEL COMMUNITY ECSC	EUROPEAN ECONOMIC COMMUNITY EEC	EUROPEAN ATOMIC ENERGY COMMUNITY EURATOM

POLITICAL EXECUTIVE

Council of Ministers 6 members, one each from national governments	Council of Ministers 6 members, one each from national governments	Council of Ministers 6 members, one each from national governments

ADMINISTRATIVE EXECUTIVE

High Authority 9 members, appointed by national governments	Commission 9 members, appointed by national governments	Commission 9 members, appointed by national governments

CONSULTATION

1. Consultive Committee
   51 members

1. Economic and Social Committee
   101 members
2. Economic Policy Committee
   21 members
3. Monetary Committee
   14 members
4. Transport Committee
   30 members

2. Scientific and Technical Committee
   20 members

ADMINISTRATIVE DEPARTMENTS

1. Administration and Finance
2. Economy and Energy
3. Coal
4. Steel
5. Industrial Reorganization
6. Finance and Investments

1. External Relations
2. Economic and Financial Affairs
3. Internal Market
4. Competition
5. Social Affairs
6. Agriculture
7. Transport
8. Overseas Countries and Territories
9. Administration

1. Research and Instruction
2. Industry and Economy
3. External Relations
4. Security
5. Information
6. Radiation Control
7. Administration and Personnel
8. Budget and Finance

SPECIAL AGENCIES

1. Mines Safety Commission
2. Transport Commission

1. European Investment Bank
2. European Social Fund
3. European Development Fund

1. Central Nuclear Measurements Bureau
2. Joint Nuclear Research Center
3. Supply Agency

SOURCE: *The European Markets: A Guide for American Businessmen* (The Chase Manhattan Bank, New York, 1964), p. 17.

It is important to note, however, that many of its members speak with authority in their national parliaments and can influence the ministers in this way. The Assembly's importance may grow, since the Treaty calls for its eventual election by universal vote within the Community. This body, representative of all the people, might then assume some of the powers of the Council—perhaps evolving into a federal legislature for the Six.

The fourth branch of the EEC is a Court of Justice, which interprets the Treaty in cases brought by member governments or the Commission. It also hears appeals from firms or persons affected by the decisions of the Commission or Council. Up to now the Court has exercised few of its interpretative powers, but within its jurisdiction it is the court of final appeal, taking precedence over the various national courts.

Several consultative committees round out the institutions of the European Economic Community. Of particular interest is the Economic and Social Committee, made up of representatives from industry, labor, consumers, and agriculture in each member country. Like the Assembly, it serves as a sounding board for the Commission and gives these special interest groups an opportunity to express themselves independently of national controls.

This division of powers among branches of the Common Market government provides a weak system of checks and balances at best. The give-and-take on policy within the Community is brought about by the distribution of powers among the member states. During Stage One of the transition period, virtually every important decision was made subject to the unanimous approval of the Council of Ministers. And before the Common Market could move on to Stage Two—where some important decisions could be made by majority vote—the Council had to vote unanimously that it was ready.

This vote in many ways held the key to the whole elaborate timetable of the Common Market. Without a unanimous vote, the Common Market would be stalled only one-third of the way to its goal. Once it was taken, however, the Treaty provided no way for a single member state to halt the Community's progress. The Treaty said that only a majority of the member states could *prevent* the transition from Stage Two to Stage Three from taking place on schedule, four years later. Figuratively, any single nation could stamp on its own brake pedal during Stage One and stop the bus. When it agreed to pass into Stage Two, it threw the brake out the window. Thereafter it could attempt to steer but not to stop the Community in its progress toward economic union.

The Common Market's search for an agricultural policy, which hinged on this vote, provides a good example of this unique system of government at work. It demonstrates the dominance of the national representatives—the Council of Ministers—in the governmental system of the EEC and, at the same time, shows how much real influence lies with the supranational Commission. Most important, it shows how much can be accomplished by compromise among sovereign governments if stimulated by the common desire to make the Common Market work.

Four Years of Industrial Growth

In the industrial sector, the Common Market's early success was dramatic. The first tariff cuts were made on schedule, and as tariffs among the Six came down, trade went up. In the first four years total trade among member countries increased by no less than 73 percent.[3] Capital investment across national boundary lines also increased, and more than 500,000 Italian workers moved into Germany, thus helping to alleviate Italy's unemployment problem and Germany's pressing labor shortage at the same time.

Germany's "economic miracle" continued through the four years, with industrial production climbing by 3 percent in 1958, 6.5 percent in 1959, 11 percent in 1960, and another 5.5 percent in 1961. Unemployment fell to less than 1 percent of the labor force. Family income went up by nearly 50 percent. The number of automobiles on the roads increased from two million in 1957 to more than five million in 1961. In France, where industrialists had been anxious because of German competition, production rose by 4 percent in 1958, 3.5 percent in 1959, more than 11 percent in 1960, and nearly 5 percent in 1961. French exports to Germany actually increased faster than German exports to France. In Italy, where levels of protection had been highest, improvement in the economy was greatest of all, with production increasing by 3 percent in 1958, more than 10 percent in 1959, 15 percent in 1960, and another 10 percent in 1961. As a result, Italy entered upon an economic miracle of its own. Unemployment, which had been a chronic problem in the Italian south, fell from 2,000,000 to less than 1,400,000 in the four years. The Benelux countries gained nearly as rapidly, their combined national income increasing by nearly 20 percent. Altogether the Six rang up the most impressive four years of economic growth in modern history.[4]

The precise connection between the EEC's tariff-cutting and the growing economic prosperity enjoyed by its people is hard to establish—it might have occurred without the Common Market. In European minds, however, there was a clear enough connection between the two to make the Common Market a great popular success. When a Paris department store tagged imported merchandise "Champions of the Common Market," marking prices down in accordance with the tariff cuts, the promotion drew crowds of shoppers. And polls showed that the man in the street was aware of the EEC and generally in favor.[5]

Considering the Common Market's astounding early success, it may be hard to see how a single issue—agriculture—could come close to wrecking it. But a look at the farm situation in Europe explains it.

---

[3] *Foreign Trade Monthly Statistics,* no. 4 (European Economic Community, Statistical Office, Brussels, 1962), p. 9.

[4] *General Statistics, 1958–1962* (Organization for Economic Cooperation and Development, Paris, 1963).

[5] New York *Times,* March 20, 1962, p. 49.

Europe's Agricultural Problem

Europe's farm problem has its roots deep in the political and military history of the Continent, as well as in its geography. The typical European farm is small, so small that it is hard to justify the purchase of tractors and other machinery which might improve farm efficiency. (About three out of four farms are smaller than twenty-five acres. By comparison, only one out of four is less than twenty-five acres in the United States.)[6] Furthermore, many of Europe's farms have been split over the generations into even smaller plots, often irregularly shaped, and sometimes separated by considerable distances. In West Germany, by 1949 the average farm holding was split into eleven fragments, averaging about two acres in size.[7]

The small size and crazy-quilt fragmentation of European farms have curtailed the farmer's efficiency and held down his income. This, in turn, has forced him to grow many crops for his table, rather than concentrate on the one or two that he might best be able to grow for the market.

Some of the inefficiency in European agriculture was war-induced—self-sufficiency is a strategic advantage if foreign trade is disrupted—but most of the subsidies, prohibitions on imports, minimum pricing schemes, price supports, and high tariffs have reflected simply a desire to protect domestic farmers from foreign competition. And the consumer pays the bill. At about the time the Rome Treaty was signed, the price paid by the government to German wheat farmers ran about 35 percent higher than the price of Argentine or Australian wheat landed in Bremerhaven or Hanover, and a loaf of white bread cost half as much again as in Great Britain, where prices are not supported. A dozen eggs cost twice as much in Paris as in London, and a pound of sugar costs more than twice as much in Rome as in London.[8]

This situation stems from the fact that farmers have even more political power in the Common Market countries than in the United States, where they comprise only 8 percent of the labor force. Comparable figures for the EEC range from a low of 10 percent in Belgium, through 12 percent in Holland, 15 percent in West Germany, 25 percent in France, and about 30 percent in Italy.[9] Political realities dictated that the leaders of the European movement, no matter what their personal convictions about the farm problem, handle the common agricultural policy with kid gloves. No logical economic theory could be sure of ratification by the national parliaments of the Six if it might later be blamed for causing hardship to the farmer.

---

[6] Frederick Dewhurst et al., *Europe's Needs and Resources* (Twentieth Century Fund, New York, 1961), p. 507.

[7] *Agricultural Integration in Western Europe,* vol. XXIX, no. 470 (Political and Economic Planning [PEP], April 18, 1963), p. 112.

[8] *Food Prices and The Common Market,* Occasional Paper no. 13 (PEP, London, May 29, 1961), pp. 7–11.

[9] *Report on Western Europe,* no. 9 (Chase Manhattan Bank, August–September, 1960).

The diplomats who met in Rome were restrained by more than political vote-counting, however. After the war, national governments had instituted plans to encourage a more rational approach to agriculture, and they were sincerely reluctant to abandon them. Industrial growth was encouraging farmers to migrate to the cities, which also helped to alleviate the problem.

As might be expected, France placed great importance on extending the Common Market to farm goods. French industry was nervous about opening the doors to German competition; losses were expected. Only through a vigorous boost to the farm sector did France expect to gain more than she gave up economically from the Community. Holland also favored the common agricultural policy, feeling that it would help the export of meat and dairy products. Italy had mixed feelings, fearful lest a flood of foreign grain and meat products hurt Italian farmers but hopeful that such a policy would expand the market for exported fruits and vegetables. Belgium's farm population was so small and voiceless as to count for little in agricultural policy. West Germany, with its highly protected and inefficient farm sector, was least anxious to open its gates to foreign farm products. Adenauer would have preferred a strictly industrial Common Market, but he realized that a strong German stand on this point might kill the infant EEC altogether.

Chancellor Adenauer's Dilemma

As an example of the political and patriotic considerations that motivated national leaders, Germany's problem is worth looking at a bit more closely, particularly because German farmers had the most to lose from an extension of the Common Market to agriculture. Chancellor Adenauer had mixed feelings about the common agricultural policy. He believed devoutly in the need for a united Europe and for German participation in it. The new markets of western Europe would occupy the attention of German industry, which had rebuilt itself into an efficient and competitive machine. Unemployed manpower from Italy could find work in Germany, replacing the slackening inflow from East Germany. Finally, the challenge of a united Europe would occupy the intellectual energies of statesmen and students who might otherwise pin their future hopes on a resurgence of German nationalism. The Common Market provided, in Adenauer's mind, an outstanding opportunity for working the new Federal Republic into an appropriate and proper position in the postwar world.

Up to a point, this plan matched the political philosophy of Adenauer's party, the Christian Democratic Union (CDU). A towering achievement of the Christian Democrats' administration had been the "economic miracle" engineered by Adenauer's economics minister, Ludwig Erhard. Erhard's economic policy was based on free competition and included unilateral re-

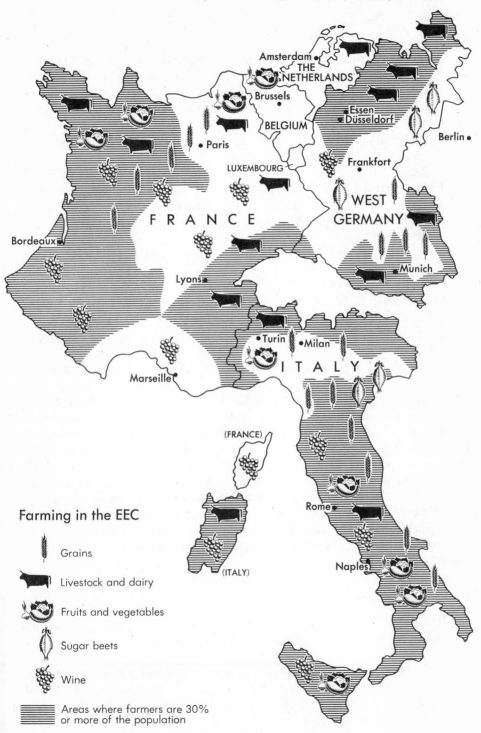

Farming in the EEC

Grains

Livestock and dairy

Fruits and vegetables

Sugar beets

Wine

Areas where farmers are 30% or more of the population

Drawn by Harry Scott.

ductions in German tariffs on industrial products. In one particular, however, the Common Market clashed with the CDU platform. This issue was agriculture. In 1957 farmers accounted for some 20 percent of the Christian Democrats' total membership, and the Farmers' Union held an influential seat in the party caucuses. Further, the CDU is a church party, and the agrarian virtues—thrift, respect for property, individualism—were seen as a bulwark against the socialist way of life.

Before EEC farm policy became an issue, Adenauer and the Farmers' Union coexisted peacefully enough under the roof of the CDU. Germany's industrial boom was drawing marginal farmers off the land more effectively than any deliberate program could. For those that remained, the government offered low-cost financing for farm improvements and even served as an impartial arbiter in land swaps, so that farmers with many parcels of land could exchange some of them for plots closer to home. The government also offered a few incentives to bring industrial plants into farm regions but deliberately soft-pedaled the program out of deference to the Farmers' Union. As a result, German farm efficiency was improving, and as long as prices remained high, the Farmers' Union was content to go along with Adenauer's farm policy.

With a loyal electorate—one-fifth of which were farmers—a working policy on agriculture, and the conviction that the German economy was progressing as satisfactorily as could be hoped, Chancellor Adenauer and his government were less than overjoyed at the prospect of coming bluntly before the people with a plan to eliminate the protection of the German farmer —even over a long transition period. Yet just such a plan was implied in the Common Market. French newspapers stated with perfect clarity that French agriculture—more efficient than that of Germany—could be expected to gain markets in Germany. In fact some papers, in Germany as well as France, called the Rome Treaty a swap of the German farm market for the French industrial market. The German dilemma was to influence the fortunes of the Common Market throughout its first four years.

The Community Approach

The Rome Treaty had spelled out the objectives of the common agricultural policy in general and slightly ambiguous language:

1. To increase agricultural productivity by developing technical progress and by promoting the rational development of agricultural production and the optimum utilization of the factors of production, particularly labor.

2. To ensure thereby a fair standard of living for the agricultural population, particularly by raising the individual earnings of persons engaged in agriculture.

3. To stabilize markets.
4. To guarantee regular supplies.
5. To ensure reasonable prices of supplies to consumers.

To the leaders of the European movement, a step removed from the accountabilities of domestic politics, objectives 1 and 2 were the heart of the design. The common policy should increase farm efficiency, promote higher yields per acre, and encourage farmers to specialize in the products they could grow best.

Objectives 3 and 4 were a nod to the political realities of reaching agreement among six countries with large and inefficient farm populations, which were well aware of the uses of the ballot. Clearly some authority would have to keep farm prices from falling, regardless of the other objectives of the policy. Further, the Community must always be able to supply enough wheat and sugar for its people—just in case imports should become "irregular." In other words, specialization could be carried on within the Common Market, but only so long as European farmers were given an environment in which they could continue to till the soil and sell their products within the Community.

Objective 5 was a sop thrown in for members like the Dutch, who imported large quantities of food at cheap world market prices. It was also designed to head off the criticism by urban voters throughout the Six that the common agricultural policy, in its solicitude for the farmer, might result in higher grocery bills for them.

The Rome Treaty's ambiguity on agriculture was no accident. Agriculture was recognized from the first as a stumbling block in the path of unity. The wording of the Rome Treaty was aimed first at circumventing the stumbling block and only second at unifying the agricultural policies of the Six. Far down on the list of priorities was the desire to transform European agriculture into a body capable of sustaining itself in free competition with the world market.

Stresa: A Job for the Commission

It was plain to all the signers of the Treaty that the agriculture problem could be hedged but not avoided. To measure the task of uniting their agricultural policies, the Six called a conference at Stresa, in northern Italy, during the month of March, 1958. The conference was attended by more than a hundred delegates, including the agricultural ministers and representatives of farm organizations from all six countries.

The Stresa Conference brought the first open discussion of escape clauses —parts of the Treaty that had been inserted to cushion the impact of the common policy on the protected farmers. One clause provided for a system of "countervailing duties" that could be applied against state-subsidized competition from another member state. When the French wheat monopoly, for example, sold wheat to Germany at a price judged to be artificially low, Germany could impose a duty to offset the artificial advantage. Another clause proposed a system of minimum prices below which restrictions might be imposed on imports from other member countries. The Treaty charged the Commission to draw up "objective criteria" for these minimum prices—in other words, conditions under which they should be imposed and what they should be.

Stresa also opened the economic question of surpluses. Immediately after the war, with people starving in the streets, it had been a universal policy in Western Europe to try to increase agricultural production. By the late fifties, however, food was no longer scarce. Some economists felt that Europe's problem, like that of North America, would be too much production rather than too little. The representatives at Stresa showed concern in their final resolution about the problem of a balance between supply and demand for foodstuffs. The task of measuring and prescribing for this problem was left to the Commission.

The Stresa Conference also left to the Commission the job of working out a "structural policy" for the Community. This term included the consolidation of fragmented land holdings, provision for rural electrification, better roads, and easier credit for farm improvement. The conference recognized that this policy would require money, and left it to the Commission to propose a suitable method for carrying it out.

The Mansholt Plan for a Common Agricultural Policy

The Stresa Conference had given a clear mandate to the Commission, and the Commission took on the job of framing an acceptable policy. The direction of this effort fell to a Dutch economist, Sicco Mansholt, vice president of the Commission and its director for agriculture. The plan that he worked out was a mixture of theoretical economics and practical politics. Mansholt attempted to create a broad agricultural market of western Europe, based on the principle of free competition but responsive to the needs of France and Germany. The result was complicated and satisfied no one in all its particulars, but it was the basic document from which the policy steadily developed over the next four years.

Speaking of the Mansholt Plan, Dr. Walter Hallstein remarked: "Indeed, [it is] under fire from critics of all complexions; some say we are too protectionist, others that we are too liberal; some say that we are too interventionist, others that we are too laissez faire. Perhaps this means we have struck the happy medium—or perhaps the unhappy medium."[10]

Spearheading the policy was a far-reaching program for structural reform to be coordinated by the Commission on a Community-wide basis. Mansholt emphasized the consolidation and grouping of land holdings and the increase of efficiency through mechanization and fertilizers. He also stressed the need for some farmers to give up farming, proposing industrial development of rural areas and improved education so that young farmers would be better equipped to find jobs in industry. Specifically, Mansholt called for a European Fund for structural improvements in agriculture, to be subscribed by contributions from member countries and dispensed by the Commission. He also called for an annual review of national measures concerning structural policy by the Council of Ministers, and suggested that the Commission make annual recommendations that would include "proposals for more action and financial aid by individual member states."

The Commission recognized, however, that structural reform alone could not solve Europe's farm problem. Of more immediate importance was the coordination of the complex and protectionist marketing systems in use in each member country. Although Mansholt's proposals for structural policy did not include much political leavening, he realized that a practical market policy would have to be a balanced blend. This was apparent from the Commission's explanation of the policy, which spoke of giving farmers "a fair rate of income approaching that earned in other sectors of the economy."[11]

Common pricing was to be the backbone of the Common Market in agriculture. If the government of one member were authorized to support prices at a level higher than that of other member countries, that nation's farmers would be gaining an unfair advantage—just as a manufacturer would profit from special tariff protection. During the transition period member countries would gradually have to bring their prices closer and closer to a common level. At the same time, other protective devices would have to be reduced —step by step—until ultimately the German, French, and Italian farmer would find their prices supported at the same level, with no administrative restrictions on competition throughout the Common Market.

To the farmer, this was a matter of grave concern. Unless he could compete successfully with other farmers all over the EEC, he stood to gain little from the reductions in national protective barriers—and he could lose everything. Furthermore, he was sure to express his concern vehemently at the polls. This, of course, made prices a vital matter to the Council, for ministers who do not heed the will of the voters do not remain ministers long. There was one important escape, however, not among those discussed at Stresa.

[10] Speech before the Defense College of the North Atlantic Treaty Organization (Paris, January 23, 1961).

[11] *Bulletin of the EEC* (Secretariat of the Commission, Brussels, December, 1959), p. 13.

This was the price level. Agricultural markets in the Six were all more or less controlled by the respective governments. If the administered price of the farmer's products was pegged by the Common Market Commission at the same level that it had been pegged at by the national government, the common agricultural policy—for all its talk of increased competition—would not affect him at all. For example, if wheat were pegged at $3 a bushel, it would make no difference to the farmer whether he sold his wheat to the German government or to the Common Market government, as long as some government agency would take it off his hands for $3.

The problem was the Common Market could not have supported wheat at that price without encouraging surplus production. France already grew more wheat than it consumed. Furthermore, the French support price for wheat was about $2 a bushel—and a $1 rise in the guaranteed price would have made French farmers plant more wheat, using land that they had not considered worth the effort of working when the guaranteed price was only $2. A Common Market government, supporting wheat at $3 a bushel, would find itself having to buy, store, and periodically dispose of a growing surplus. Clearly a high support price for wheat would run into direct conflict with the Rome Treaty's goal of economic efficiency.

On the other hand, if the Common Market had set the support price at $2, many of the German farmers who had managed to eke out a living on small, fragmented plots when prices were higher would have found it impossible and would have been forced to shift to some other activity. But this would have been certain to have political repercussions in Germany, and might even have driven the Federal Republic out of the Common Market, thereby defeating the basic purpose of the European movement.

Faced by this dilemma the Mansholt Plan confined itself to stating that prices must be brought to the same level by the end of the transition period; it left the determination of that level for the future. The plan made one sally in the direction of price setting: Starting with the 1961–62 harvest year, the Commission proposed that the national governments adjust their support prices on wheat toward each other slightly (Germany was to reduce its price by one mark per one hundred kilograms, France to raise its price by one mark),[12] and suggested similar moves for prices on sugar, corn, and barley.

External Protection: The Variable Import Levy

As for the protection from wheat grown outside the Common Market, the issue was not nearly so touchy. The Commission recognized the need to cushion the Community against wide fluctuations of world market prices. The most common device for protecting a market from foreign competition is the tariff. But the tariff, being a fixed amount or percentage of value, can

---

[12] *Ibid.,* June–July, 1960, p. 41.

often be overcome by foreign producers, especially with farm products, where price fluctuations are sometimes very wide. When used, tariffs are usually supplemented by rules which call for sealing off the national market completely if the tariff does not succeed in protecting it. As a result, the typical European system of agricultural protection had become a mixed bag of restrictive laws and international agreements, all of which added up to a mutual understanding that no one would disrupt the others' farm markets by selling them cheap food.

To accomplish all this in a much more simple and direct manner, Mansholt chose the variable import levy, a protective system introduced by Sweden. The variable levy is defined as the amount of duty needed to bring the price of imported goods up to the target price set for the domestic market. If the internal price has been set at $3.00, and foreign wheat can be landed and sold at $2.80, the levy is $0.20. If the world has a bumper harvest and foreign producers are willing to sell their wheat at $1.75, the variable levy automatically rises to $1.25. In this way, the domestic farmer can forget about the world market price and rest contented that come what may, he will collect his $3.00 a bushel—insulated from the competition of foreign producers.

Similar policies were recommended for coarse grains, sugar, and dairy products. To effect these policies, European Market Organizations—with power to intervene in the internal markets of the member countries—and a levy system at the Community frontier to insulate Common Market farmers from the competition of the world market were set up. For beef, pork, poultry, and eggs, the Commission proposed a looser market organization. Protection would be provided by a mixture of tariffs, quantitative restrictions, and, again, a variable levy, based on the price of grains used for feed, which could be adjusted as needed to keep foreign produce from selling below the price guaranteed to domestic growers. For fruit, vegetables, and wine, the principal external protection was to remain the tariff.

Through the technicalities, five points show clearly from this first concrete expression of the Commission's agricultural policy:

1. The principle of a free flow of farm goods inside the Community. The Commission's proposals called for the complete abolition of intra-EEC restrictions on trade and paid scant attention to escape clauses. It planned for the first movements toward a common support price to begin by 1961 and foresaw that the transition period should be completed in only six years.

2. Emphasis on structural policy. Although preoccupied as to detail by the pressing problems of market organization, the Commission placed primary emphasis on the long-range program of helping European farming to become efficient.

3. A goal of reasonable price levels. The Commission did not tackle the pricing problem directly, but sought to establish a precedent for levels close to the average for the Six, rather than near the highest level.

4. Protection from world market prices. The Commission's proposals for protection against nonmember countries in the farm sector were frankly aimed at holding down imports to the level needed to fill out the Community's needs—considerably smaller needs than those of the individual member countries.

5. Firm policy administration. The Commission sought to insulate itself from domestic pressure groups and also staked a claim to an independent source of revenue—the European Agricultural Alignment and Guarantee Fund.

A true Common Market in agriculture, with the Commission itself playing the key role, is at the core of this summary. Hardships caused by this Common Market would be borne, as much as possible, by outsiders rather than by voting members of the EEC.

Out of the Incubator: Changes in the Mansholt Plan

For the rest of 1959 and early 1960, the Community's governmental apparatus worked over the Commission's proposals. The Economic and Social Committee came forth with several recommendations, which were duly passed on to the Council of Ministers. The final version of the Commission's proposals, refined by debate in the Economic and Social Committee, was submitted to the Council of Ministers on June 30, 1960. It differed from the original Mansholt Plan in three important particulars.

First, the Economic and Social Committee suggested that consultative committees be set up to help the Commission draw up its detailed proposals for marketing important commodities—such as grains, sugar, vegetables, dairy products, and wines. These committees, comprising representatives of the interested farm organizations and consumer groups, would then work closely with the regular Community institutions to carry out the policy. Although these committees would reduce the Commission's own authority, they were "European" and not purely national pressure groups. The Commission accepted the recommendation.

Second, the Commission recommended dropping some of the provisions for protecting the Common Market farmer from foreign competition, and it placed greater emphasis on the levy system. Originally the variable import levy was to have been backed up by the use of quantitative restrictions on imports. As the efficiency of the levy system became understood, however, these devices were considered superfluous. The concept of minimum prices, which had been dealt with at length during the Stresa Conference, was also judged an unnecessary complication, and the Commission proposed that it be dispensed with.

Third, the Commission incorporated the Economic and Social Committee's proposal to develop a comprehensive "social policy" to improve the lot of farmers and farm labor. Some of its objectives overlapped with those already implied in the structural policy, and some were added. The objectives of the social policy read like a political platform, which in part they were: better social security for farmers, educational opportunity for farm children, "assistance to young farmers seeking independence," aid in shifting to other occupations, better housing, aid to elderly farmers, and better social and cultural conditions. The basic aims of the Mansholt structural policy persisted, but inside a candy coating.

The Commission stuck by its guns as far as the length of the transition period was concerned, stating that the six-year deadline should be maintained to encourage the agricultural sector to adapt itself to changes and to avoid inappropriate investments.

Speeding Up the Timetable

While the Commission had been refining its proposals, the Common Market had moved ahead on another front. On May 10, 1960, the Council of Ministers decided to speed up the timetable for transition to a full Common Market. The Rome Treaty had allowed twelve years for the gradual reduction of intra-EEC trade barriers and the adoption of common policies. It had provided, in fact, that the transition could be slowed down to fifteen years. But the Common Market's spectacular early success in the industrial sector had kindled a general desire to get on with the tariff-cutting; because there was an atmosphere of rapid economic growth, member governments were now agreed that many other measures for economic integration—such as freeing the movement of capital and labor—could be taken faster than had been foreseen by the men who drew up the Rome Treaty.

On May 10, 1960, the Six agreed to make their next scheduled tariff cuts ahead of schedule and to work toward bringing the Common Market into full effect by about 1967, instead of 1972 as planned. There was little disagreement over this among the Six. The French insisted, however, that a speedup in the industrial timetable must be matched by steady progress in the agricultural sector. Tariffs on farm goods must be reduced ahead of schedule too, and there must be steady progress toward a common agricultural policy.

The acceleration decision of May 10 imparted a new urgency to the agricultural agreement. Germany and France—the two most important members —were pulled in opposite directions by internal politics regarding agriculture. Yet the positions of these two countries would have to be reconciled before the Common Market had gone very far along in its course.

A few news items from the New York *Times* show how seriously the

French were taking their farm problem at that time. At Amiens on February 11, at least one hundred people were injured in protests over a minor revision of the government's price formula. On February 25 the National Federation of Agricultural Organizations pressed for better price supports at its national convention. On March 16 a majority of the National Assembly defied President de Gaulle by asking for a special parliamentary session to consider rural unrest. On April 7 mass farmer demonstrations were held in eighteen towns, and violence erupted in two. Farmers in Quimper, Brittany, tried to block trains moving their produce to market. And on May 5—less than a week before the acceleration decision—opposition groups in the Assembly failed in an attempt to censure the de Gaulle government for its handling of the farm crisis.

The Council of Ministers received the Commission's proposals on agriculture at a time when its attention was focused on the acceleration of the timetable. Knowing that the two issues were inextricably interwoven, the Council appointed a Special Committee on Agriculture to study the Commission's proposals. This committee, unlike the Commission or the Economic and Social Committee, was not a supranational body. Its members reported to the national governments and were responsible for seeing that their countries' interest was being carried forward by the policy.

In July the Commission concluded another study of far-reaching importance. Seven months earlier the Council of Ministers had told the Commission to investigate a complaint by the German government that bread and fondant paste (used in making candies) from Holland and fondant paste from Belgium were entering Germany under unfair conditions. The Germans claimed that Dutch and Belgian producers were buying low-cost raw materials from suppliers outside the EEC and were, therefore, able to ship the finished product into Germany at prices so low as to be unfair. They asked the Commission to allow a special tax to be levied on these imports to raise their prices to the German level. The Commission decided that the Dutch and Belgian producers did indeed have an unfair advantage and that the Germans could apply a special import levy equal to the savings that Dutch and Belgian producers realized from buying raw materials outside the Community. This decision opened the door to other complaints by Germany, Italy, and France on various processed products. Its effect was to cancel the price advantage of imports and encourage EEC producers of processed foodstuffs to switch to high-cost wheat or sugar grown in the Community.

A hint of counterpressure came at nearly the same time from the United States, as the Secretary of Agriculture, Ezra Taft Benson, made a visit to Brussels. European unity had been an appealing idea to Americans ever since the Marshall Plan, and the Common Market drew almost universal applause in the United States. The Eisenhower administration's view was that the EEC would strengthen Europe economically and politically, and that

Illingworth in the London *Daily Mail* (Ben Roth Agency), approximately May 16, 1961

Committee for Economic Disarmament

Keith Temple in the New Orleans *Times-Picayune*, September 6, 1962

International Reactions to the Common Market Debates

Juhl for the Copenhagen P.I.B. (Ben Roth Agency), approximately July 11, 1962

Camel- and Needle's-Eye Problem

COLONISTS IN EUROPE

"It's not exactly beautiful, but we all wish to preserve our national characteristics. . . ."

this stronger, more stable ally would be worth some loss in U.S. exports to the EEC due to tariff discrimination. Further, it was expected (correctly, as it turned out) that any such losses would be offset by gains caused by Europe's growth in import demand.

This was all very well in the abstract, but U.S. farm groups saw real losses and no offsetting gains for themselves as they speculated on the Commission's agricultural proposals. Holland and Germany, for example, imported large quantities of grain from the United States, but the variable import levies seemed to promise French growers an unassailable position in these markets. Furthermore, 1960 was an election year in the United States, and neither party could afford to turn a deaf ear to farm protests.

In Brussels, Benson talked with Mansholt, to whom he expressed his "concern over the direction the agricultural policy appears to be taking." Mansholt emphasized that the Commission was aiming at a liberal trade policy for farm products and added that its proposals were more liberal than most member's present national policies. This seems to have satisfied Benson, who was quoted on his departure as saying that the talks had "completely put my mind at rest, since the EEC is aiming at readaptation aid to farmers in certain regions on a temporary basis, for a limited period, and on a limited scale to assist them in giving up unprofitable production so as to improve their income."[13]

The Democrats, too, stepped carefully to avoid stirring up the issue of U.S. farm exports to the EEC. Their platform "welcomed" the Common Market and also promised the American farmer "new high levels of food consumption both at home and abroad."[14] Indeed, the Trade Expansion Act, which followed Kennedy's election in November, was passed on the assumption that the EEC would eventually modify the principle of Community preference in farm goods, although neither the Commission's proposed policy nor the realities of Common Market politics justified any such conclusion.

Even more serious than the apprehensions of American farmers were the British objections to the agricultural policy. Although Britain had turned a cold shoulder toward the Six at Messina and Rome, a growing body of British opinion now favored some form of association with the Common Market. Most Europeans expected that Britain would eventually join, and many were anxious for it. But the agricultural policy loomed as an important obstacle to British entry.

Britain imports most of its food from the Commonwealth, and the economies of Australia and New Zealand would suffer greatly if food from EEC countries were to receive preference in the British market. Furthermore, former British colonies such as Ghana and Nigeria count heavily on the

---

13 *Ibid.*, August–September, 1960, p. 33.
14 New York *Times*, July 13, 1960, p. 19.

British market for tropical food products; yet these developing nations would lose their preferred position in Britain to the ex-French Associated Overseas Countries, whose right of access to EEC markets had been expressly spelled out in a protocol to the Rome Treaty. How could the trade split in Europe be healed if EEC agricultural policy made no allowance for Britain's relationships with the Commonwealth?

These pressures added to the Commission's headaches but did not change the fact that their agricultural policy would stand or fall on its reception by the Council of Ministers.

Guidelines for a Common Agricultural Policy

By the end of 1960, the Council of Ministers had begun to speak. The Special Committee of the Council led off with its report, which endorsed most of the Mansholt market policy but downgraded the politically unattractive structural policy. The committee endorsed free movement of farm products within the Community "under conditions similar to those which govern an internal market." It also endorsed the idea of a common price level and stressed the need for a common commercial policy toward nonmember countries.

The Council itself followed with an opinion on the levy system. It, too, generally concurred with the Commission's recommendations. On trade among the member states, the Council agreed that the levies should be gradually reduced to zero, but balked at the Commission's proposal to remove other forms of protection as the levies were introduced. As for trade with nonmembers of the EEC, the Council endorsed the levy system wholeheartedly. In fact, it suggested that the levies should do more than just "equalize" import and EEC prices; import prices should be a bit higher, to ensure that member countries would have an advantage over imported produce.

This first encounter between the Commission philosophy—governed mainly by economics—and the Council's—governed mainly by politics—was a fair indication of things to come. Each member of the Council was answerable to a national electorate. All had national goals to pursue, and within the framework of the Treaty, they pursued them. The Commission, effectively insulated from national politics, recommended bold plans. It was soon faced, however, with the choice of insisting on its plans or yielding to national pressures in the interests of preserving the cooperative spirit that sustained the Common Market itself.

The Commission chose to yield on most issues. As the body empowered to write the proposals, it tried to write them in a way that would shave the national objectives of the Six as closely as they could be shaved without drawing blood. If they were shaved too close, the Council would fail to agree; and if the Council failed to agree on the agricultural policy, there would be no Common Market.

The Institutions at Work

Through the early months of 1961, the institutions of the Community concerned themselves with details of the policy. Following the Council's instructions, the Commission submitted proposals on a system of applying minimum prices, and this was debated—paragraph by paragraph—in the parliament. The Commission, meanwhile, was meeting periodically with the Council's Special Committee on Agriculture, and it adopted only those parliamentary amendments that seemed likely to meet with the Special Committee's approval. To cite one example, the parliament recommended that minimum prices applied by a member state as a means of keeping out imports should not exceed the support price. The Commission, which had opposed minimum prices altogether in its first proposals, recommended that member states be allowed to fix such minimum prices at 5 percent above the support price.

The parliament also debated the levy system, approving it without significant reservations, and it continued throughout the spring and summer to advise the Commission on its agricultural proposals as they were prepared. The Economic and Social Committee also became increasingly active as the Commission's detailed proposals for the Common Market in pork, grains, and other products, as well as their recommendations on minimum pricing, began to take shape.

In March the European Court of Justice entered the agricultural picture for the first time. The Commission had accused Italy of restricting imports of pig meat from other member countries in violation of the Treaty. Italy countered by invoking an escape clause. The Commission retorted that Italy could not invoke the escape clause unilaterally, but had to ask the Commission's permission. Nine months later the Court ruled in favor of the Commission and made the Italian government pay court costs. This case provided the Common Market's judiciary with its first slim volume of precedent, establishing the principle that the EEC was the custodian of its own Treaty and that member states could not interpret parts of the Treaty in their own interest and invoke them unilaterally.

The Real Debate

It became more and more apparent, however, as the spring turned to summer and the summer turned to fall, that the debates in the European Parliament and the Economic and Social Committee and even the deliberations of the Court of Justice provided a decorative edging rather than the warp and woof of the Common Market fabric. The Commission took note of their recommendations but paid considerably more attention to the recommendations of the Special Committee for Agriculture.

The real debate over the common agricultural policy was beginning to take shape inside the Special Committee among the member countries themselves. The Parliament and the Economic and Social Committee continued to function as sounding boards, but the real differences of opinion were not between branches of the Common Market government; they were between the member states. As the year grew colder, the national positions began to congeal. Substantial progress toward an agricultural policy had to be made before the end of the year if the Six were to keep moving ahead of schedule in the industrial sector, and the French government made it clear that agriculture could not be bypassed.

In the French view, moving to the second stage without truly substantial progress toward a Common Market in agriculture would violate the spirit of the Treaty. Furthermore, it would be against the interests of France, and France was prepared to use its veto in the Council of Ministers to prevent the move to Stage Two, if necessary. Some 23 percent of the French population were farmers and dependents, and yet they earned only 13 percent of French national income. Although the first three years of the Common Market had brought prosperity to the country as a whole, the farmers had seen little of it. French plans for building up the agricultural sector were based on a broad EEC market, free of restrictions against French farm products but protected against imports from outside the Six. The Commission's proposed levy system and Agricultural Guidance and Guarantee Fund would provide a large part of the funds France would need for structural reform.

The German position was at the other extreme of the debate. While the Germans recognized that a real Common Market would have to include agriculture, they opposed the French view that agricultural integration should proceed at the same pace as industrial. The Germans felt that the more difficult problems of implementing a common agricultural policy should be attacked more deliberately and that a more gradual transition should be allowed than in the freeing of trade in industrial products. This thinking was conditioned by the poor competitive position of German agriculture and by the pressures exerted by the Farmers' Union on the Adenauer government.

During the summer the Commission had not been unduly concerned about the German position obstructing the progress of the Common Market. Adenauer's government was facing elections, and it was thought that his recalcitrance on the common agricultural policy reflected a wish to avoid stirring the issue and would disappear soon after election day. The industrial boom was continuing, and leaders of the Christian Democratic party had been swinging around to the view that the affluent new middle class—peo-

ple with their own homes, bank accounts, and shares of Volkswagen stock—
might prove to be as strong a bulwark against socialism as the traditional
farm families. Posters emphasizing the high cost of farm supports to the consumer had even begun to appear on city billboards. While Adenauer was
shifting his party's base of power, however, he could not be expected to hand
his political opponents an issue likely to reduce the CDU's majority of the
farm vote. As soon as the elections were past and the CDU was firmly en-
trenched for another four years, it was thought, the Germans would stop
dragging their feet and an agricultural policy acceptable to the French could
be negotiated.

The German elections produced a surprise, however. Instead of being
returned to power with a large majority in the legislature, the Christian
Democrats lost ground to a third party, the Free Democrats, and found
themselves unable to muster a parliamentary majority without the Free
Democrats' support. Adenauer suddenly found himself in the trickiest kind
of political situation—dependence on a coalition government. Instead of
being more free to lead Germany to a compromise with the French, Adenauer found himself less free. The German position on agriculture hardened.

The other member states had various special interests to pursue in framing the common agricultural policy, but all wished to push on with it, especially if failure to do so would result in a French veto of the move to Stage
Two. By the fall, though, another issue had intruded. Britain had at last applied for admission to the Common Market. On October 10 in Brussels
Edward Heath, in charge of negotiating British membership, told the Six,
"We desire to become full, wholehearted and active members of the European Community in its widest sense and to go forward with you in the building of the new Europe." But he added, "Australia, New Zealand and Canada,
in particular, have vital interests in [agriculture] for which special arrangements must be made. . . . We shall no doubt have to consider a whole
range of possibilities, including duty-free, levy-free, or preferential quotas,
market-sharing arrangements, and long-term contracts."[15] The smaller countries, who were most anxious for Britain to join, now sought to ensure that
the common agricultural policy would be sufficiently flexible to permit it.
But France and Germany remained the dominant contenders, and they were
not greatly influenced by concern for Britain's problems.

Up until the first of December most of the controversy between France and
Germany had taken place in the meetings of the Special Committee for
Agriculture. A special meeting of the Council of Ministers itself was called
for November 29–December 3. It was hoped that by then the Special Com-
mittee would have achieved compromise on all but a few points and the
Ministers themselves could then reach full agreement.

By November the Commission's main worry over the policy went far

---

[15] *Economist*, London, December 2, 1961, p. 876.

beyond agriculture. It was becoming apparent that without a fairly detailed agricultural agreement there would be no move to Stage Two. The French were not to be satisfied with agreements in principle, since they felt that the principles were amply stated in the Treaty itself. They had to be satisfied that a common agricultural policy would be carried out in practice within a short period of time. And under the Treaty the French could legally block virtually all progress in the Common Market's timetable during Stage One simply by saying no. The French gave no indication of throwing away this legal club. On November 16 President de Gaulle told Walter Hallstein, President of the Commission, that pressure from French farmers was mounting. He implied that the French government's support for the Common Market could not be taken for granted if the EEC temporized much longer.

On November 21 Economics Minister Erhard spoke to the European Parliament at Strasbourg and assured its members that Germany would not allow the agricultural dispute with France to impede the Common Market's progress into the second stage. This was widely interpreted as a sign that Germany was now ready to compromise. The delegates awaited with some optimism, therefore, the opening speech of the November 30 meeting to be given by the German Agriculture Minister, Werner Schwarz.

As Schwarz began to speak, all optimism faded. He was presenting, he said, a final program that had been approved two days before by the West German cabinet. Germany would agree to the proposed system of target prices and variable levies, Schwarz said, but only in exchange for three important concessions. First, Germany must be allowed to grant transportation and other subsidies to wheat farmers in order to help them compete against the French. Second, the principle of Community preference, which was drawing an increasing amount of criticism from America and the British Commonwealth, would have to be dropped and Germany allowed to keep bilateral trading agreements with other countries. Third, the Commission's plans for financing export subsidies with revenue collected from import levies would have to be scrapped, and any money for Community export subsidies would have to be raised in the regular way, through a proportionate contribution of the national budgets. Schwarz went on to indicate that this was a package deal, and any attempt to modify any part of it might result in Germany's withdrawing the offer altogether.[16]

The reaction to the Schwarz Plan was strong and negative. The French Minister of Agriculture, Edgard Pisani, suggested that Germany was rejecting the whole idea of a common agricultural policy. The Commission was disappointed. Mansholt, whose agricultural policy was battered but still recognizable, suggested that escape clauses should take care of the German objections, but the German delegation was intractable. After two days of argument and discussion of the Schwarz Plan, the meeting broke up with a

---

[16] *Financial Times,* London, November 30, 1961.

call to reconvene December 12. The Commission, with some forced optimism, said that at least the issues had been clarified.[17]

The meeting on December 12 produced no breakthrough. Mansholt suggested that the Special Committee on Agriculture and the Commission meet jointly during the following week to submit new proposals to the Council on December 18. Two days afterward, on December 14, Mansholt spoke before the Western European Union in Paris and told the British not to expect a longer transition period than the original members if Britain joined the EEC. He said that any bulk contracts to import grain from the Commonwealth would be allowed only temporarily, but went on to say that the Six must not set their target prices high enough to encourage EEC farmers to produce all their own foodstuffs.

The German Farmers' Union had participated in talks with British farmers' unions a few days before, however, at Agriculture House in London, and the two groups had agreed that the transition period should take "substantially longer than at present contemplated in the Commission Proposals."[18] It was clear that the national pressure groups were not ready to accept the Commission's leadership unless forced, and where would Mansholt find the force?

The Eleventh Hour

As the last scheduled meeting of the Council of Ministers drew near, the Commission realized that it was running out of time. Between December 18 and 21, the Council would have to throw aside its disagreements and reach common decisions on dozens of points that had evaded compromise for eighteen months. The Six still had to accept the principle of the levy system and write it into marketing regulations for cereal grains, pork, poultry, and eggs. The Dutch government, feeling that the time was ripe for decision on its own prime export crop, had added dairy products to the agenda. Regulations for the fruit, vegetable, and wine sectors also had to be adopted. The issue of minimum prices remained to be settled. A dispute had arisen over the application of Common Market anticartel policy to farm organizations and national marketing organizations. A firm regulation of the tariff protection and countervailing charges applicable to processed foodstuffs was still not set. Finally, there was no agreement on the responsibilities of the various Community institutions in carrying out and, particularly, in financing the common policy.

Erhard was in the chair on December 18 as the Council opened its last scheduled meeting. At the outset Erhard stressed that the time was ripe for a

[17] *Ibid.*, December 1, 1961.
[18] *Ibid.*, December 11, 1961.

political decision, and the three days passed with frantic efforts at compromise. The Commission submitted six detailed proposals, but the Ministers soon got embroiled in technicalities. Then the Commission took a new tack aimed at compromising eight "points of policy." This produced limited agreement on target prices and market organization. On the twenty-first, German Deputy Economics Minister Mueller-Armack remarked that the agenda still looked as though it would take six or seven more meetings to get through, but Pisani, who had not been noted for his optimism, said, "The European atoms, which moved along parallel lines yesterday, are now beginning to fuse."[19] The Council meeting, originally scheduled to end on Thursday, the twenty-first, finally disbanded Saturday morning, the twenty-third, at 3:00 A.M. with a call to reconvene in emergency session December 29. Dejected and weary, the ministers went home for Christmas. After fifty strenuous hours of debate, they had not yet reached agreement on principle.

In the ebb and flow of debate, it was becoming apparent that no single point of disagreement could be definitely settled until all were settled. One delegate told a London *Financial Times* reporter, "We thought we had settled escape clauses this morning, but we spent an hour and a half on it again this afternoon, getting nowhere."[20] Like a tower of cards, the elements of a "package deal" were painstakingly laid one atop the other, until a slip would send the entire package tumbling in a heap.

Not only the Commission, but the ministers themselves spent the Christmas holidays in a last effort to wrap up the elusive "package deal." The day after Christmas, Belgian Deputy Foreign Minister Henri Fayat asked the ambassadors of the other five member countries to visit him separately. He handed each a typewritten set of proposals for breaking the deadlock and emphasized the "imperative necessity" of moving on to Stage Two. At the same time Spaak wrote a memo to the effect that the Treaty did not require that the agricultural policy be definitely set in order to move on to Stage Two. Pisani and French Foreign Minister Maurice Couve de Murville met with Premier Michel Debré, however, and agreed to hold the line that the Community was an indivisible whole, and that agriculture must be settled before France would vote to pass on to Stage Two. Rumor in Bonn had it that Adenauer had heard directly from de Gaulle.

The last meeting of the Council of Ministers got off to a slow start on December 29. Erhard was still in the chair, and Couve de Murville was on hand to head the French delegation. The day was spent in the familiar dispute over financing. The French wanted the receipts from the variable import levies to be used to pay export subsidies on a Community basis immediately; the Germans wanted these receipts to be applied in the importing country for as long as possible. The indefatigable Commission was ready with a com-

---

[19] *Ibid.,* December 23, 1961.
[20] *Ibid.,* December 27, 1961.

promise: In the first year—1962—the Commission would handle one-sixth of the expenses for export subsidies, price supports, and structural improvements. The funds needed would come from the member states as budgetary contributions, except for one-tenth, which would come from the receipts of the variable import levies. Each year both fractions would double, so that Germany would have more than half of its levies to apply nationally for three years, but the Community would take over completely within five years.

By the end of the day Erhard was hopeful for accord on financing, but he declined to comment on the chances of entering Stage Two. Couve de Murville said only that the Six were very far apart, and agreement might take a very long time.[21] With only one working day to go, and only two before the clock ran out, it seemed clear by nightfall that the Six would not make the deadline. No package deal had been wrapped up, and detailed negotiations over individual Commission proposals had scarcely begun.

Under these circumstances it is not surprising that the leaders of the European movement looked around for a loophole. French parliamentary practice sanctions the custom of "stopping the clock" at times when important deadlines are in danger of being missed. The body may rule that a session once started can be continued indefinitely, and the effect of any decisions ultimately reached may be dated back to the beginning of the session.

When the Council sat down for its last workday before the new year, the French delegation pressed the others not to force a vote, but to stop the clock. The Dutch quickly agreed. Although Erhard was not happy with this subterfuge, he agreed that it could be done if there was reasonable prospect of success in a few days. The ministers concluded the rest of their year-end business, reluctantly postponed the 10 percent tariff cut that was expected to take place with the conclusion of the agricultural agreement, and recessed for the New Year holiday, to reconvene January 4.

The Thirteenth Hour

When the ministers returned to the Palais de Justice on January 4, they knew that the Common Market's moment of truth was near. The French and German positions on agriculture remained far apart, and the negotiations themselves were continuing on borrowed time.

This was an anxious moment for the "Europeans." Four years of hard work on the European Economic Community had been crowned with phenomenal success. The member countries had cut industrial tariffs among themselves by 40 percent, trade among them had expanded by 73 percent, living standards within the Community were at an all-time peak, and unemployment had practically vanished. Progress had been made in drafting

---

[21] *Ibid.*, December 30, 1961.

"harmonized" laws for the Six countries in fields as diverse as fringe benefits for workers and antitrust policy. The structure of a European Political Union had become a serious topic of debate. The EEC had been recognized by the superpowers to east and west: the United States now maintained a special embassy to the Community in Brussels and the Kennedy administration treated it as the most important force in Europe, while the Soviet Union gave recognition to the EEC's success by a thunderous and ineffectual propaganda campaign. Even Britain, whose delegates had not bothered to attend the Messina Conference, had petitioned for negotiations with a view to joining. And the United States talked of a new Atlantic partnership, with Washington and Brussels as its poles.

Yet the Community, with all its promise, had bogged down over agriculture. The negotiations with Britain had reached a standstill because the Six could not negotiate about policies they did not have. Efforts to conclude trade agreements with the United States were bogging down for the same reason. To the Commission it must have looked as though the whole edifice of the European Economic Community were about to turn back into a pumpkin.

The national delegates, too, were becoming acutely conscious of what they were about to lose. Germany, by continuing to hold out against the principles of common grain pricing and Community preference, might be about to lose the tangible benefits of a booming industrial economy and even jeopardize its newly won respectability among the nations of western Europe. France, by continuing to insist on iron-clad assurance of a protected market for its farm surpluses, might lose that market altogether—along with other benefits ranging from Germany's subscription to the African development fund through France's newly won leverage in world affairs.

On the fifth the German position began to crack, as Schwarz accepted the levy system and the principle of Community preference. By Monday the eighth, however, the entire house of cards began to quiver as the Germans again refused to meet French demands for the harmonization of support prices. The deadlock persisted through the ninth, although the Commission bombarded the ministers with a steady stream of compromise proposals. The waning hopes of all were expressed by the Italian delegation, who flatly announced that they intended to return to Rome by the end of the week.[22]

The simple finality of the Italians' announcement came as a shock. It jarred both the French and German delegations into the realization that they must find common ground quickly if they were to find it at all. Suddenly the rest of the jigsaw puzzle began to fall into place. France and Germany approved the Commission's regulations for poultry, processed foods, and wine. Late in the evening of the eleventh, the Six accepted a Commission draft on the criteria for establishing minimum prices. By noon on the twelfth

[22] *Ibid.,* January 10, 1962.

France had agreed to a looser clause on the harmonization of grain prices, and the policies for cereals and pork had been approved. Later in the day the problem of escape clauses, which had tangled the discussions for months, was solved by a general clause which allowed a member state to apply "special measures" to protect its domestic market as it saw fit, but empowered the Commission to approve or disapprove the action.

By the thirteenth it was apparent that the long-sought "package deal" was in the ministers' grasp. Technical points of difference remained, but all the principal issues which had eluded compromise throughout December had been settled. By 5:30 A.M. on the fourteenth the last *i* had been dotted and the last initials scribbled on the last document.[23] The Commission had proposed and the Parliament had recommended, and now the Council of Ministers had made its decision.

The agricultural agreement of January 14, 1962, was the result of hundreds of hours of negotiation by the Council and tens of thousands of hours of staff work by the Commission and its staff. Actually it involved nine separate regulations, three resolutions, and two decisions, ranging in context from the quality of wine to the mechanics of financing export subsidies. Basically, however, it was a political decision. The secret ingredient that made agreement possible was the political will of the member states to move ahead into Stage Two and fulfill the EEC's early promise of building a united Europe.

After the Agreement

The rising sun on January 14, 1962, came up over the same European countryside on which it had set the evening before. But the relationship of the European governments had changed significantly during the night. The national governments of the Six—once at the point of rejecting a supranational Europe altogether—had reaffirmed their confidence in the Common Market and given it a new lease on life.

What had the long wrangle over agriculture proved? Probably the most obvious point was that the nations were still the main seats of power. The Council of Ministers thought of their countries first and the Community second, and the Council made the decisions. Despite the important work of the Commission and the contributions of the Parliamentary Assembly and the Court of Justice, the agricultural agreement was basically an agreement between the two big countries—France and Germany. The predominance of the nations was shown even more clearly a year later, when President de Gaulle barred British entry into the EEC over the objections of all five of France's fellow members.

But the agricultural agreement had one vitally important ingredient that

---

[23] *Ibid.*, January 15, 1962.

would not have been present in a simple Franco-German trade treaty. In the end both nations made agricultural concessions in order to preserve the wider national benefits flowing from the Common Market. It is unlikely that an agreement could have been reached at all without the deadline imposed by the move to Stage Two and the fear that failure to meet it would have dealt the entire Common Market a crippling blow.

The role of the Commission should not be underestimated. Although nations follow the dictates of their own interests, the essence of supranationalism is the welding of these interests to the common good. By tireless staff work and imaginative drafting of proposals, the Commission secured approval of an acceptable policy, even though it lacked traditional executive powers.

The agricultural agreement illustrates how the Six may back into political union through the coordination of economic policies. While the Commission was modifying its proposals, while the Special Committee for Agriculture and the Council of Ministers itself were debating them, and even during the final stage of give-and-take after New Year's Day, a common topic of speculation in Europe was the possibility of a formal "political" Community of the Six. The "political" Community, like the Defense Community of the early 1950's, cuts across too many national traditions to be widely popular. Few issues, however, could be more "political" in their implications than the common agricultural policy, which is gradually being coordinated under the guise of economic integration. "Gentlemen," Dr. Hallstein has said, "We are not in business; we are in politics."

The main content of the agreement had been economic, but the concept behind it was a political one. Europeans and overseas observers alike had hung on the decision because its core was the movement toward political unity through economic integration. It is clear that neither political unity nor economic integration was achieved by the step that took the Common Market into its second phase. This fact was to be reemphasized by the subsequent refusal to admit Britain. The view that remained dominant was that of de Gaulle's *l'Europe des Patries,* the Europe in which countries worked together but did not submerge their right to make ultimate decisions in a supranational, or federal, structure such as Jean Monnet desired. But nevertheless there had been a significant move toward majority, in place of unanimous, decisions.

In the long discussions that culminated in the historic agreement on a common agricultural policy (hedged though it was by reservations), the advantages of supranational working together had triumphed over the pressures of national interest groups, even those of the farm groups in the two major countries of France and Germany. The degree to which the Commission through the Mansholt Plan had been able to turn sensitive domestic issues into international technical ones had been a strong factor in its success. The negotiations, like subsequent ones, demonstrated that advances could be achieved only if national parties and parliaments supported the efforts of the European Economic Community. They also showed that a dedicated international staff could think supranationally and transmit tangibly something of its own conception of the advantages of multinational arrangements.

To move forward significantly on the road pointed out by the "Europeans" would seem to require an agreement to merge the executives of the three supranational executives, those of the European Economic Community, the Iron and Steel Community, and Euratom; to provide a single physical center for them; to arrange for regular meetings; to provide diplomatic representation both to and from them; and to advance steadily toward financial, defense, and political integration. For the latter, a directly elected European Parliament might well be essential. But it is worth recalling that the Treaty setting up the European Economic Community presages such an Assembly that might have its own legislative powers and not merely opportunities for debate and advice as has the present body. It is also significant that in as far as the Treaty has been accepted by member states of the EEC, its provisions have become part of their national law and cannot be abrogated or superceded by purely national action. The Treaty is not only an international convention; it is also a code of rules and a constitution.

The agreement on agricultural policy sheds particular light on the EEC's emerging economic philosophy. In the industrial sector—dominated in Europe as in America by private enterprise—the EEC had shown a readiness to slash trade barriers and welcome international competition. In the government-administered agricultural sector, however, it was clear that protectionism still prevailed. Despite Mansholt's emphasis on efficiency, the Council of Ministers' first concern was to protect farm income—and farm votes. It is also significant that the Six, when confronted with an impasse in the negotiations, tended to sidestep the strongest points of disagreement and to compromise whenever possible at the expense of outsiders. Thus the Six did not agree on the level of a common wheat price before moving to Stage Two (and did not until nearly two years later) but reached accord on export subsidies, Community preference, and the levy system.

The Community's new import policy got its first test late in 1963, with the imposition of variable levies on imported poultry. As European living standards had risen in the late fifties, U.S. chicken-growers had developed a brisk business exporting to the Six. By early 1962 volume had risen to an annual rate of more than $50 million, but in the twelve months following imposition of the variable levies, those exports fell by 40 percent. The United States charged a violation of the General Agreement on Tariffs and Trade, and the EEC's reply defended the principle of Community preference. The sequence of charges and countercharges became so bitter that it was dubbed the "Chicken War" and was sent by the U.S. and EEC governments before a panel of experts from the General Agreement on Tariffs and Trade to determine the extent of U.S. injuries arising from the imposition of the levies. Although the United States and the EEC accepted the board's compromise decision, the issue remains unresolved, and American objections to Community preference hang over the EEC's plan to impose variable levies on grains and other farm products.

Because Europe is such an important market for agricultural products from North America and the developing nations as well, the EEC's Community preference has made it plain that agricultural trade problems can be solved only in a worldwide framework. Thus the Common Market's own success plus its protectionist farm policy may lead to a worldwide approach to the rational use of land and farm labor. In the meantime, however, it encourages Community self-sufficiency and tends to depress agricultural trade.

Handicapped as it is by a weak "constitution" and a vague political apparatus, the Common Market is still a long way from fulfilling the hopes of the "Europeans." If the Community's "government" is to have lasting influence, its institutions must develop and assume powers now exercised by the national governments. It is too early to tell whether this will take place. If not, the European Economic Community will retain historical importance as the matrix that held together the nations of Continental Western Europe during their transition from postwar dependence on America to the strength and political independence of the mid-1960's. If the EEC's institutions do accumulate new powers as they gain experience, then this experiment in economic integration may reach its true goal—a politically united Europe.

DEGREES OF AGRICULTURAL SELF-SUFFICIENCY IN THE COMMON MARKET COUNTRIES

(Domestic Production as a Percent of Consumption)

	FRANCE	GERMANY	ITALY	NETHER-LANDS	BELGIUM-LUXEMBOURG	COMMON MARKET
Sugar	116	93	97	107	119	103
Potatoes	101	98	103	115	100	100
Wheat	113	70	93	32	69	91
Other grains	106	77	72	35	43	77
Beef and veal	102	87	74	105	95	93
Pork	100	94	94	154	101	100
Poultry	101	51	93	336	102	93
Cheese	103	78	99	209	33	99
Butter	102	94	84	192	97	101

SOURCE: *Statistical Information,* no. 1 (European Economic Community, 1964).

Selected Bibliography

Listed below are some additional sources covering the subject of this article. Of the many books describing the birth of the Common Market and the working of its institutions, I believe the following are among the best:

AMERICAN MANAGEMENT ASSOCIATION. *The European Common Market*, AMA, New York, 1958.
CAMPBELL, A. C., and THOMPSON, D. C. *Common Market Law*, Stevens, London, 1962.
THE CHASE MANHATTAN BANK. *The New European Markets*, CMB, New York, 1964.
EUROPEAN ECONOMIC COMMUNITY. *General Report*, EEC, Brussels, Annual.
HUMPHREY, DON D. *The United States and the Common Market*, Praeger, New York, 1962.
MOORE, BEN T. *NATO and the Future of Europe*, Harper, New York, 1958.
NUTTING, SIR ANTHONY. *Europe Will Not Wait*, Hollis and Carter, London, 1960.
SHANKS, MICHAEL, and LAMBERT, JOHN. *The Common Market Today and Tomorrow*, Praeger, New York, 1962.

For a more detailed description of European agriculture and its problems, the following books and papers are recommended:

DEWHURST, FREDERICK, ET AL. *Europe's Needs and Resources*, Twentieth Century Fund, New York, 1961.
ECONOMIST INTELLIGENCE UNIT. *The Commonwealth and Europe*, EIU, London, 1960.
POLITICAL AND ECONOMIC PLANNING (PEP), London, Occasional Papers:
Agricultural Integration in Western Europe, 1963.
Agricultural Policies in Western Europe, 1959.
Agricultural Policy in the European Economic Community, 1958.
Commodity Agreements and EEC Farm Policy, 1964.
Food Prices and the Common Market, 1961.
YATES, LAMARTINE. *Food, Land, and Manpower in Western Europe*, Macmillan, New York, 1960.

For a factual report in English of the events leading to the adoption of the common agricultural policy, one may refer to the *Bulletin of the European Economic Community*, which is published monthly in Brussels, and the *Financial Times*, which appears daily in London. The author also drew material from the New York *Times* and from statistical sources published by the European Coal and Steel Community, European Economic Community, and Organization for Economic Cooperation and Development. Some information also came from conversations with European and American businessmen and officials.

Study Questions

1. Under the Rome Treaty, which powers are assigned to supranational institutions and which to the Council of Ministers? In what ways does the supranational Commission influence Common Market policy? As time passes, would you expect the influence of the supranational institutions to grow or shrink? Explain.

2. Why was agriculture a more difficult subject on which to secure international agreement than industry?

3. What role did national political parties play in the European Common Market conflicts? In what ways did the differences in the organization of European institutions and those of a national state influence the outcome of negotiations?

4. How did Britain's decision to consider joining the Common Market affect the agricultural negotiations among the Six? How would British membership have complicated the task of finding a common agricultural policy?

5. Why has it been easier to develop "functional" supranational organizations in Europe (like the Coal and Steel Community) than political ones (such as a United States of Western Europe)? To what extent does this ease of development depend on post-World War II factors such as the spread of prosperity to middle and working classes, mobility of persons throughout western Europe, and the rise of a "new European culture"?

5

USSR

Legality vs. Terror
The Post-Stalin Law Reforms

Harold J. Berman

On March 6, 1953, Joseph Vissarionovich Djugashvili died. Known to the world by his party name, Stalin ("man of steel"), he had ruled the Soviet state for more than twenty-five years and had forged it, by the most ruthless means, into the second greatest industrial and military power in the world. Feared and worshiped by his people, hated and adored, he had put his stamp on every aspect of their lives. His death left a void, an abyss. Could the Soviet system of government survive without the man who had made it what it was?

This case describes the struggle of legality against terror in the Soviet Union during the decade following Stalin's death. Stalin left the legacy of a dual state, founded on both law and terror. The executors of his "will," appointed by him, sought to eliminate the terror. But could they do so without also eliminating themselves as Stalin's executors? The case of legality vs. terror thus raises the question of whether the Stalinist dualism is ineradicably built into the Soviet political system.

Many outside observers of Soviet events had anticipated that when Stalin died there would be a bloody struggle for personal power among those whom he had raised to high places. Many had thought also that such a personal struggle would be associated with a "class" struggle among the various bureaucracies of Soviet society—the Communist party apparatus, the secret police, the army, the economic administrators, the governmental hierarchy. To a very limited extent these anticipations were fulfilled. But the real crisis

Acknowledgement is gratefully made to the Harvard University Press for permission to draw upon the author's book, *Justice in the U.S.S.R.: An Interpretation of Soviet Law* (rev. ed., 1963), in various portions of the present chapter. Citations and additional bibliographical references may be found in that book.

precipitated by Stalin's death was not a struggle for power; it was, rather, a crisis in the whole structure of authority and in the whole system of ideas by which the Soviet polity had been governed in the Stalin era: Could Stalin's tyranny be replaced as a basic principle of order and a basic driving force in Soviet society? Could the Soviet political, economic, and social system operate without the fear and the faith that he had inspired? Could the sacrifices necessary to achieve the universal goals of the Great October Revolution be wrung from the Soviet people without the terrible and wonderful image of Stalin as the symbol of those goals?

These questions may not seem very real to people who live in peace and comfort and who are content to keep what they have and stay where they are. They are meaningful questions, however, to a people living in the throes of war and revolution, a people who are asked to suffer for big ideas and who must feel that their suffering is justified. Millions of Soviet soldiers went to their death in World War II shouting *Za Stalina, Za Rodinu!*—"For Stalin, For the Motherland!" Twenty million Soviet citizens—possibly twenty-five million—lost their lives in that war. But it was not only in the period from 1941 to 1945 that sacrifices had been demanded: there was also the period of prewar preparations from 1939 to 1941, the period of mass purges from 1934 to 1938, and the period of violent collectivization of agriculture from 1930 to 1933; and before that there was the famine and mass typhoid epidemic of the early 1920's, which had resulted, in turn, from four terrible years of civil war following the 1917 Revolution; and before that was World War I, in which Russian casualties had equaled those of all the other warring countries put together. At least forty million—perhaps sixty million—persons had perished because of these catastrophes in the one generation from 1914 to 1945. Yet in 1945, when the Soviet Union had won the war and an exhausted people were looking forward to a relaxation of tensions and controls, Stalin demanded renewed economic sacrifices and discipline—a remobilization—in order that Soviet power in the world might be maintained.

De-Stalinization Begins

In March, 1953, Stalin's successors did not resign the positions that they had achieved under his leadership. They were his men, placed by him, obedient to him. They, too, had worshiped and feared him, loved and hated him. Yet not one of them except, possibly, Lavrenti Beria, head of Stalin's secret police, could even think of assuming his authority: and Beria was executed by the rest of them for allegedly trying.

Lacking the capacity and the will to attempt to create a new image of an almighty and infallible leader, Stalin's successors ultimately took the opposite course—they denounced their former master for creating that image of himself. In February, 1956, at the Twentieth Congress of the Communist party, Nikita S. Khrushchev, who a year earlier had succeeded Georgii M. Malenkov as *de facto* head of the Soviet state, accused the dead Stalin of having exalted himself above the party and of having committed terrible crimes against prominent party officials. At the Twenty-second Party Congress in October–November, 1961, the charges against Stalin were multiplied, and his mummified body was ordered removed from the mausoleum in Red Square where it had lain in state alongside Lenin's. Just as in his lifetime only the good things of Soviet life had been credited to Stalin, so now only the bad things were attributed to him. Above all, he was denounced for establishing the "cult of personality" (*kul't lichnosti*). The "personality" referred to was his own, but the phrase was also identified more generally with arbitrariness, irrationality, and the naked exercise of personal power.

A Stalinist Trick?

Yet the denunciation of Stalin and his methods could not in itself provide an adequate alternative to the leadership that Stalin had exercised; nor could it overcome the widespread belief that Stalin's methods were essential to the very system of Communist party control which his successors were perpetuating. It would, indeed, be a typical Stalinist trick for the new leader, Khrushchev, to use anti-Stalinism as a pretext for establishing a new form of Stalinism under his own leadership.

After the removal of Stalin's body from the mausoleum and its reburial next to the Kremlin wall alongside that of Mikhail Kalinin and other former Soviet leaders, the following story circulated among Muscovites: "Well, Comrade Stalin," Kalinin said, "I did not expect to see you here. How long do you expect to stay?" "At least until the next Party Congress," Stalin replied. "Where will you go then?" asked Kalinin. "I shall go wherever the party sends me," answered Stalin.

Socialist Legality

Without a Stalin, however, Stalinism was not a viable system of party control. Nor was Khrushchev willing—at least in the first decade after 1953—to risk the charge of neo-Stalinism. Instead, he and his associates sought to find genuine alternatives to terror as an instrument of government. Above all, they sought to replace terror with the principles of what they called—and what Stalin had called—"socialist legality." Stalin, they charged, had systematically violated in practice the principles of socialist legality that he had proclaimed in theory.

By restoring the practice of socialist legality, as well as by strengthening its theory, the post-Stalin leadership hoped (1) to discredit the old regime and legitimate its own authority, (2) to unite potentially hostile factions under its own banner, (3) to overcome the deadening effects of terror upon individual and group initiative, and (4) to give a new direction to the Soviet social order.

It is important to note that none of these four objectives could be achieved overnight, no matter what the new leadership said or did. Stalin had been too greatly revered simply to be cast aside at once. Moreover, the attack upon him by his successors—who had been his faithful servants while he lived—was too obviously self-serving to be accepted unquestioningly by the entire Soviet people.

In addition, there were important divisions among various groups within the party and within the country generally—resentments harbored by the less privileged against the more privileged—which had been submerged under Stalin's powerful rule but which now came to the surface and would not easily be downed. Each group was glad to have legality applied to it, but many were eager to see poetic justice applied to others. The secret police were hated. The peasantry was bitter. The industrial managers chafed at the tight controls imposed by the planning authorities. There were sharp racial antagonisms toward Georgians, Armenians, Jews, and other minority Soviet nationalities.

Above all, a long time had to elapse before that great enemy of change—fear—could begin to disappear. In Moscow in 1962, a Soviet professor said to the author: "I am not proud of the book I wrote in 1952. But you must remember that in those days if you said anything favorable about the West, you would be told: 'Enough!' And if you persisted, you might disappear." Then he added, "And you know, nine years is a very short time in the perspective of history"—for his more recent books were not much better.

Stalin's Heirs

Finally, apart from those who feared that the terror might return, there were those who had a strong stake in the old methods. These were "Stalin's heirs," as the young Soviet poet Yevgeny Yevtushenko called them in 1962, some of whom, in his words,

> . . . cut roses in retirement
> but secretly consider this a temporary retirement.
> Others even curse Stalin from the rostrum
> but at night long for the old days.
> The heirs of Stalin . . .
> do not like a time when the camps are empty
> and the halls where people listen to poetry
> are overfilled. . . .

Stalin's heirs occupied leading posts in every hierarchy, including the Presidium of the Central Committee of the Communist party of the Soviet Union. The task that confronted Khrushchev and his followers was to rid every organization of those leaders who, whether by experience or belief, were committed to Stalinism, that is, who accepted the necessity of arbitrariness and terror as primary instruments of Soviet rule. Everyone above the age of forty was a Stalinist by appointment; the task was to oust those who were also Stalinists by conviction. In some organizations it was necessary to remove the entire leadership apparatus twice in succession in order to achieve a clean sweep.

Masters and Servants

Thus, even with the utmost determination, the Soviet rulers would require many years to erase the legacy of illusion, distrust, fear, inertia, bureaucratism, and ruthlessness that Stalin had left. But the difficulties that they faced were compounded by an even more serious factor—namely, the ambiguities inherent in their position as leaders both of the Soviet state and of the Communist party. As leaders of the Soviet state they were servants of the law of that state, which, like the law of other countries, speaks in universal terms and purports to regulate all aspects of public life in their society. As leaders of the Communist party, however, they were the masters of the Soviet legal system and not its servants. They could change it at will, without effective control by the legislature or the electorate; and they themselves were elected not by legal procedures but by informal and secret means. Moreover, as leaders of the Soviet state they were committed to maintaining law and order within their own country and lawful, orderly relations with other states; as leaders of the Communist party, however, they were committed to bringing about the rapid transformation of their country into a new type of social order called communism and to striving for the spread of Communist party influence throughout the world.

These ambiguities are inherent in the phrase "socialist legality." The adjective "socialist" is intended to distinguish Soviet legality from that of non-socialist countries; it implies the absolute authority of the Communist party over all aspects of political, economic, and social life; it implies a planned economy and a common ideology of discipline and service; it implies a dynamic, collective movement forward to a classless utopia in which the entire coercive apparatus of state authority, including the legal system itself, will die out. Thus socialism is a philosophy that subordinates formal legal processes and norms to informal political, economic, and social pressures and to utopian social ideals. It is in tension with the concept of legality (in Russian, *zakonnost'*), which signifies not only the observance of laws (*zakony*) but also the observance of the spirit of laws, "due process of law," those principles which give laws their morally binding force.

Thus the replacement of the "cult of personality" with "socialist legality" was no easy task. In addition to the obstacles imposed by the legacy of Stalinism, there were obstacles inherent in the very nature of the Soviet political, economic, and social system. Put bluntly, if the campaign for legality were carried too far, it might call into question the very authority of Khrushchev and his colleagues and the very purpose of the Revolution. Moreover, it would not be easy to place limits upon law reform, since law is a highly technical and complex institution which is fully understood only by a professionally trained class of people. If the jurists were not carefully controlled, they might introduce new legal standards and procedures that would embarrass not only the various organizations charged with governing the different aspects of Soviet society, but also the Communist party leadership itself.

Six Tendencies in Law Reform

Soviet law reform in the decade after Stalin's death was marked by six major tendencies that, in part, conflicted with each other. The character of the Khrushchev era was to be molded by their interaction. The first four tendencies were toward (1) elimination of terror, (2) liberalization both of procedures and substantive norms, (3) systematization and rationalization of the legal system as a whole, and (4) decentralization and democratization of decision-making.

The latter two tendencies pressed in other directions as well—(5) toward the introduction of popular participation in law enforcement and the administration of justice, and (6) toward a return to harsh criminal and administrative penalties against persons who defied what may be called "the Soviet way of life."

1. The Elimination of Terror

The first indication that Stalin's successors did not intend to pursue his policy of terror came less than a month after his death; on April 3, 1953, charges that had been made in January against fifteen Kremlin doctors were exposed as a frame-up. The doctors, most of whom were Jewish, had been accused of a Zionist conspiracy to murder, by medical means, a whole series of top Soviet leaders. It was widely feared that the accusations signaled a return to the mass purges of the late 1930's. Now, however, with Stalin dead, security officials were charged with "impermissible procedures" in extorting confessions from the accused doctors. In connection with this there appeared a series of articles in the press proclaiming the "inviolability" of Soviet law.

On July 10, 1953, it was announced that Beria, Minister of Internal Affairs since 1938, had been arrested as an "enemy of the people." Beria and six associates were reported on December 24, 1953, to have been executed after a secret trial. Other officials of the Ministry of Internal Affairs, henchmen of Beria, were executed in 1954, 1955, and 1956. Since May, 1956, there has been no evidence of the execution of any Soviet political leader, although many have been denounced and sent into retirement.

Following the arrest of Beria, important steps were taken to eliminate those features of Soviet law which permitted terror to be disguised in legal form.

First, the Special Board of the Ministry of Internal Affairs was abolished in September, 1953. It was this Special Board which had been the chief instrument of terror. It was a three-man administrative committee—the Russians called it a troika—which was empowered by a 1934 statute to send people to labor camps without a hearing, after a secret administrative procedure, without right of counsel and without right of appeal. The significance of the abolition of the Special Board is indicated by the fact that it was not publicly announced in the Soviet press until January, 1956, four months after news of it, given by Soviet legal officials to the author of the present article, was published in the American press.

Second, the security police were deprived of the power to conduct investigations of crimes under their own special rules without supervision by the Procurator General of the U.S.S.R.

Third, the special procedures for court cases involving the most serious antistate crimes were abolished. The laws of 1934 and 1937 permitting persons charged with certain such crimes to be tried secretly, *in absentia,* and without counsel, were repealed.

Fourth, the military courts, which had previously had a wide jurisdiction over civilians, particularly in the case of political crimes, were deprived of all jurisdiction over civilians except for espionage.

Fifth, the law permitting punishment of relatives of one who deserts to a foreign country from the armed forces—though they knew nothing of the desertion—was abolished.

Sixth, the prominent jurist Andrei Y. Vyshinsky's doctrine that confessions have special evidentiary force in cases of counterrevolutionary crimes —based on the transparently false notion that people will not confess to such crimes unless they are actually guilty—was repudiated; confessions were now treated as having no evidentiary force in themselves, and the matters contained in a confession must be corroborated by other evidence.

Seventh, Vyshinsky's doctrine that the burden of proof shifts to the accused in cases of counterrevolutionary crimes was also repudiated. In 1958 new criminal legislation placed the burden of proving the guilt of the accused squarely on the prosecutor. Although the phrase "presumption of innocence" is avoided in the codes, all that American jurists generally mean by that phrase was spelled out in Soviet law.

Eighth, Vyshinsky's broad definition of complicity, borrowed from the Anglo-American doctrine of conspiracy, was repudiated. Persons could no longer be held liable for acts of their associates unless they intended those acts to take place.

Ninth, the law on so-called counterrevolutionary crimes was slightly narrowed and made a little less vague. The term "counterrevolutionary" was eliminated and the term "state" (i.e., antistate) substituted. The crime of "terrorist acts," which hitherto had been interpreted to include any violent act against a state or party official or, indeed, his close relatives, whatever the motive, was restricted to murder or serious bodily injury to the official himself, committed for the purpose of overthrowing or weakening Soviet authority. The law on state secrets was substantially relaxed—though it was still far wider in its scope than most Americans would consider tolerable— and a new list of what constituted a state secret was drawn up, which is less broad and more precise than the earlier list.

Finally, there took place from 1955 to 1957 a systematic reexamination of all cases of persons previously convicted of counterrevolutionary crimes and the release from labor camps of the overwhelming majority of such persons, with cancellation of their criminal record.

The gradual restoration of procedural due process of law in political cases was a signal achievement of the first decade of the post-Stalin regime. The Soviet citizen was now protected against police terror, false charges, and faked trials to a far greater extent than ever before in Soviet history. No longer did he need to fear the midnight knock on the door as a prelude to being transported to a Siberian labor camp without a fair hearing.

Yet one cannot speak of the total elimination of political terror so long as open opposition to Communist party policy—the "party line"—could lead to criminal sanctions, however "objectively "and "correctly" imposed. The 1958 Statute on State Crimes, carried over from the earlier law on counterrevolutionary crimes, contained a provision against "agitation or propaganda" directed against the Soviet system. Under that statute, to defame the Soviet political and social system for the purpose of weakening Soviet authority, or even to possess written materials of such a defamatory nature, is punishable by imprisonment for up to seven years.

The law against anti-Soviet agitation and propaganda is only one of many features of the Soviet political, economic, and social order that keep alive the fear among Soviet citizens that the terror may return. The fear of a return to terror is itself a form of terror. Therefore, one must view the developments of the ten years after Stalin's death as reflecting only a tendency, though an extremely important tendency, toward the elimination of terror.

2. The Liberalization of Soviet Law

Apart from political crimes, Soviet law underwent substantial liberalization in the decade after Stalin's death. To understand the extent and significance of this liberalization, it is necessary to trace briefly the development of Soviet law in the Stalin and pre-Stalin periods.

In the early 1920's, Lenin (who was himself originally a lawyer) sponsored the enactment of a series of Soviet codes (a Judiciary Act, Civil Code, Criminal Code, Land Code, Labor Code, and others) which gave Soviet Russia a legal system similar in its main outlines to that of the countries of Continental Europe, including prerevolutionary Russia. This was part of the "breathing spell" introduced by the New Economic Policy (NEP), after the bankruptcy of the earlier period of War Communism. It was viewed as a temporary concession to capitalism. At the same time the NEP codes contained certain provisions which reflected the revolutionary goals of the new Soviet system. In civil law it was provided that any legal transaction "directed to the obvious prejudice of the state" shall be invalid and that any profits which have accrued from such a transaction shall be forfeited to the state as unjust enrichment. Moreover, article 1 of the Civil Code stated that "Civil rights shall be protected by law except in instances when they are exercised in contradiction to their socioeconomic purpose." Thus a man could own his house, but if he had an extra room in it, he could be required to take in a tenant; a mill could be leased to a private individual, but if he failed to operate it for a certain period in order to avoid taxes, it could be taken away from him. In criminal law, the doctrine of analogy was formulated: abandoning the French Revolutionary principle of "no crime, no punishment without a [previous] law," the Soviet Criminal Code permitted a court to sentence a man for an act not directly prohibited but analogous to an act so prohibited. Under this provision, for example, a Mohammedan who performed the rite of circumcision upon a 12-year-old boy was sentenced under the article of the Code prohibiting rape, and managers who intentionally committed serious violations of economic regulations were punished, by analogy, under the provisions on counterrevolutionary crimes.

Such "escape clauses" in the NEP codes were conceived as harbingers of the time when classless socialism would be ushered in and law itself would begin to "die out," together with all other instruments of state coercion. And with the abandonment of the NEP compromise in 1928 and the introduction of the Five-Year Plans, that time was thought to be at hand. Within seven or eight years, it was thought, Soviet society would be able to realize the Marxist-Leninist dream of a society in which, in Engel's words, "the public power will lose its political character." In the new planned economy, money would be transformed into a mere unit of account; private property and private rights generally would be swallowed up in collectivism; the family would disappear as an economic and legal entity; crime would be exceptional and would be treated as mental illness. There would be no need of either the compulsion or the formality of state and law. Socioeconomic expediency would be the ultimate criterion for all decisions; disputes would be resolved on the spot by "the whole people." Meanwhile, the "bourgeois" law of the NEP period was viewed as rapidly becoming obsolete, and there was no thought of replacing it with "socialist law," since that was considered to be a self-contradiction.

In 1936, however, Stalin proclaimed a new doctrine: he announced that socialism had finally been achieved, that the first transition period was over at last, and that only friendly classes now existed in the Soviet Union. But instead of the dying out of state and law, of money and property, of the family, of criminal sanctions, and the rest, there was to be a wholesale restoration of these institutions on a new socialist basis. Nor would they disappear when the Soviet Union moved from socialism—the first stage of the classless society, in which each "receives according to his work"—to communism—the final stage, in which each will "receive according to his need."

"We need stability of laws now more than ever," Stalin said in his report on the draft Constitution in December, 1936. With "stability of laws" as their slogan, Soviet jurists denounced the radical ideas of the first phase of the Revolution and restored conservative, even conventional doctrines and practices, proclaiming them to be truly "socialist."

After 1936 serious efforts were made to eliminate the loopholes of socio-economic expediency in the NEP codes, pending the enacting of new codes. Stalin became an ardent spokesman for "socialist legality." Yet the practice of force and violence survived; indeed, 1936 and 1937 were the years of the worst terror. Officially, the Soviets saw no contradiction in this. Vyshinsky, Stalin's spokesman in the field of law, wrote in 1938 that "suppression and the use of force" were "still essential" so long as communism was not world-wide; against "class enemies," no holds were barred. But where there was no question of political opposition, due process of law was to apply.

Thus Stalin's system from the mid-1930's on was based on a coexistence of law and terror. Law was for those areas of Soviet life where the political factor had been stabilized. Where the stability of the regime was thought to be threatened, law went out the window. No fundamental legal opposition was tolerated. Where real opposition was even suspected, it was dealt with by "suppression and the use of force." The Soviets had the delicacy at least not to call this law. Yet the line was not always easy to draw, and the inherent conflict between law and force resulted in some strange paradoxes. The law punished discrimination on the basis of nationality, yet the Ministry of Internal Affairs removed and dispersed whole national groups that were considered insufficiently loyal—the Volga Germans, the Crimean Tartars, the Karachais, the Kalmucks, the Chechen and Ingush, and the Balkars. Anti-Semitism was a crime in law, but Jewish "cosmopolitans" were sent to labor camps as counterrevolutionaries. Legal guilt was purely personal, but political guilt could be avenged against relatives and friends.

The spheres of law and terror were not easy to keep separate. In the first place, the borderline between them often shifted: the crime of theft of state property, for example, which was supposed to be dealt with by due process of law, could easily merge with counterrevolutionary crimes and thereby become subject to repression by the secret police. In the second place, even though terror diminished after 1938, it continued to have a deleterious effect on the legal system itself. Urgently needed law reforms were delayed and sidetracked because of people's fear of being labeled "deviationist." Thus, although Stalin in 1936 had called for new all-union codes to replace the republican codes of the NEP period, and although many drafts of such codes were prepared, none were adopted, and only piecemeal legislation was enacted to reflect the new conditions.

It was only with Stalin's death that the time became ripe for bringing the hastily enacted codes of the early 1920's up-to-date and, at the same time, for eliminating many of the harsh rules that had been introduced by special laws in the 1930's and 1940's.

It would be impossible to list the hundreds, indeed thousands, of needed reforms that were introduced from 1953 to 1963. A brief account of some of the most important may suffice, however, to indicate the direction and scope of the tendency toward liberalization.

In criminal law and procedure the "tightening up" of the rules with respect to burden of proof, the evaluation of confessions, and the doctrine of complicity, which have already been mentioned in the discussion of political crimes, gave increased protection to persons accused of nonpolitical crimes as well. In addition, the doctrine of analogy, which had already been criticized and limited while Stalin lived, was finally abolished. Also, the right of an accused to counsel prior to trial, though still limited, was significantly extended; time for supervisory review of an acquittal in a criminal case, formerly unlimited, was reduced to one year; powers of search and seizure were somewhat restricted; penalties were substantially lightened for many crimes—for example, new laws imposing lighter sentences for petty rowdyism ("hooliganism") and petty theft of state or public property eliminated the spending of many long years in labor camps for such trivial offenses. Some offenses were eliminated as crimes altogether, such as abortion, absenteeism from work, and quitting one's job without permission. Large-scale amnesties in 1953 and 1957 released all except those sentenced for, or charged with, the most serious offenses.

One of the most significant reforms in Soviet criminal law—and one that bears upon both the elimination of terror and upon liberalization generally —has been the narrowing of responsibility for so-called official crimes. Intentional or negligent abuse of office is a crime under both the old and the new law; but under the old law virtually any employee—a waiter in a restaurant or a milkmaid on a collective farm—was considered to be guilty of an abuse of "office" for improper performance of duties. An Amnesty Edict of March 27, 1953, three weeks after Stalin's death, specifically singled out persons sentenced for official and economic crimes as subject to amnesty, and also called for the substitution of administrative and disciplinary responsibility for criminal punishment of less dangerous official crimes. The 1960 RSFSR (Russian Soviet Federative Socialist Republic) Criminal Code limits the applicability of punishment for official crimes to persons acting as representatives of state authority or occupying offices connected with the fulfillment of regulatory or administrative obligations.

With respect to the system of detention, a 1957 law eliminated the term "labor camp," substituting "labor colony" for all places of confinement (except prisons, which are used only for temporary detention or, very rarely, for the most serious crimes) and introduced a new regime for prisoners

At work

*Problems of Socialist
Legality as Reflected
in the Soviet Press*

I. Scmenov

and at home

[At the top the speaker is
hailing the resolutions and
decrees of the Twentieth
Party Congress; at the bottom
he is kneeling before Stalin.]

E. Shcheglov

[The scene is the Comrades' Court.] "I think, comrades, that we
will not be strict, taking into consideration the heart-felt repen-
tance of Citizen Bottlekin!"

Boris Leo

DON'T TOUCH! FATAL!

[On the electrified safe a portion of the Edict of Strengthening the
Struggle Against Especially Dangerous Crimes is reproduced:] "to
permit the application of the death sentence—shooting—for theft
of state or social property in especially large amounts. . . ."

which permitted them far more lenient treatment. Those convicted of lesser crimes were permitted to have their wives (or husbands) visit and stay with them from time to time; they were paid substantial wages for their work (with deductions for food, clothing, and other expenses) and were required to send allotments home to their dependents. Also, liberal parole provisions were introduced.

Liberalization was not confined to criminal policy. After 1953, and especially after 1955, there was a reexamination of every branch of law and a weeding out of many of the harshest features. For example, a new civil right was created, the right to obtain a court order for public retraction of a newspaper libel. In labor law, the rights of trade unions were enhanced and the procedures for settlement of workers' grievances were improved. Similar examples could be adduced from many other fields of law.

In 1961, 1962, and 1963 in certain areas there was a contrary trend—which we shall discuss below—away from liberalization. These backward steps, however, did not stop the liberal momentum of the post-Stalin reforms.

3. Systematization and Rationalization

The tendency toward liberalization of law generally is, of course, an important buttress for the tendency toward elimination of political terror. For such tendencies to have permanence, however, deep foundations are required in the legal system as a whole. From this standpoint, the efforts of the post-Stalin regime to systematize and rationalize the Soviet legal system are of great significance.

The Stalin Constitution of December, 1936, and the Vyshinsky jurisprudence that surrounded it, rehabilitated the various republican codes—criminal, civil, labor, and family—of the NEP period of the twenties that had largely fallen into disrepute in the years between 1928 and 1936. Of course the NEP codes, designed for a transition period of mixed capitalism-socialism, were inadequate for the new period of full socialism with its planned economy. The Stalin Constitution, therefore, called for the creation of all-union codes to replace the earlier republican codes. But until such all-union codes were adopted, the earlier ones were to prevail, together with the thousands of statutory and administrative changes introduced into them.

During the remaining sixteen years of Stalin's reign, as was mentioned before, no all-union codes were adopted, although many drafts were produced. Only with the removal of the political and ideological pressure of Stalinist autocracy did it become possible to introduce new codes and, together with them, a reorganization of the entire system of legal administration. The first major event in this development was the adoption in August, 1955, of a new Statute on Procuracy Supervision. The Procuracy, an historic Russian institution reestablished by Lenin in 1922, is the cornerstone of the Soviet legal system. It combines functions of our Department of Justice, congressional investigating committees, and grand juries. It not only investigates and prosecutes crimes, but it supervises the entire system of administration of justice, and has the power to investigate and protest to higher authorities (whether administrative or judicial) any abuse of law that comes to its attention. Until 1955 it operated on the basis of a 1922 statute that was encrusted with many legislative and administrative modifications. The 1955 statute clarified and consolidated the supervisory powers of the institution over judicial and administrative acts. Incidentally, the new statute also added sanctions against officials of the Procuracy for negligence in failing to expose illegal practices in places of criminal detention.

The second major event was the removal of certain aspects of control by the Ministry of Justice over the courts and the reorganization of the Supreme Court of the U.S.S.R., as well as the republican and regional courts. This took place in 1956 and 1957. The result was a streamlining of the court system and an increase in its independence.

In December, 1958, the Supreme Soviet of the U.S.S.R. adopted a series of fundamental principles of various branches of law—Fundamental Principles of Criminal Law, Fundamental Principles of Criminal Procedure, and Fundamental Principles of Court Organization—together with new comprehensive statutes on state crimes, military crimes, and military tribunals. Subsequently, in December, 1961, the Supreme Soviet adopted Fundamental Principles of Civil Law and of Civil Procedure. As of 1963, Fundamental Principles of Family Law and of Labor Law were in preparation; indeed, the Statute on the Procedure for the Hearing of Labor Disputes adopted in 1957 was itself a systematization of many aspects of labor law. On the basis of the various fundamental principles, the republics adopted their own new judiciary acts, codes of criminal law and criminal procedure, and codes of civil law and civil procedure.

Of the many other important pieces of legislation in the first post-Stalin decade, mention should also be made of the 1961 Statute on Administrative Commissions of Local Municipal Councils, which restricted the powers of administrative bodies to impose fines and established a procedure for appealing such fines; the 1960 Statute on State *Arbitrazh,* which reorganized the procedures for hearing the hundreds of thousands of contract disputes that arise each year among state economic enterprises; and the new statutes on the organization of the legal profession in the various republics, which strengthen the independence of the advocate and his responsibility to his client.

Two other items deserve mention in connection with the systematization of Soviet law. The Juridical Commission of the Council of Ministers of the U.S.S.R. was given the function of determining which laws have lost their force in the light of the new legislation. In the twenty-one years between 1937 and 1958, the U.S.S.R. Supreme Soviet enacted over 7,000 statutes, edicts, and decrees, while the Council of Ministers issued about 390,000 decrees and regulations. Few of these approximately 397,000 normative acts were formally declared to have lost their force. Yet in 1960 only about

15,000 of them actually remained in force. The Juridical Commission has attempted to cleanse the Augean stables of Soviet legislation by systematically listing, little by little, those laws and other normative acts which are no longer valid.

In connection with this effort, it is important to note a 1958 law on the publication of laws. Of the more than 7,000 laws of the Supreme Soviet enacted between 1937 and 1958, only some hundreds were published. Of the 390,000 decrees and regulations of the Council of Ministers, only a few thousand were published. The rest were merely distributed to the appropriate officials concerned with their enforcement and to other authorized persons. The 1958 law attempted to increase the publicity given to laws by requiring that all laws and acts of the U.S.S.R. Supreme Soviet and all edicts and decrees of its Presidium which have "general significance" or are of a "normative character" be published in the journal of the Supreme Soviet. Also, decrees of the Council of Ministers which are of general significance or have a normative character were required to be published in the *Collected Decrees of the Government of the U.S.S.R.*

The systematization and rationalization of Soviet law was not something that could be accomplished in a few years. Indeed, it is something that must go on continually. The recognition of its importance and the very great efforts devoted to it were an encouraging sign of the determination of the post-Stalin regime to establish a far higher degree of legal security than had existed in the past.

4. The Decentralization and Democratization of Decision-Making

Implicit in the tendencies toward an all-embracing, liberalized, and systematic legality was the belief in the possibility of a wide decentralization of decision-making and a still wider participation of the public in the formulation of issues for decision.

Two qualifications must be made at the outset, however, in discussing the tendency of the post-Stalin period of Soviet history toward greater decentralization and democratization. The first is that there was no sign that the new Soviet leadership had any intention of allowing this tendency to extend beyond its power to control it. The limits of decentralized decision-making and democratization were set by the central authorities. The second qualification is that the theory of "democratic centralism"—centralization of authority combined with decentralization of operations—had also been Stalin's theory. The difference after his death was a difference in degree.

The tendency toward decentralization and democratization was greatly accelerated after Stalin's death, however, by the very nature of the tendencies toward elimination of political terror, toward liberalization, and toward systematization and rationalization of the law. Apart from all other considerations, the effectuation of these tendencies required the participation of hundreds of thousands of people at various levels of the official hierarchy and in various parts of the Soviet Union. In addition, one of the main purposes of these efforts—that of overcoming the rigidities of the system inherited from Stalin, thus to stimulate local and individual initiative and enthusiasm—necessitated the enlistment of maximum cooperation from a maximum number of people.

When one thinks of the United States, one thinks of 180 million people of diverse outlooks, diverse traditions, and diverse interests, scattered across a great continent that includes not only New York City and Washington, D.C., but also Texas and California and Mississippi and Vermont and a host of other very different kinds of community. But too many, when they think of the Soviet Union, stop with the Kremlin. Needless to say, even if one imagined the entire Soviet population to be a disciplined army, the commander in chief would be greatly in need of subordinate units of command with considerable autonomy of action. He could not run the lives of 220 million people—including thirty or forty major nationalities, spread across one-sixth of the earth's surface—by push button from Moscow. When the author presented the "push button" theory to a leading Soviet jurist some years ago, he merely replied: "It would take too many push buttons."

This is not to say that centralization is not the major fact of the Soviet political and economic system. "Bolsheviks are centralists by conviction," said John Maynard in 1948. Under Stalin this Bolshevik conviction was strengthened by fear of "the leader" (*vozhd'*), who often urged decentralization but did not hesitate to crack down when it tended toward deviation.

The decision in 1957 to abandon the rule of the 1936 Constitution calling for all-union codes and to substitute a rule calling for separate codes in each of the fifteen Soviet republics to be based, however, on All-Union Fundamental Principles; the earlier decision to dissolve the All-Union Ministry of Justice into separate republican ministries of justice and the later decision to do the same with the Ministry of Internal Affairs; and, most important, the decision in 1957 to split the economy of the country into about one hundred economic regions, each with its own Council of National Economy, and to divide among these regional councils some of the functions of the former economic ministries that had their central offices in Moscow—these decisions in the direction of decentralization were called for by the enormous bureaucratization of Soviet social and economic life, which had become almost too stifling to endure.

Yet decentralization in itself is not democratization; it may be, and to a certain extent it was, simply a moving of the center to the localities, a stretching of the chain of command. It was also more than that, however. The lower links in the chain were unquestionably given more initiative. And even where ultimate decisions were reserved for Moscow, a far greater hearing was given to the voices of the localities.

This trend is illustrated by the process of law reform itself. Khrushchev and his immediate associates could give the word that the time had come for substantial law reforms and could indicate the lines along which the reforms should run, but the word could not become a reality without an enormous effort on the part of the people who would be directly affected by these reforms. These included not only the professional lawyers who would have to draft them and the officials who would have to administer them, but also the various people who would have to live under them.

The comprehensive legislation enacted in the late 1950's and early 1960's was worked on by representatives of hundreds, indeed thousands, of organizations. All the major governmental agencies expressed detailed views on the various provisions. There was endless discussion in the universities, in research institutes, in economic organizations of various kinds, in scholarly journals, and in the daily press.

In addition, popular participation in lawmaking was stimulated by the expansion of the committee system of the Supreme Soviet of the U.S.S.R. and of the Supreme Soviets of the fifteen republics. Tens of thousands of expert consultants reported to these committees. And apart from major all-union and republican legislation, there was a substantial increase in the powers of the local municipal councils and a vast amount of activity on the part of local governmental organizations, involving the participation of literally hundreds of thousands of Soviet citizens.

It would be a mistake to suppose that Soviet federalism and Soviet democracy involve—as ours do—a struggle between opposing political units and groups, a competition for political leadership. In the Soviet Union all power resides in the Communist party, which remains, as stated in the Constitution, the "central core" of all organizations, whether they be state or social. Despite the development of greater intraparty democracy after 1953, the party remained a disciplined elite, subservient to its leadership. Decentralization and democratization of decision-making in the spheres of government, law, and economic administration were not a threat to party supremacy; indeed, they were required by the party as a means of maintaining its supremacy.

Yet party control was, in a much deeper sense, challenged by the development of autonomous centers of discussion and initiative, even though it remained the "central core" of such centers. The cohesion of Soviet jurists, for example, is striking. Whether they are judges, procurators, Ministry of Justice officials, law professors, research workers, legal advisers to state institutions and enterprises, advocates, or notaries, the more than eighty thousand jurists in the Soviet Union are bound together by the closest professional ties. They work together; they meet in many different kinds of activity; they discuss and debate common problems; and they are bound not only by their common legal education but also by their common vested interest in the preservation of legality. As a class, they grew greatly in importance during the years after Stalin's death.

5. Popular Participation in the Administration of Justice

In describing the movement away from political terror, harshness of punishment, chaos and irrationality of legislation, and overcentralization of decision-making, one runs the risk of leaving the false impression that the Soviet legal system was becoming just like that of the United States. It is true that Stalin's successors sought to eliminate the dualism of law and terror which formerly characterized the Soviet system, and in so doing they took important steps in the direction of a more humane, rational, and democratic legal system. Yet they sought to do this without abandoning the dynamic revolutionary development of the Soviet state and of Soviet society; indeed, their purpose was to instill new vitality into that revolutionary development by softening the motive force of fear and strengthening that of common effort, common struggle, common enthusiasm. The Soviet people were now being asked to make sacrifices voluntarily that formerly had been evoked from them in part by threat of force. No doubt both the leaders and the people were greatly relieved at the decrease in emphasis upon terror and coercion and the increase in emphasis upon the liberal, rational, and democratic elements in their legal system. But these elements were not—for the leaders, at least—ends in themselves, but rather a means of lifting their society to new heights of economic progress, political power, and social solidarity.

Law was conceived as a major instrument for achieving these goals. It was seen, above all, as a means of educating Soviet people to be the type of socially conscious, dedicated members of society who were required if socialism was to be maintained and if communism was to be achieved.

This concept of the dynamic function of law in molding not merely the conduct of men but also their morality and their very characters was perhaps the greatest challenge that Soviet law presented to the West in the post-Stalin decade. One aspect of this concept was the greatly increased participation of ordinary Soviet citizens—of society, the public (*obshchestvennost'*, as Soviet terminology has it)—in the administration of justice.

In Soviet theory the functions of state organizations (which operate in part by coercion) will, under communism, be turned over entirely to social organizations (which operate only by persuasion). In anticipation of this glorious day, the role of social organizations was greatly increased from about 1959 on. Neighborhood and factory meetings were convened for a variety of purposes and were given certain semijudicial functions. Also, a voluntary auxiliary police force was organized—the so-called *druzhiny,* or people's guards—to help keep order; they directed traffic, took drunks into custody, and attempted in general to enforce law and order among the people on the streets. In addition, many special volunteer commissions were formed and given semiofficial status; they were organized to observe conditions in the labor colonies and to make recommendations, to report to municipal councils on housing questions, to report on local observance of "socialist legality," and to perform a host of similar functions. Trade unions and the Young Communist League (Komsomol) were also considered to be social organizations, and their functions were extended.

Many of the functions of Soviet social organizations are also performed in the United States by volunteer workers and social organizations. Indeed, probably no country in the world can match the United States in the amount of public-spirited activity by volunteer social organizations. Yet there is a difference in kind between Soviet social organizations and their American counterparts—a difference that is striking. In part it is a difference in the scope of the activities of Soviet social organizations, especially their power over the lives of their members; in part it is a difference in the amount of official pressure than can be brought upon them, pressure that results from their links with the state through the Communist party.

For example, in the period after 1958, the Komsomol organizations in the universities called for student volunteers to work during the summer holidays in the so-called virgin lands of the East. The volunteers were recruited, however, by lists posted on bulletin boards, and refusal to go courted expulsion from the Komsomol and probably—at least it was so assumed by the students—from the university.

A second example may be found in the activities of the "Comrades' Courts," operating under a 1961 statute, amended in 1963, which met in apartment houses or in factories to consider minor offenses committed between neighbors or fellow workers. Their punitive powers were limited to a ten ruble fine (in 1960 the ruble was officially revalued at $1.11) and to a sentence of up to fifteen days of menial physical work. Mostly they issued reprimands and warnings. They could also, however, recommend eviction from the apartment or disciplinary action (including demotion and, in some cases, discharge) by the factory management. Such eviction or disciplinary action could be resisted through regular court proceedings, but nevertheless, the recommendation of the Comrades' Court was a serious matter.

One other example: Soviet courts sometimes go "on circuit," so to speak, to apartments or factories, to hear criminal cases involving persons in those places. The purpose is to demonstrate to the entire "collective" and to the public the social danger in the offenses charged and to educate people in the requirements of the law. But the tendency to convict and to mete out harsh punishment is very strong when such an educational purpose is in the forefront of the procedure itself. In the late 1950's and early 1960's, there was increased pressure for such demonstration trials.

Western students of the Soviet scene have emphasized the evils of this new kind of "social justice." To evaluate them properly, one must put oneself in the Soviet situation, where true social cooperation in informal voluntary groups, entirely independent of the state, hardly existed. The Comrades' Courts in action impressed outside observers by the good spirit in which they were received. Especially important is the fact that their powers were very limited, and that these limits were enforced by the courts and the legal system.

The great danger, of course, was the potentiality for abuse of these social organizations by the Communist party and the state. A still greater danger was the dream of a far-off time when there would be no legal system and no state but only one vast social organization, one vast Communist party. It was, no doubt, a dream that could never be realized; but so long as it was held, it inhibited the achievement of true legal security.

6. The Return to Harsh Criminal and Administrative Penalties

A sixth major tendency in Soviet law in the first post-Stalin decade was the return in 1961, 1962, and 1963 to harsh criminal and administrative penalties against those who refused to cooperate in building communism.

In May and June, 1961, the three largest republics, comprising three-fourths of the Soviet population, finally enacted the notorious antiparasite law that had first been proposed for public discussion in 1957 and later adopted by the smaller republics during 1957 to 1960. This law, in its final form, provided for "eviction" (*vyselenie*) to "specially designated localities," for two to five years, of persons who "are avoiding socially useful work and are leading an antisocial parasitic way of life." Money or property acquired by such persons "by nonlabor means" was subject to confiscation. Persons could be sentenced under this law by the judges of the regular courts in a summary procedure, without the usual guarantees of the criminal law and without right of appeal, or else by general meetings in the factories or collective farms with review by the local municipal council.

To a Western lawyer, and—judging from private conversations—to many Soviet lawyers as well, the antiparasite laws contradicted the provision of the 1958 Fundamental Principles of Criminal Procedure which stated that no person may be punished for a crime except by sentence of a court. Official Soviet doctrine, however, reconciled these laws with the Fundamental Principles on the more-than-tenuous theory that the offender was not being punished for a crime, nor was he being confined; he was simply being "evicted" to another place where he must take a socially useful job. This was considered an "administrative," not a "penal," measure.

In the first year of the operation of this law in the RSFSR, according to a statement made by the Minister of Justice at a public lecture in Moscow in May, 1961, ten thousand people in Moscow were charged under the antiparasite law; of these eight thousand, he said, received only warnings while two thousand were sent out of Moscow.

Also, the extension of the death penalty in 1961 and 1962 to a wide variety of crimes, many of them economic crimes not involving violence, reflected the regime's determination to take extreme measures against those who most flagrantly violate the tenets of Communist morality. In May, 1961, the death penalty (which had been abolished altogether in 1947 and restored in 1950 for treason, espionage, wrecking, terrorist acts, and acts of banditry, and in 1954 for murder committed under aggravating circumstances) was extended to stealing state or social property in especially large amounts, counterfeiting money or securities for profit, and the commission of violent attacks in places of detention by especially dangerous recidivists or persons convicted of serious crimes. In July, 1961, the death penalty was expanded to include speculation in foreign currency. In February, 1962, it was extended to attempts upon the life of a policeman or volunteer auxiliary policeman (*druzhinnik*) on duty, to rape committed by a group or by an especially dangerous recidivist or entailing especially grave consequences or committed on a minor, and to the taking of bribes under aggravating circumstances by an official who holds a responsible position or who has been previously tried for bribery or taken bribes repeatedly.

In a case tried in July, 1961, the statute imposing the death penalty for foreign currency speculation was applied retroactively by a special decree of the Presidium of the Supreme Soviet which authorized the retroactive application "as an exception" in the specific case. (The decree was never published as it was not considered to be "of general significance.") There is reason to believe that there were other such cases of retroactive application of the death sentence specially authorized by similar edicts. The 1961 decree was the first example of a Soviet criminal law expressly made retroactive, so far as the author has been able to discover, since 1929.

Judging from Soviet press accounts of individual trials, many hundreds—possibly six or seven hundred—of Soviet citizens were executed for economic and other crimes in 1961–63. One can only say "possibly" because Soviet crime statistics are a state secret. (In 1961, forty-three persons were executed in the United States.)

This harsh policy was also reflected in increased penalties for lesser crimes. Soviet jurists publicly criticized the tendency of some procurators and courts to treat the imposition of the death penalty for serious crimes as a signal for reversing the entire trend toward liberalization.

What significance should we attach to these developments? As is so often the case with violations of basic principles of judicial procedure, the particular victims do not command our affection. They were, presumably, scoundrels. Rather, it is the abuse of the integrity of the legal process that concerns us, for one abuse suggests another.

During the years after Stalin's death, much was heard of "the thaw"—to use the title of Ilya Ehrenburg's 1954 novel—that is, the unfreezing of Soviet life, the reduction of terror, the increased freedom to criticize, the greater encouragement of individual initiative, the relaxation of tensions. But the *long-range* problem of government in the Soviet Union is whether the Soviet leaders are willing and able to establish not merely a season, or a climate, or a policy of freedom and initiative, but also a legal and institutional foundation that will make freedom and initiative secure from their own intervention. Until that problem is solved, the fear of a return to Stalinist terror will haunt the Soviet people, particularly the intellectuals. In research institutes and universities, as well as among educated people generally, debates raged in 1961 and 1962 over the "liquidation of the consequences of the cult of personality," which was party jargon for preventing a recurrence not only of violence, but also of all the rigidities that went with it. Nobody—presumably from Khrushchev on down—wanted such a recurrence. But nobody could guarantee that it would not happen.

In 1957, Deputy Procurator General P. I. Kudriavtsev, responding to a series of questions on guarantees against a return to Stalinist terror, said to the author: "Do not forget that we have in the Soviet Union the dictatorship of the proletariat, and that law must serve the state authority." To the question "Suppose the law conflicts with the interests of the state; which prevails?" he replied, "The interests of the state." He amplified: "Compulsion may be necessary. The Special Board of the MVD [Ministry of the Interior] was necessary in its time, in the late thirties. Only it was later abused. The Cheka, which Lenin introduced, was entirely justified. No revolution is bloodless—ours is the most bloodless revolution in history, far more bloodless than the French or English Revolutions." I asked: "When will your revolution be over?" He replied: "We live in an age of war and revolution. The revolution goes on." And then, to make crystal clear the connection between this basic historical perspective and the law reforms we had been discussing, he said: "If it becomes necessary, we will restore the old methods. But I think it will not be necessary."

In addition to preserving the possibility of a return to physical terror "if it becomes necessary," Khrushchev replaced the Stalinist dualism of law and terror with a new dualism of law and social pressure: one was free from arbitrary arrest by the secret police, but one was not free from the social pressure of the "collective"—whether it was the more innocuous pressure of the collective of neighbors in the crowded apartment houses or the less innocuous pressure of the factory, one's coworkers, or the local party organization. The new dualism still stood in the shadow of the old.

Yet it would be a great mistake to assume that the "thaw" ended with the harsher methods adopted in 1961–63. Such an assumption underestimates the importance of the legal and institutional changes that had in fact taken place. The law reforms had already made their influence felt. They had acquired a momentum that was hard to stop. A vast structure of procedures and rights had been built, and though its foundations needed to be greatly strengthened, it was not something that could easily be toppled.

Can the Paradox Be Resolved?

The development of Soviet law in the first decade after Stalin's death was a measure of the paradoxes of the Soviet political system in that period. On the one hand, the law reforms reflected a new political climate that was far more tolerant of experimentation and dissent. They reflected a much more mature and efficient approach to the conduct of public affairs, and a much more democratic one. They served as a strong deterrent to the forces of arbitrariness, irrationality, and ruthlessness that Stalin had represented. On the other hand, Soviet law remained totalitarian in the sense that it still sought to regulate all aspects of economic and social life, including the circulation of ideas, while leaving the critical questions of political power to be decided by informal, secret procedures beyond the scrutiny or control of either legislative or judicial bodies. Soviet law remained the law of a one-party state. It remained the law of a centrally planned economy. It remained a law whose primary function was to discipline, guide, train, and educate Soviet citizens to be dedicated members of a collectivized and mobilized social order.

The law reforms did not directly affect the powers of the top leaders of the Soviet state, including their power to recruit new leaders. The Presidium of the Central Committee of the Communist party, and the Central Committee itself, operated under their own rules, outside the legal system; and it was they who dictated to the Supreme Soviet what legislation should be enacted. Nevertheless, as the competence of the Supreme Soviet and other state agencies increased, they achieved a certain amount of *de facto* independence. This was particularly true at the intermediate and lower levels of government: the local soviets, the procuracy and courts. The other institutions of administration and enforcement of law continued to be, in a general sense, under the control of the party; but as they were given more and more to do, it became harder for the party to interfere directly.

Yet the party apparatus could not complain of any erosion of its power, for under Stalin it had been completely under the dictator's thumb. The Khrushchev regime had not only liberated the institutions of the state but it had also liberated the party. Indeed, nobody could complain that his authority had been hurt by the strengthening of legality, except the many lesser Stalins who had been eliminated from positions of leadership. With the gradual decline of these lesser Stalins, and the denunciation of their former mentor, everyone else seemed to have more importance than before.

The lawyers, certainly, were happier. It is true that they had not yet come to positions of political power. Only one of their number, Roman A. Rudenko, the Procurator General of the U.S.S.R., was in the Central Committee of the party. But they had become essential to the implementation of party policy. The leading party and government journals—*Pravda, Izvestia, Kommunist,* and others—were continually publishing articles proclaiming the importance not only of law and legality, but also of procurators, judges, and lawyers, for the proper functioning of a socialist society.

Indeed, nobody could seriously oppose the idea of law reform. The controversial political issues of the decade after Stalin's death were of a different sort: they were issues of foreign policy, of the organization of industry, of the organization of agriculture, of priorities for investment in heavy industry and in consumer goods, and of greater freedom for artists and writers to break away from the rigid formulas of the past. Yet the increased emphasis upon law and legality had an important, although indirect, bearing on these issues, too. Once the party leadership made it clear that nobody was to be whisked away and shot for saying the wrong thing, and that power was to be exercised within the limits laid down by law, then it became more apparent that these issues of foreign and domestic policy must be resolved peacefully, on the basis of the right of conflicting groups to be heard. An increased faith in the possibility of negotiating reasonable settlements, an increased belief in the feasibility of principled compromise between opponents both at home and abroad, is implicit in the post-Stalin law reforms; and this was the key difference between Khrushchev and Stalin as well as between Khrushchev and his living antagonists who, in 1957, sought to oust him but instead were ousted by him—Vyacheslav Molotov, Lazar Kaganovich, Georgii Malenkov, and their supporters.

Outside the Soviet Union, however, there were complaints. The Chinese Communist leaders and their friends in Asia and elsewhere denounced Khrushchev's doctrine that the end of the dictatorship of the proletariat had been reached and an "all-people's state" introduced—in other words, the replacement of terror by law. The Soviet system, they said, had lost its revolutionary zeal. In the West, on the other hand, it was generally charged that the Soviet law reforms had not gone far enough, that they were only a temporary retreat, another breathing spell; they paid lip service to legality, it was charged, but they did not truly challenge the autocratic features of the Soviet system or the utopianism that serves as their justification.

Both these types of complaint looked primarily to the future. If one looks to the past, it is apparent that the Soviet legal system of 1963 differed from that of 1953 more than the Western critics, and less than the Eastern critics, were willing to admit.

What had happened was that the tendency toward elimination of terror had led to liberalization, this in turn to systematization and rationalization, this in turn to decentralization and democratization, and finally to popular participation. But challenge to the system had become acute, and there was a return to harsh penalties and administrative resettlement of parasites, which is not terror in the Stalinist sense but yet suggests terror and the possibility of a return to terror.

What then is the judgment in the case? Stalin's successors *were* able to eliminate terror without eliminating themselves, and terror is *not* built into the system; a meaningful legal order, secure from arbitrary interferences, *is* possible within the structure of Soviet politics. But there are several important qualifications: (1) The choice of leaders remained beyond the reach of legal processes. (2) The basic policies chosen by the leaders were not subject to legal challenge. (3) The threat of a return to terror remained as a form of terror. The change—and it was a very significant change—was, in the first post-Stalin decade, one of degree, but not of kind.

Selected Bibliography

The following general works on Soviet law may be consulted for background: Harold J. Berman, *Justice in the U.S.S.R.: An Interpretation of Soviet Law*, Harvard U. Press, Cambridge, and Vintage (Random), New York, 1963; Kazimierz Grzybowski, *Soviet Legal Institutions*, U. of Michigan Press, Ann Arbor, 1962; John N. Hazard, *Settling Disputes in Soviet Society: The Formative Years of Legal Institutions*, Columbia U. Press, New York, 1960; Glenn G. Morgan, *Soviet Administrative Legality: The Role of the Attorney General's Office*, Stanford U. Press, Stanford, 1962; Jan F. Triska and Robert M. Slusser, *The Theory, Law, and Policy of Soviet Treaties*, Stanford U. Press, Stanford, 1962.

Soviet cases and excerpts from statutes and treatises are collected in John N. Hazard and Isaac Shapiro, *The Soviet Legal System: Post-Stalin Documentation and Historical Commentary*, Oceana, Dobbs Ferry, N.Y., 1962. It also contains an excellent bibliography of Soviet and non-Soviet books and articles on various aspects of Soviet law.

An analysis of the dualism of law and social pressure may be found in Harold J. Berman and James W. Spindler, "Soviet Comrades' Courts," *Washington Law Review*, vol. 38, pp. 842–910, 1963.

Study Questions

1. This case concludes by stating that Soviet law reforms after Stalin's death constitute a change "of degree, but not of kind." This suggests that the Stalinist legacy of terror either (a) has been preserved despite the reforms or (b) was not an essential element of Soviet politics under Stalin. Does the case, as presented, provide a basis for accepting either or both of these alternatives?

2. Does the discussion of Soviet law create difficulties in your mind because of the absence of certain elements associated with the concept of due process of law as understood in the United States? In particular, is it possible to speak of law, or legality, in reference to a system in which there is (a) no opportunity for free, public debate of proposed legislation within the supreme legislative agency (the Supreme Soviet), (b) no right to circulate information or ideas that challenge the foundations of the prevailing political system, (c) no power in the judiciary to refuse to apply statutes that violate the constitution, (d) no constitutional prohibition against the enactment of retroactive criminal laws, (e) no restrictions against bills of attainder?

3. In 1964 Khrushchev was removed from his position as First Secretary of the Central Committee of the Communist party of the Soviet Union by a vote of the Central Committee, and from his position as Chairman of the Council of Ministers of the U.S.S.R. by a vote of the Presidium of the Supreme Soviet of the U.S.S.R. (later ratified by the Supreme Soviet). What additional facts would have to be adduced in order to show that not only the form of law but also the spirit, or substance, of law was applied in the transfer of supreme political authority?

4. Does the case suggest that there are pressure groups in the Soviet system? If so, how would you compare their organization, mode of operation, access to decision-making bodies, and power to accomplish or defeat change with those of pressure groups in Western parliamentary systems?

5. Each successive phase of Soviet legal development—under War Communism, the New Economic Policy, collectivization of agriculture and the first Five-Year Plans, the second stage of development of the Soviet state (from 1936 on), the liquidation of the consequences of the cult of personality (after 1953)—has been justified by the Soviet leadership as a reflection of Marxist-Leninist principles. Is there any common thread of Marxist-Leninist theory that runs through this entire history? Do the post-Stalin law reforms reflect a Marxist-Leninist theory of the role of law in society?

6. Given the increasing power of the central government in the American political system, and the increasing liberalization, rationalization, and democratization of Soviet political and legal institutions, is one justified in suggesting that the two systems are moving closer toward each other and will finally meet?

B   6
C   7
D   8
E   9
F   0
G   1
H   2
I   3
J   4

DATE DUE

MAY 14 1974			
DEC 14 1974			
GAYLORD			PRINTED IN U.S.A.